D0044703

CONTOURS OF DESCENT

CONTOURS OF DESCENT

U.S. Economic Fractures and the Landscape of Global Austerity

ROBERT POLLIN

VERSO

London • New York

First published by Verso 2003
© Robert Pollin 2003
All rights reserved

The moral rights of the author have been asserted

1 3 5 7 9 10 8 6 4 2

Verso
UK: 6 Meard Street, London W1F 0EG
USA: 180 Varick Street, New York, NY 10014-4606
www.versobooks.com

Verso is the imprint of New Left Books

ISBN 1-85984-673-4

British Library Cataloguing in Publication Data
A catalogue record for this book is available from the British Library

Library of Congress Cataloging-in-Publication Data
Pollin, Robert,
Contours of descent: U.S. economic fractures and the
landscape of global austerity/Robert Pollin.
p. cm.
Revision of paper in the volume entitled:
The economics of the third way, published in 2001.
Includes bibliographical references.
ISBN 1-85984-673-4
1. United States–Economic policy–1993–2001. 2. United States–Economic
policy–2001. 3. United States–Economic conditions–1981–2001.
4. United States–Economic conditions–2001. 5. Recessions. 6. Financial crises.
7. International economic relations. I. Title.

HC106.82.P65 2003
330.973–dc21   2003057189

Typeset in Ehrhardt
Printed in the USA by R.R. Donnelley & Sons.

TO MY WIFE SIGRID MILLER POLLIN,

AND TO MY PARENTS ABE POLLIN AND IRENE POLLIN,

WITH LOVE AND GRATITUDE

CONTENTS

PREFACE AND ACKNOWLEDGEMENTS

This book began its incubation as a conference paper for the January 2000 Allied Social Science Association meetings on the reality behind the 1990s economic boom under President Bill Clinton. My paper was part of a larger project organized by Professors Philip Arestis of the Jerome Levy Economics Institute and Malcolm Sawyer of the University of Leeds, which sought to examine the situation in which traditional left-of-center parties were reaching power in North America and Europe, but, once in power, were pursuing a policy agenda that was more consonant with the center-right. Clinton himself had termed this policy approach a "third way." The "first way" approach, in Clinton's view, was committed to free markets and big businesses, while the "second way" referred to the remaining legacy of "big government" in something like the form of Roosevelt's New Deal and Johnson's Great Society.

At the time I wrote the paper, the U.S. economic boom under Clinton was being held up as the single strongest piece of evidence on behalf of the superiority of this "third way" approach. Opinion polls were giving Clinton approval ratings well above 60 percent with respect to his handling of the economy. But my review of the basic facts in the U.S. about economic growth, living standards, and not least, the fragility of the financial system over the 1990s, convinced me that the accolades being showered on Clinton and his third way approach were undeserved. The paper first appeared in the June 2000 issue of *New Left Review* and subsequently, in somewhat different form, in the excellent volume edited by Professors Arestis and Sawyer, *The Economics of the Third Way: Experiences from Around the World*.

One of the major themes I emphasize in this book is the absolutely dismal recent performance of economists in the realm of forecasting. I would therefore ask that readers grant me the indulgence of quoting the prediction that I myself made as the concluding sentence of the June 2000 *New Left Review* paper – that "Clinton will hand over to his successor the most precarious financial pyramid of the post-war epoch." Using the Standard and Poor's 500 as our reference point, my assessment was published two months before the stock market bubble had reached its August 2000 peak. I would hasten to add that, amid the relentless cheerleading at that time on behalf of what many economists claimed was a "new economy" impervious to massive financial market misjudgments and recessions, there were still thoughtful analysts providing informed and realistic assessments of the situation at hand. I learned substantially from such people, and I refer to the work of many of them in the chapters that follow.

Shortly after the paper appeared in *New Left Review*, George Galfalvi at Verso, the magazine's book publishing affiliate, contacted me, proposing that I consider writing an expanded version of the paper as a book for Verso. Other commitments prevented me at the time from taking George up on what was nevertheless a very intriguing offer. But I began thinking about the idea again by the end of the year. By this point, two people whose opinions matter a lot to me had also urged me to write the book. One was Noam Chomsky, whom I have never met, but don't need to meet to know that one should listen seriously when he offers advice. The other person was my wife Sigrid, who, in our more than a quarter of a century of sharing everything, has never led me astray.

By the time I had decided to accept Verso's offer, the U.S. Supreme Court had thrown the 2000 presidential election to George W. Bush. It was clear that, if I were aiming to produce a work that would be current in its assessments, the subject matter would need to expand to encompass not just the Clinton years, but the initial initiatives of the incoming Bush administration as well. Of course, it is difficult to evaluate policy measures as they unfold, as I have done with much of my discussion of the Bush economy. But the challenge has been simplified by the Bush Administration's relentless predictability in advocating tax cuts for the rich as its universal economic cure-all.

In its initial conception then, this book was meant to be about U.S. economic policy and the state of the U.S. economy – that is, both the initiatives taken as well as the outcomes produced – under Clinton and Bush. But then September 11 happened. I'm not convinced that "September 11 changed everything," as some observers argue. But it did certainly force me to change my plan for this book. Of course it's perfectly reasonable to address a given problem, such as the fiscal crisis of state and local governments in 2002, without considering global issues, if it is evident that the role of global forces in contributing to the problem has been small. But if the aim of this book was to tell a story about the effects of U.S. economic policies broadly, it seemed, after September 11, that I couldn't do a minimally decent job if I was neglecting the situation in less developed countries. After all, in the immediate aftermath of September 11, there was a near-universal consensus – including public pronouncements by President Bush and Secretary of State Colin Powell – that one of the main causes of terrorism such as we experienced on September 11 is the deep and pervasive poverty in less developed countries. As such, even keeping in mind the initial focus of the book on the U.S. economy and U.S. policies, it became clear that I needed to also give attention to problems of poverty and instability in the less developed world, as well as the connections between these and the sources of terrorism. Fortunately, these were also questions that, broadly speaking, I had researched in the past and was examining in ongoing studies.

These, then, were the fits and starts that I experienced in conceptualizing this book. But these problems quickly faded in significance when I was confronted with the real task at hand, which, of course, was to transfer my still inchoate thoughts into something worthy of a reader's attention. And while I was the only one that pushed my pen across the page and cursor across the computer screen, many people deserve thanks for helping me to produce the book you hold.

First, I want to acknowledge my editors at the *New Left Review* and Verso, including Perry Anderson, Tariq Ali, and Sara Barnes. I especially thank George Galfalvi, who both hatched the plan then stuck with me as the scope of the project widened. Kim Weinstein did an excellent job, as usual, in producing the finished camera-ready copy from typescript form. The Ford and Rockefeller Foundations provided generous financial support for much of the research that undergirds this book.

I am greatly in debt to my graduate students at University of Massachusetts-Amherst. As Robert Heilbroner aptly observed, economics is widely practiced in a manner that produces "rigor, but alas also *mortis.*" But the graduate students at U Mass create an environment in which one would feel truly foolish if one didn't at least try to deploy the techniques of economic analysis toward a deeper purpose, which is to shed light on the most pressing human and ecological issues before us. It would make no sense to single out names in sustaining this vibrant intellectual environment at U Mass. However, three people in particular shared important insights from their dissertation research that I have incorporated into this book – Dr. Lawrance Evans Jr. of the U.S. General Accounting Office on the U.S. stock market; Professor Minqi Li of York University on the contemporary Chinese economy; and Vamsicharan Vakulabharanam, who is still completing his thesis on peasant agricultural conditions in India. In addition Sevinc Rende wrote an excellent econometric paper on wages and the inflation/unemployment trade-off in the U.S. and extended her paper further at my request.

I have pestered lots of knowledgeable people, and they have been generous in sharing their knowledge. These include: U Mass colleagues Michael Ash and Jim Crotty on the Clinton economy; Doug Henwood on the IMF; Jane D'Arista and Tom Schlesingeer of the Financial Markets Center on financial markets and the Fed; Max Sawicky of the Economic Policy Institute and my colleague Elissa Braunstein of the Political Economy Research Instutute (PERI) at U Mass on the fiscal crisis of state and local governments; Bob Sutcliffe of the University of the Basque Country, Sanjay Reddy of Barnard College, Robert Wade of the London School of Economics, and Christian Weller and Adam Hirsh of the Economic Policy Institute on global inequality and poverty; and C.P. Chandrashakar, Jayati Ghosh and Utsa Patnaik of Jawaralalel Nehru University on the suicides by peasant farmers in India.

I presented preliminary versions of Chapters 2 – 4 at seminars before the Economics Departments of the University of California-Riverside and University of Tel Aviv. I gained much from the comments of the seminar participants, including especially Gary Dymski, David Fairris, Keith Griffin, Aziz Khan and Victor Lippitt at UC-Riverside, and Chaim Ferstman, David Frankel, Eddie Deckel, June Flanders and Alex Cuikerman at Tel Aviv.

Dean Baker of the Center for Economic and Policy Research read a previous draft of Chapters 2 and 3 and made extremely valuable comments. Andrew Glyn of Oxford University did the same with the entire manuscript. Jerry Epstein, the Co-Director of PERI along with myself, also went through the entire manuscript carefully. Jerry also provided continued encouragement in the midst of our daily joint efforts to build PERI into something valuable.

My greatest intellectual debt on this project is to Professor James Heintz of PERI. James worked with me closely on virtually every aspect of the book and also provided incisive comments on the entire manuscript. The great professional golf champion of the 1940s and 1950s Ben Hogan once said about the role of luck in his success, "I've been very lucky in golf. And I've found that the more I practiced, the luckier I got." In a similar vein, I found that the more I consulted with James on this book, the better I got at writing it. I am fortunate to be collaborating with him on several other projects with PERI, and look forward to many more joint efforts.

I rely on the love and support of my parents Irene and Abe Pollin. I also now have an answer to their regular question, "When is the book going to be done?" My two daughters Emma and Hannah Pollin are my well-springs of sustenance, with this book and everything else, even though, in their current status as full-fledged independent adults, they have abandoned their childhood job of distracting me when I didn't feel like working. Still, along with Brian Warwick, they deserve credit for helping me come up with the book's title, through a process of eliminating almost every conceivable alternative combination of words. Sigrid Miller Pollin told me to write this book, and then told me how to do it in ways that a non-specialist might care. She certainly knows how to achieve this when she designs buildings, so I'm counting on her skills being transferable.

CONTOURS OF DESCENT

CHAPTER ONE

Neoliberal Consensus:
Clinton, Bush, Greenspan, IMF

> *"The disposition to admire, and almost to worship, the rich and the powerful, and to despise, or, at least, to neglect persons of poor and mean condition, though necessary both to establish and to maintain the distinction of ranks and the order of society, is, at the same time, the great and most universal cause of the corruption of our moral sentiments."*
>
> — ADAM SMITH, *THEORY OF MORAL SENTIMENTS*

In July 2002, the cover article of the leading economics newsweekly *The Economist* blared out: "American Capitalism Takes a Beating." This was amid the collapse of the U.S. stock market bubble, the recession, and the wave of corporate accounting scandals. But as *The Economist* cover suggested, the tribulations of that moment were not simply confined to a few failing corporations, dishonest accountants, overzealous market speculators, or the normal bruises of a recession. Deeper vulnerabilities were being exposed, problems of *American capitalism itself* – the system as a whole.

Such headlines in the serious mainstream press would have been unthinkable only 18 months earlier, when Bill Clinton stepped down from the presidency with a lofty 65 percent approval rating. Then, the press was awash with reports about a New Economy, turbo-driven by the Internet, globalization and business-friendly government policies in the U.S. and throughout the world. The Clinton administration had generated three straight years of fiscal surpluses between 1998–2000, a feat that the U.S. government had not previously accomplished since the Harry Truman administration in 1947–49. Alan Greenspan was being hailed as a *maestro* for having tamed inflation even as unemployment also remained low, and for presiding over the most formidable growth in stock market wealth in U.S. history.

What happened in the ensuing 18 months? Of course, George W. Bush replaced Bill Clinton as President, and the U.S. was attacked by terrorists on September 11, 2001. These were both important for understanding the beating American capitalism was taking as of mid-2002. From its first days in office, the Bush administration pursued an unwavering agenda favoring big business and the rich. This overarching Bush commitment prevented him from advancing anything close to a serious program for either preventing a recession or shifting the economy toward a healthy growth track once the recession had begun. Bush did regularly offer proposals for fighting the economic downturn, but these lacked credibility. His most ambitious such initiative, announced only one month into his term of office, was a program of tax cuts, in which 65 percent of the cuts went to the richest 20 percent of households and a full 45 percent went to the richest one percent, while, at the same time, *none* of the cuts were to take effect in 2001, the year when the recession was taking place.

But the Bush administration cannot be held responsible for the severe financial imbalances that had been building throughout the 1990s, or the recession that had actually begun before Bush took office. We also cannot blame Bush alone for the accounting scandals and other fraudulent corporate practices that began coming to light after the high flying Texas energy company Enron collapsed in disgrace in the fall of 2001, taking their Big Five accounting firm Arthur Andersen with them. The Enron scandal was followed in quick succession by the similarly ignominious demise of WorldCom, Global Crossing, Tyco International and other major U.S. corporations. The fact is that the loose accounting standards that led to these scandals were widely known and broadly accepted throughout the 1990s market bubble. Thus, a *Business Week* cover story in October 1998 titled "Earnings Hocus-Pocus," documented how, with the assistance of creative accounting firms, "companies come up with the numbers they want." This is exactly what Dick Cheney himself was referring to when, as Chairman of another Texas energy firm Halliburton before becoming Vice President, he said in a 1996 promotional video for the Arthur Andersen accounting firm "I get good advice…over and above the just sort of normal by-the-book auditing arrangement."[1] These same loose accounting standards were responsible for George W. Bush, as a private citizen, being let off the hook by government regulators for his illegal insider trades as a director of yet another Texas energy company, Harken Energy Corporation, in July 1990. The point is that shady accounting was standard operating procedure throughout the 1990s bubble economy, and neither Wall Street nor the regulators under Clinton much cared as long as the market continued rising. The market's collapse caused the accounting scandals, in other words, not the other way around.

The September 11 terrorist attacks were a horrible human tragedy that also created immediate economic costs to the travel and tourism industries while also spreading a sense of vulnerability among investors. At the same time, the increase in military spending at the federal level, and, even more so, in civil defense spending at the state and local government levels, injected around $100 billion of additional demand into the economy in 2001. This provided a major counterforce to the collapse of private investment spending associated with the recession. On balance, American capitalism's economic beating as of mid-2002 was not being inflicted by Osama bin Laden.

More than anything else, the causes of the stock market collapse, corporate scandals and recession were the result of economic imbalances that had been built during the Clinton years. Clinton and his supporters claimed to have pursued a new direction in economic policy – what Clinton himself termed a "Third Way" between "those who said government was the enemy and those who said government was the solution" – an information-age government that "must be smaller, must be less bureaucratic, must be fiscally disciplined and focused on being a catalyst for new ideas."[2] But in fact, Clinton's government in most respects represented a conventional center-right agenda, akin – as Clinton himself once put it – to an Eisenhower Republican stance updated to the post Cold-war epoch. Clinton's administration was defined by across-the-board reductions in government spending as a share of the economy's total spending, virtually unqualified enthusiasm for free trade, only tepid, inconsistent efforts to assist working people in labor markets, and the deregulation of financial markets – with Alan Greenspan providing crucial leadership in granting to financial traders the leeway they had long sought to freely speculate with other people's money.

Moreover, U.S. economic performance under Clinton was far more mixed than acknowledged by boosters of his "Third Way." The overall figures on GDP and productivity growth for the full Clinton presidency were middling in comparison with the Kennedy-Johnson, Nixon-Ford, Carter and Reagan-Bush years (as needed for clarification, we will refer to the presidency of Bush the father as Bush-1). Unemployment and inflation did both fall, but this was due in large measure to the declining ability of workers to secure wage increases even at low unemployment rates. Finally, the real gains in investment and productivity that occurred in the second half of the Clinton presidency rested on what many observers even at the time could see was a fragile foundation – a stock market in which prices had exploded beyond any previous historical experience, inducing an enormous expansion of, first, private consumption spending, then investment spending. But because neither household incomes nor corporate profits rose at anywhere near the pace of the stock market boom, the result was unprecedented borrowing to pay for the spending spree. The springs of economic growth under Clinton came from a levitating stock market setting off a debt-financed spending boom. It should have been no surprise when this all began unravelling even before Clinton left office.

In addition, a fair evaluation of economic performance under Clinton, or any other recent U.S. president, cannot focus only on the U.S. economy. Especially as regards the less developed economies of Latin America, Africa and Asia, the parameters of acceptable economic policy are established in Washington D.C., no matter which political grouping happens to hold office within a given country. This generalization applies even to such large and diverse less developed countries as Argentina, South Africa and Indonesia. The U.S. government exerts its influence both directly – through its policies on government spending, financial markets, international trade, labor standards and immigration – and at one step removed, through its control over the International Monetary Fund and World Bank. The IMF and World Bank are physically located across the street from each other in Washington, and the U.S. government controls the major voting bloc at both institutions. The late Rudi Dornbusch of MIT, arguably the most influential international economist of his generation, summarized the relationship between the IMF and U.S. government aptly in saying, "The IMF is a toy of the United States to pursue its economic policy offshore."[3]

Not surprisingly therefore, both the IMF and World Bank have aggressively supported a policy agenda very similar to that practiced by the Clinton administration in the U.S., including free trade, a smaller government share of the economy and the deregulation of financial markets. Indeed, it was during the Clinton years that the term "Washington Consensus" began circulating to designate the common policy positions of the U.S. administration along with the IMF and World Bank. This policy approach has also become widely known as *neoliberalism*, a term which draws upon the classical meaning of the word *liberalism*.

Classical liberalism is the political philosophy that embraces the virtues of free market capitalism and the corresponding minimal role for government interventions, especially as regards measures to promote economic equality within capitalist societies. Thus, a classical liberal would favor minimal levels of government spending and taxation, since private individuals, rather than governments, should be "free to choose" as the Nobel Prize winning classical liberal economist Milton Friedman puts it, how they spend their income. Moreover, as private individuals, we spend our own money in a much more efficient way than when the government spends on our behalf, since a government cannot possibly care as much as we do about how to make the best use of what we earn.

A classical liberal would correspondingly favor minimal levels of government regulation over the economy, including financial and labor markets. Businesses should be free to operate as they wish, and to succeed or fail as such in a competitive marketplace. Meanwhile, consumers rather than governments should be responsible for deciding which businesses produce goods and services that are of sufficient quality as well as reasonably priced. Businesses that provide overexpensive or low-quality products will then be out competed in the marketplace regardless of regulatory standards established by governments. Similarly, if businesses offer workers a wage below what the worker is worth, then a competitor firm will offer this worker a higher wage. The firm unwilling to offer fair wages would not survive over time in the competitive marketplace.

This same reasoning also carries over to the international level. Classical liberals favor free trade between countries rather than countries operating with tariffs or other barriers to the free flow of goods and services between countries. Restrictions on the free movement of products and money between countries only protects uncompetitive firms from market competition, and thus holds back the economic development of countries that choose to erect such barriers.

Neoliberalism, and the Washington Consensus dominant within the U.S. government as well as the IMF and World Bank, are contemporary variants of this longstanding political and economic philosophy. The major difference between classical liberalism as a philosophy and contemporary neoliberalism as a set of policy measures is with implementation. Washington Consensus policy makers are committed to free market policies when they support the interests of big business, as, for example, with lowering regulations at the workplace. But these same policy makers become far less insistent on free market principles when invoking such principles might damage big business interests. Federal Reserve and IMF interventions to bail out wealthy asset holders during the frequent global financial crises in the 1990s are obvious violations of free market precepts.

Broadly speaking, the effects of neoliberalism in the less developed countries over the 1990s reflected the experience of the Clinton years in the U.S. A high proportion of less developed countries were successful, just in the manner of the U.S. under Clinton, in terms of reducing inflation and government budget deficits, and creating a more welcoming climate for foreign trade, multinational corporations, and financial market investors. At the same time, most of Latin America, Africa and Asia – with China being the one major exception – experienced deepening problems of poverty and inequality in the 1990s, along with slower growth and frequent financial market crises, which in turn produced still more poverty and inequality.

The administration of George W. Bush also follows an essentially neoliberal agenda of less government management of the capitalist marketplace, both for less developed countries and with respect to the U.S. itself. To the extent that Bush-2 continues to succeed in delivering massive tax cuts for the rich, it follows that funds to support government social programs will disappear, especially given that Bush is also intent on spending without restraint on his diplomatic doctrine of pre-emptive attacks against hostile regimes. Alan Greenspan still runs monetary policy under Bush, just as he did under Clinton, Bush-1 and Reagan. The Washington Consensus still holds at the International Monetary Fund and World Bank under Bush, and this also means that neoliberal policies are being applied selectively. As one glaring example of selective application, the Bush administration, through the IMF, refused to provide Argentina with emergency loans in 2001, but provided a $30 billion bailout for Brazil only months later, reversing its own stated policies for Brazil itself in doing so. As the *New York Times* explained, "American banks like Citigroup, FleetBoston and J.P. Morgan Chase have much greater exposure to Brazilian loans than to Argentine ones. Brazil has also been a big magnet for American industrial investment...and a Brazilian meltdown would turn those into white elephants, (8/9/02, p. C1)."

Of course, even making allowances for flexibility in the application of neoliberal principles, significant differences do exist between Clinton and Bush. The general requirement of product differentiation in an electoral market entails that at the margin any Democratic President will offer more social concessions than a Republican of the same cohort. Unlike Clinton, Bush is unabashed in his efforts to mobilize the power of government to serve the wealthy. But we should be careful not to make too much of such differences in the public stances of these two figures, as against the outcomes that prevail during their terms in office. It was under Clinton that the distribution of wealth in the U.S. became more skewed than it had been at any previous time in the previous forty years – with, for example, the ratio of wages for the average worker to the pay of the average CEO rising astronomically from 113 to 1 in 1991 under Bush-1 to 449 to 1 when Clinton left office in 2001.[4]

Plan for the book

Thus, the basic issue for understanding both the beating taken by American capitalism in 2002 and the more punishing economic travails of the less developed countries is not the Clinton program per se, the Bush program per se, or the IMF agenda for the less developed countries. It is rather the common set of neoliberal policy assumptions that constitutes the center of gravity for policy formation in all three cases. This book is an attempt to excavate that center of gravity. It does so through describing how increasing inequality and instability have resulted from the specific policy choices advanced under both Clinton and Bush and through the implementation of neoliberalism in various less developed countries.

Chapter 2 provides an overview of the economic experience under the team of Clinton and Greenspan, examining both the main policy measures and the economy's performance under Clinton. The discussion ends, as did the Clinton years themselves, just as the economic boom began unraveling and the descent into recession had begun. In Chapter 3, I then examine in more depth the three extraordinary economic developments under Clinton: the attainment of balance, and then a surplus, in the Federal Budget; the simultaneous declines in unemployment and inflation, in direct contradiction to the predictions of mainstream economic theory; and the historically unprecedented stock market boom. Explaining these three developments is central for understanding how the Clinton economy could have appeared to be performing so well even as problems of inequality and financial instability were deepening.

Because I am writing only a bit more than two years into Bush's term of office, it is impossible to provide a full evaluation such as that in Chapters 2 and 3 for Clinton. But as far as possible, Chapter 4 tells the story of how, under Bush, American capitalism was taking a beating through 2002 without clear signs as to when exactly this beating would end. Of course, a major element of this story is the stock market collapse, and the implications of the market's collapse for more fundamental concerns about the health of the real, tangible economy of business investments, jobs and wages, and the viability of the public sector. Because the stock market boom was crucial to growth under Clinton, the basic Bush problem was finding some alternative engine of economic growth. Alan Greenspan attempted to move the economy forward through interest rate cuts, but these proved insufficient, in no small part because he was operating within a highly speculative, deregulated financial market that he helped create. As we discuss, the only serious contenders Bush offers as a growth agenda is to lower taxes for corporations and the rich, or to increase spending for the military, to pay for wars against Al Queda, Iraq, and perhaps other countries within what Bush terms the "axis of evil."

Chapter 5 is about neoliberalism in the less developed countries. I present both general patterns regarding economic growth, inequality and poverty under neoliberalism, and some specific experiences. The specific stories include the tragic pattern of mass suicides among destitute farmers in India, the financial collapse and depression in Argentina, and the spread of sweatshop working conditions throughout the less developed countries. I also consider the situation with international aid to poor countries. Of course the poor countries would benefit substantially through an increase in foreign aid to a level that reached even half the amount that that the rich countries had pledged back in the early 1970s. The rock star Bono, lead singer of the group U2, deserves credit for bringing much greater attention to the efforts of the United Nations and activists around the world as they try to increase the amount of foreign aid provided by the rich countries. But I also show that, even if foreign aid were to increase to something approximating that level of generosity supported by the United Nations, Bono and other activists, its positive effects are still more than countered by the regime of slow economic growth fostered by neoliberalism.

Overall then, these chapters attempt to do just what the subtitle of the book suggests: to delineate both the root causes of U.S. economic fractures under Clinton and Bush as well as the landscape of austerity in the less developed world. But these chapters also aim to provide some useful guideposts for constructing a renewed viable egalitarian policy framework, which I sketch in the book's closing Chapter 6. This chapter briefly considers policies in three crucial areas: macroeconomic interventions targeted at increasing opportunities for decent jobs, rather than simply targeting inflation; labor market regulations also aimed at improving conditions for working people and the poor; and financial market regulations aimed at controlling financial speculation and channeling credit to productive uses. This chapter builds from many of the concerns that have been raised effectively in recent years by progressive political movements around the world, including the living wage movement in the U.S. and elsewhere, the movement to tax and regulate speculative currency markets (the "Tobin Tax" movement), and, more generally, the movement fighting global neoliberalism under the bracing idea that "another world is possible."

The overall approach

As with all works of political economy, this book proceeds from a fairly simple set of underlying ideas. These ideas will form the basis for my critique of neoliberal policies in both the U.S. and developing countries. It will be helpful to sketch these ideas at the outset just as I have briefly outlined the basic tenets of classical liberalism and neoliberalism. To begin with, there is no question in my view that free markets create powerful incentives for people to work hard and innovate, just as the classical liberal view would suggest. The leaders of the ex-Soviet Union and other Communist governments made a massive historical error by denying or repressing this fact. The market system achieves these important aims through two simple means. The first is to allow people to pursue their own self-interest in their working lives. The second is that this self-interested behavior will be held in check by competition in the market – that is, even if a baker wants to charge $10 for a loaf of bread, she will not be able to do so because her competitors down the street will get all of her business by charging $1 a loaf. These two simple market forces, self-interest and competition, are wellsprings for the prodigies of effort and material abundance that are so evident in the United States and other advanced capitalist countries.

However, if free market capitalism is a powerful mechanism for creating wealth, why then does a neoliberal policy approach, whether pursued by Clinton, Bush or the IMF, also produce severe difficulties in terms of inequality and financial instability, which in turn diminish the market mechanism's ability to even promote economic growth? It will be helpful to consider this in terms of three fundamental problems that result from a free-market system, which I term "the Marx problem" "the Keynes problem" and "the Polanyi problem." Let us take these up in turn.[5]

The Marx problem

Does someone in your family have a job and, if so, how much does it pay? For the majority of the world's population, how one answers these two questions determines, more than anything else, what one's standard of living will be. But how is it decided whether a person has a job and what their pay will be? Getting down to the most immediate level of decision making, this occurs through various types of bargaining in labor markets between workers and employers. Karl Marx argued that, in a free market economy generally, workers have less power than employers in this bargaining process because workers cannot fall back on other means of staying alive if they fail to get hired into a job. Capitalists gain higher profits through having this relatively stronger bargaining position. But Marx also stressed that workers' bargaining power diminishes further when unemployment and underemployment are high, since that means that employed workers can be more readily replaced by what Marx called "the reserve army" of the unemployed outside the office, mine, or factory gates.

Neoliberalism has brought increasing integration of the world's labor markets through reducing barriers to international trade and investment by multinationals. For workers in high-wage countries such as the United States, this effectively means that the reserve army of workers willing to accept jobs at lower pay than U.S. workers expands to include workers in less developed countries. It isn't the case that businesses will always move to less developed countries or that domestically produced goods will necessarily be supplanted by imports from low-wage countries. The point is that U.S. workers face an increased *credible* threat that they can be supplanted. If everything else were to remain the same in the U.S. labor market, this would then mean that global integration would erode the bargaining power of U.S. workers and thus tend to bring lower wages.

But even if this is true for workers in the U.S. and other rich countries, shouldn't it also mean that workers in poor countries have greater job opportunities and better bargaining positions? In fact, there are areas where workers in poor countries are gaining enhanced job opportunities through international trade and multinational investments. But these gains are generally quite limited. This is because a long-term transition out of agriculture in poor countries continues to expand the reserve army of unemployed and underemployed workers in these countries as well. Moreover, when neoliberal governments in poor countries reduce their support for agriculture – through cuts in both tariffs on imported food products and subsidies for domestic farmers – this makes it more difficult for poor farmers to compete with multinational agribusiness firms. This is especially so when the rich countries maintain or increase their own agricultural supports, as has been done in the U.S. under Bush. In addition, much of the growth in the recently developed export-oriented manufacturing sectors of poor countries has failed to significantly increase jobs even in this sector. This is because the new export-oriented production sites frequently do not represent net additions to the country's total supply of manufacturing firms. They rather replace older firms that were focused on supplying goods to domestic markets. The net result is that the number of people looking for jobs in developing countries grows faster than the employers seeking new workers. Here again, workers' bargaining power diminishes.

This does not mean that global integration of labor markets must necessarily bring weakened bargaining power and lower wages for workers. But it does mean that unless some non-market forces in the economy, such as government regulations or effective labor unions, are able to counteract these market processes, workers will indeed continue to experience weakened bargaining strength and eroding living standards.

The Keynes problem
In a free market economy, investment spending by businesses is the main driving force that produces economic growth, innovation and jobs. But as John Maynard Keynes stressed, private investment decisions are also unavoidably risky ventures. Businesses have to put up money without knowing

whether they will produce any profits in the future. As such, investment spending by business is likely to fluctuate far more than, say, decisions by households as to how much they will spend per week on groceries.

But investment fluctuations will also affect overall spending in the economy, including that of households. When investment spending declines, this means that businesses will hire fewer workers. Unemployment rises as a result, and this, in turn, will lead to cuts in household spending. Declines in business investment spending can therefore set off a vicious cycle: the investment decline leads to employment declines, then to cuts in household spending and corresponding increases in household financial problems, which then brings still more cuts in business investment and financial difficulties for the business sector. This is how capitalist economies produce mass unemployment, financial crises and recessions.

Keynes also described a second major source of instability associated with private investment activity. Precisely because private investments are highly risky propositions, financial markets have evolved to make this risk more manageable for any given investor. Through financial markets, investors can sell off their investments if they need or want to, converting their office buildings, factories and stock of machinery into cash much more readily than they could if they had to always find buyers on their own. But Keynes warned that when financial markets convert long-term assets into short-term commitments for investors, this also fosters a speculative mentality in the markets. What becomes central for investors is not whether a company's products will produce profits over a long term, but rather whether the short-term financial market investors *think* a company's fortunes will be strong enough in the present and immediate future to drive the stock price up. Or, to be more precise, what really matters for a speculative investor is not what they think about a given company's prospects per se, but rather what they think *other investors are thinking*, since that will be what determines where the stock price goes in the short term.

Because of this, the financial markets are highly susceptible to rumors, fads and all sorts of deceptive accounting practices, since all of these can help drive the stock price up in the present, regardless of what they accomplish in the longer term. Thus, if U.S. stock traders are convinced that Alan

Greenspan is a *maestro*, and if there is news that he is about to intervene with some kind of policy shift, then the rumor of Greenspan's policy shift can itself drive prices up, as the more nimble speculators try to keep one step ahead of the herd of Greenspan-philes.

Still, as with the Marx problem, it does not follow that the inherent instability of private investment and speculation in financial markets are uncontrollable, leading inevitably to persistent problems of mass unemployment and recession. But these social pathologies will become increasingly common through a neoliberal policy approach committed to minimimizing government interventions to stabilize investment.

The Polanyi problem

Karl Polanyi wrote his classic book *The Great Transformation* in the context of the 1930s depression, World War II and the developing worldwide competition with Communist governments. He was also reflecting on the 1920s, dominated, as with our current epoch, by a free-market ethos. Polanyi wrote of the 1920s that "economic liberalism made a supreme bid to restore the self-regulation of the system by eliminating all interventionist policies which interfered with the freedom of markets."[6]

Considering all of these experiences, Polanyi argued that for market economies to function with some modicum of fairness, they must be embedded in social norms and institutions that effectively promote broadly accepted notions of the common good. Otherwise, aquisitiveness and competition – the two driving forces of market economies – achieve overwhelming dominance as cultural forces, rendering life under capitalism a Hobbesian "war of all against all." This same idea is also central for Adam Smith himself, as should be evident from the quotation that opens this chapter. Smith showed how the invisible hand of self-interest and competition will yield higher levels of individual effort that increases the wealth of nations, but that it will also produce the corruption of our moral sentiments unless the market is itself governed at a fundamental level by norms of solidarity.

In the post-World War II period, various social democratic movements within the advanced capitalist economies adapted the Polanyi perspective. They argued in favor of government interventions to achieve three basic ends: stabilizing overall demand in the economy at a level that will provide for full employment; creating a financial market environment that is stable and conducive to the effective allocation of investment funds; and distributing equitably the rewards from high employment and a stable investment process. There were two basic means of achieving equitable distribution: relatively rapid wage growth, promoted by labor laws that were supportive of unions, minimum wage standards and similar interventions in labor markets; and welfare state policies, including progressive taxation and redistributive programs such as Social Security. The political ascendancy of these ideas was the basis for a dramatic increase in the role of government in the post-World War II capitalist economies. As one indicator of this, total government expenditures in the United States rose from 8 percent of GDP in 1913, to 21 percent in 1950, then to 38 percent by 1992. The International Monetary Fund and World Bank were also formed in the mid-1940s to advance such policy ideas throughout the world – that is, to implement policies virtually the opposite of those they presently favor. John Maynard Keynes himself was a leading intellectual force contributing to the initial design of the International Monetary Fund and World Bank.

But the implementation of a social democratic capitalism, guided by a commitment to full employment and the welfare state, did also face serious and persistent difficulties, and we need to recognize them as part of a consideration of the Marx, Keynes and Polanyi problems. In particular, many sectors of business opposed efforts to sustain full employment because, following the logic of the Marx problem, full employment provides greater bargaining power for workers in labor markets, even if it also increases the economy's total production of goods and services. Greater worker bargaining power can also create inflationary pressures because businesses will try to absorb their higher wage costs by raising prices. In addition, market-inhibiting financial regulations limit the capacity of financial market players to diversify their risk and speculate.

As we discuss further in Chapter 6, corporations in the U.S. and Western Europe were experiencing some combination of these problems associated with social democratic capitalism. In particular, they were faced with rising labor costs associated with low unemployment rates, which then led to either inflation, when corporations had the ability to pass on their higher labor costs to consumers; or to a squeeze on profits, when competitive pressures prevented corporations from raising their prices in response to the rising labor costs. These pressures were compounded by the two oil price "shocks" initiated by the Oil Producing Exporting Countries (OPEC) – an initial fourfold increase in the world price of oil in 1973 then a second fourfold price spike in 1979.

These were the conditions that by the end of the 1970s led to the decline of social democratic approaches to policymaking and the ascendancy of neoliberalism. The two leading signposts of this historic transition were the election in 1979 of Margaret Thatcher as Prime Minister of the United Kingdom and in 1980 of Ronald Reagan as President of the United States. Indeed, it was at this point that Mrs. Thatcher made her famous pronouncement that "there is no alternative" to neoliberalism.

This brings us to the contemporary era of smaller government, fiscal stringency and deregulation, i.e. to neoliberalism under Clinton, Bush and throughout the less developed world. It is worth emphasizing again that the issue is not a simple juxtaposition between either regulating or deregulating markets. Rather it is that markets have become deregulated to support the interests of business and financial markets, even as these same groups still benefit greatly from many forms of government support, including investment subsidies, tax concessions and rescue operations when financial crises get out of hand. At the same time, the deregulation of markets that favors business and finance is correspondingly the most powerful regulatory mechanism limiting the demands of workers, in that deregulation has been congruent with the worldwide expansion of the reserve army of labor and the declining capacity of national governments to implement full-employment macroeconomic policies – thereby exacerbating both the Marx and Keynes problems. The aim of this book, in short, is to show in specific ways how the Marx, Keynes and Polanyi problems have deepened under Clinton, Bush and neoliberal policies in the less developed countries, and to propose an alternative policy path that can reverse the contours of descent that we observe.

Economic growth, distribution and the environment

One major economic issue that I do not attempt to tackle in this book is the environment, even though the environmental policies of Clinton, Bush and, in the less developed economies, the World Bank, have produced severe problems. The main reason for not addressing environmental issues is that it is simply beyond the range of topics that I am able to reasonably handle.

But insofar as the book criticizes policies that lead to slower economic growth and advances proposals for accelerating growth, it would seem that, at a minimum, I should briefly acknowledge the environmental issues associated with growth. Of course, to begin with, any acceleration in the rate at which economies grow will produce environmental costs. But it is also true that such environmental costs could be greatly reduced through conscious policy initiatives – in particular, if governments recognize the process of accelerated economic growth as an opportunity to replace existing, dirtier production and transportation methods with cleaner technologies. As an obvious example, expanding urban transportation systems based on rail technologies rather than clogging the already overcrowded major cities with still more private cars would promote both economic growth and a cleaner environment.

But there is an additional important consideration here, which has been emphasized by the pioneering work of my University of Massachusetts colleague James Boyce, among others – that a more equal distribution of the rewards from growth will itself contribute to a more environmentally benign growth path. The basic argument Boyce makes is straightforward: most of the benefits of degrading the environment accrue to the wealthy, while most of the costs are borne by the middle class and, especially, working people and the poor. As one important case of this, Boyce considers the experience in the Philippines under President Ferdinand Marcos.

> During the two decades of Marcos' rule, the Phillipines' rich tropical hardwood forests were rapidly felled for timber, with little effort to minimize the environmental impacts of deforestation. Exports of logs and lumber ranked among the country's top foreign-exchange

earners until the early 1980s, when revenues collapsed due to the virtual depletion of economically accessible forests. [7]

Boyce's point is that if the benefits of timber exports in the Philippines had been more equitably distributed – as opposed to being hoarded by Marcos and his ruling clique – those benefits, for any given group, would not have been so large as to completely outweigh the costs of deforestation. The long-term imperatives of environmental protection would then have outweighed the immediate income gains through deforestation.

More generally, this example shows that there are ways through which accelerating economic growth, increasing equality and environmental sustainability can become convergent – and even mutually reinforcing – policy goals. Of course, there remains the rather large question of getting from here to there. This book does not pretend to answer that question *in toto*. But we at least attempt some small steps in the right direction.

CHAPTER TWO

Clintonomics: The Hollow Boom

"Watch what we do, not what we say."

— JOHN MITCHELL, ATTORNEY GENERAL UNDER PRESIDENT RICHARD NIXON

"It's the economy, stupid," was the one memorable slogan to have emerged out of Bill Clinton's successful first run at the Presidency in 1992, and it became the overarching theme of his full eight years in office. Clinton came into office pledging to end the economic stagnation that had enveloped the last two years of the Bush-1 administration and advance a program of "Putting People First" through large investments in job training, education and rebuilding the country's public infrastructure.

But Clinton's economic program changed drastically even during the two-month interregnum between his November election and his inauguration in January 1993, as Bob Woodward of the *Washington Post* documented in compelling detail in his first Washington insider book on economic policy, *The Agenda*. As reported by Woodward, Clinton himself acknowledged only weeks after winning the election that "We're Eisenhower Republicans here … . We stand for lower deficits, free trade, and the bond market. Isn't that great?" Clinton further conceded during this same time period that with his new policy focus "we help the bond market and we hurt the people who voted us in."[1]

Clinton never abandoned the idea that "it's the economy, stupid" should remain the watchwords of his Presidency. It was just that the "Putting People First" agenda of his 1992 campaign would have to yield top priority to the prerogatives of the financial markets and the wealthy. How could Clinton have undergone such a lightening reversal from the program on which he was elected to office? The answer was straightforward, and explained with unvarnished candor by Robert Rubin, who had been Co-Chair of the premier Wall Street firm Goldman Sachs before joining the Clinton administration and who was to become Clinton's most influential economic advisor and Treasury Secretary. Still during the interregnum before Clinton's first inauguration, Rubin pointed out to members of the more populist camp within the newly forming administration that the rich "are running the economy and make the decisions about the economy."[2]

What happened when Clinton put the agenda of the financial markets at the top of his administration's concerns? There is no doubt that dramatic departures from past U.S. economic trends did occur during the Clinton era, including the simultaneous fall of inflation and unemployment; the reversal of the federal budgetary situation from persistent deficits to three years of surplus at the end of Clinton's second term in office; and the unprecedented run-up in stock prices. But these developments can themselves be adequately understood only within a broader context that includes consideration of both Clinton's main policy initiatives and the overall performance of the economy in the Clinton years – including the macroeconomic performance, the performance of the financial markets, as well as what happened to "the people" of the abandoned "Putting People First" agenda. This chapter begins by examining Clinton's main initiatives in the areas of trade policy, regulation of labor and financial markets, and fiscal and monetary policy. With this overall policy environment as background, we then evaluate the economy's overall performance in the Clinton years. In Chapter 3, we sharpen the focus of the discussion, considering in detail the three dramatic departures during the Clinton years – the simultaneous fall of inflation and unemployment, the transition from fiscal deficits to surpluses; and the stock market bubble.[3]

Economic policy under Clinton

Trade policy

The Clinton administration's position on trade was virtually identical to that of its Republican predecessors, proclaiming the universal virtues of free trade and pushing for Presidential authority to negotiate so-called "fast track" agreements to further it, by-passing normal legislative scrutiny. Gestures towards labor or environmental concerns were almost completely empty of content, including his sound-bite sop to demonstrators amid the November 1999 World Trade Organization meetings in Seattle.[4]

The Clinton Administration's actual position on trade was set out in a full chapter of the *Economic Report of the President 1998* (ERP) which, under the rubric of "Benefits of Market Opening," rehearses the most unambiguous orthodox case for free trade. According to orthodox theory (i.e. the so-called "Hecksher-Ohlin model") all trading partners will utilize their existing economic resources more efficiently after having opened their economies to free trade. These efficiency gains are then compounded over time, producing a higher rate of productivity growth for all free-trading countries. Consumers in all countries benefit through the productivity gains, since greater efficiency in production is the key to making available more goods and services at both higher quality and lower prices.

Not surprisingly, the Clinton chapter ignores longstanding critiques of the assumptions behind the orthodox model, in particular its premises that both countries always operate at full employment and utilize the same techniques of production. Without these assumptions, it does not follow even within the logic of the orthodox model itself that all countries will necessarily benefit from trade opening. Consider, for example, trade between the United States and Mexico after NAFTA, once we allow for the possibility of unemployment in the United States. It then follows that U.S. workers could become unemployed when the firms that employ them are outcompeted by cheaper Mexican producers. Overall growth would then fall in the U.S., since fewer people are working. Similarly, if we allow that Mexican corn production techniques are far less efficient than those in the United States, it also follows that, after trade opens, Mexican agriculture will be out-competed, producing a loss of livelihood for millions of Mexican workers.[5] But even if we accept these assumptions of full employment and uniform production technologies among trading partners, the orthodox model itself still predicts that opening a country to free trade will produce losers as well as winners from trade *within* any given country. For example, the orthodox model is firm that once trade opens between a high-wage country like the U.S. and a low-wage country like Mexico, average wages in the U.S. would tend to fall as those in Mexico rise (due to "factor price equalization"). Thus, even the orthodox model makes clear that for free trade to promote fairness as well as efficiency, the losers from trade need to be compensated by the winners.

It is difficult to estimate reliably what the specific impact of NAFTA, or any other single trade agreement, has been on jobs and wages for average workers in the U.S., even while theory tells us that the general direction of the effect will be negative. But another question can be dependably answered: how much did the Clinton administration – consistent with the orthodox trade theory it espoused – compensate workers on the losing end of trade opening? Rhetorical flourishes aside, it provided almost no compensatory support.[6] Rather, the 1998 ERP reiterates mainstream arguments that trade is not primarily responsible for either the long-run wage stagnation for most American workers or the increased differentials between high- and low-wage workers. It instead attributes rising inequality in the labor force to "skill-biased technological change", as the introduction of new, computer-based processes creates wage premia for workers able to handle them, while depressing the income of workers unable to do so. David Howell of the New School University has demonstrated fundamental flaws in this view, showing that increased wage inequality is actually more a reflection of social and institutional, rather than technological, changes – in particular, the steady weakening of American trade unions and growing hostility of American labor laws to the concerns of working people.[7] It follows that even if the Clinton administration had failed to address losses to U.S. workers from its trade policies, it could still have compensated them with labor market policies and measures to redistribute income. What was its record in these areas?

Labor market policy
The short answer is that the Clinton administration did almost nothing to advance the interests of organized labor or working people more generally. Long-time labor journalist David Moberg commented in 1999, "Clinton has probably identified less with organized labor than any Democratic president this century."[8] Of course, since the AFL-CIO is a permanent electoral prop of any Democratic candidate to the Presidency, its concerns cannot be

completely disregarded in the Republican manner. Clinton thus supported a two-step rise in the minimum wage in 1996–97, from $4.25 to $5.15, the rate at which it remained for the rest of the Clinton presidency (and, indeed, at the time of writing in March 2003). But this modest increment did little to reverse the precipitous fall in the real value of the minimum wage. In 1996 the real value of the $4.25 rate was more than 40 percent below its peak buying-power in 1968. When Clinton left office in January 2001, the minimum wage was at $5.15, still 35 percent below its peak real value in 1968 even though the economy had become 81 percent more productive between 1968 and 2000.[9] Clinton supporters argue that they compensated for the decline in the minimum wage through an increase in the Earned Income Tax Credit (EITC) program, which is a program of direct government income supports to low-wage workers and their families. We will examine Clinton's initiatives with the EITC program below, in the context of federal tax policies and changes in the national poverty rate.

Still focusing on labor market policies, the administration also claimed the Family and Medical Leave Act of August 1993 as a major accomplishment. The law requires employers with 50 or more employees within a 75-mile area to offer 12 weeks of unpaid leave per year for employees who have worked for the company at least 1,250 hours within the past year. Leave can be taken for health problems, the birth or adoption of a child or care for a family member. The exact boundaries of these grounds were poorly defined, as were also the conditions that employers may impose on them. For example, it was not clear whether companies could require that employees use up their sick and vacation days before taking advantage of the act. In the area of worker training, billed as a central plank of Clinton's 1992 campaign pledge to "Put People First," the Workforce Investment Act of August 1998 consolidated the forty-odd federal training programs, introduced vouchers for workers to pay for private training and created a nationwide jobs database.

Clinton proposed a Striker Replacement Act in March 1993. This would have barred companies from permanently replacing strikers in disputes over working conditions (temporary replacements and strikes over pay were not to be affected). But the administration made only token efforts to build support for this measure. Not surprisingly, it failed in Congress, receiving fewer votes in the

Senate than a similar bill under the Bush-1 administration. However, in perhaps the best example of the President's gesture politics, in March 1995 Clinton signed an executive order barring federal contracts of over $100,000 to companies that had permanently replaced striking workers. Initially the Senate threatened to block the order, but in the end it desisted, perhaps persuaded by reported administration claims that virtually no major contractors would be affected. In February 1996 the order was struck down by the District of Columbia circuit court of appeals, and the issue was dropped. During the year it was nominally in effect, not one contract was cancelled under the directive.

On the more favorable side, Clinton did veto cuts in funding for the National Labor Relations Board and Occupational Safety and Health Administration, and a bill that would have effectively legalized company unions. Appointments to the National Labor Relations Board were more congenial to trade union leaders than before. But the overall record of the administration on issues directly affecting working people was thin indeed, especially given its unqualified support for free trade in the face of labor's opposition. It should not be surprising that union membership continued its long decline during the Clinton presidency, standing at 13.5 percent of the total workforce when he left office in January 2001, more than three full percentage points below the 16.8 percent that prevailed in 1988, Ronald Reagan's last year in office. About 4.4 million more workers would have been union members when Clinton left office had the national unionisation rate only remained at the level under Reagan in 1988.

Taxation and federal expenditures

Taxation

Clinton's tax policies lessened the highly regressive effects of the Reagan–Bush years. However, the relative burden of taxation was still more regressive when Clinton left office than in 1979, prior to Reagan's 1980 election. The omnibus Budget Reconciliation Act of 1993, which raised taxes by $240.4 billion over 5 years, increased the levy on incomes over $140,000 from 30 to 36 percent, with an additional 10 percent surcharge for incomes over $250,000. It also included a higher gasoline tax, elimination of the cap on income subject to Medicare hospital insurance tax, and a substantial extension of the Earned Income Tax Credit (EITC) program. Under the EITC, which began in the Ford admin-

TABLE 2.1: Estimated effective federal tax rates on 2001 income under prevailing tax law, 1979, 1989 and 1997

	Percentage-point change	
Income group	1979–89	1989–97
Bottom four-fifths	-0.1	-0.9
First	+0.4	-2.9
Second	+0.2	-0.4
Third	-0.6	-0.1
Fourth	+0.1	+0.2
Top fifth	-2.7	+2.6
81–95 pct.	-3.8	+3.2
96–99 pct.	-5.2	+3.9
Top 1 pct.	-9.1	+5.1
All	-1.0	+1.5

Source: Mishel, Bernstein and Boushey *State of Working America 2002*, Washington: Economic Policy Institute

istration and has been supported by both Republican and Democratic administrations since, employed workers become eligible for a tax credit if their wages produce less than a certain threshold level of income to support their family.

Clinton's second major piece of tax legislation was the Taxpayer Relief Act of 1997, which reduced taxes by $290 billion over 10 years – that is, reducing by half the revenue gains scheduled in the 1993 Act. The new law combined a range of child and education tax credits with lower taxes on inheritance and capital gains. Calculations by the Citizens for Tax Justice estimate that the net effect of the 1997 Act was to reduce taxes for the upper 60 percent of the population, with the great bulk of the cuts going to the top 20 percent.

Lawrence Mishel, Jared Bernstein and Heather Boushey of the Economic Policy Institute, drawing from Congressional Budget Office data, compared the total impact of the Clinton program with the Reagan record by analysing the federal tax rates of households at 2001 income levels, under the tax laws that prevailed in 1979 (pre-Reagan), 1989 (Reagan) and 1997 (Clinton after implementation of his last major tax initiative). Table 2.1 summarizes their main findings.

As the table shows, between 1979–89, the bottom 80 percent of households experienced a slight 0.1 percent decline in their tax obligations, and a somewhat bigger decline of 0.9 percent between 1989–97. Most of the tax reductions under Clinton were concentrated among the least well-off 20 percent of households, who experienced a 2.9 percent decline in their fiscal burden – a drop primarily due to the increased income supplements channelled through the Earned Income Tax Credit. Correspondingly, the richest 20 percent of households experienced a decline in their tax rates of 2.7 percent between 1979–89 that was reversed under Clinton when their rates rose by 2.6 percent between 1989–97. By far the biggest swing here was among the top 1 percent, who experienced a 9.1 percent tax cut between 1979–89 and a 5.1 percent tax increase in the period 1989–97. Thus the Clinton administration did restore part of the progressive dimension of the tax system that was lost in the 1980s, but not all of it.

Expenditures

The overriding objective of the Clinton administration was to bring government expenditures down, in line with its broader macroeconomic priority of deficit reduction. The extent of the spending cuts is set out in Table 2.2, which shows federal government expenditure patterns between 1992, the last year of the Bush-1 administration, and 2000. Total expenditures fell as a percentage of GDP from 21.9 to 18.1 percent between these years, a decline of 17.1 percent. The most significant reduction slashed military spending from 4.7 to 3.0 percent of GDP, a drop of 36.7 percent. But there have been large cuts in other areas as well, including support for education (-23.9 percent), science (-19.1 percent), income security (-17.6 percent) and transportation (-10 percent).

The reductions in military spending, of course, reflected the end of the Cold War and consequent expectation of a widespread 'peace dividend'. While the cuts were substantial, what is more remarkable is that the annual military budget should have remained at $300 billion, after the Cold War justification for an exorbitant arms race evaporated. Spending on arms remained 5.5 times greater than federal outlays on education. It was also triple the proportion of spending relative to GDP as prevailed in the 1930s, the last decade prior to World War II and the Cold War era (and in a period when GDP was historically low). The fact is that, insofar as the end of the Cold War yielded any peace dividend under Clinton, it took the

TABLE 2.2: Federal expenditures by function 1992–2000

	Percentage of GDP		Percent change,
	1992	2000	1992–2000
Total expenditures	*21.87*	*18.12*	*-17.1*
Defense	4.72	2.99	-36.7
Social Security	4.56	4.15	-9.0
Interest	3.15	2.26	-28.2
Income Security	3.12	2.57	-17.6
Medicare	1.88	2.00	+6.4
Health	1.41	1.56	+10.6
Education	0.71	0.54	-23.9
Veterans	0.54	0.48	-11.1
Transportation	0.52	0.47	-9.6
Agriculture	0.24	0.37	+54.2
Natural Resources	0.32	0.25	-21.9
Justice	0.22	0.28	+27.3
Science	0.25	0.19	-24.0
International	0.25	0.17	-32.0

Source: OMB, Budget of the United States, Historical Tables

form of an overall decrease in the size of the federal government rather than an increase in federal support for any of the programs supposedly cherished by Clinton, such as better education, improved worker training, or poverty alleviation.

The administration's extension of the Earned Income Tax Credit was its most significant anti-poverty initiative. When the EITC program originated under Ford's Republican administration in 1975, it covered 6.2 million families for an average income supplement (in 2001 dollars) of $661 per family. The program expanded under Carter, Reagan and Bush alike (1978, 1984, 1986, 1990). By 1992, the last year of the Bush administration, it covered 14.1 million families, who received an average income supplement of $1,169 (2001 dollars). By 2000 Clinton's add-on had extended it to an estimated 19.2 million tax filers – covering now to a lesser extent individuals and couples without children as well as families – for an average supplement of $1,728 (2001 dollars).[10]

But against this EITC enlargement must be set the dismantling of welfare assistance programs – what had been called Aid to Families with Dependent

Children (AFDC), and is now termed Temporary Assistance for Needy Families (TANF). Thus, while total outlays for EITC rose (in 2001 dollars) by $17.5 billion, from $9.3 to $26.8 billion between 1992–2000, spending on "family support" grew by only $2.1 billion, from $19.1 to $21.2 billion, after having actually fallen in real dollars for most of Clinton's presidency. Moreover, expenditure on Food Stamps and other Nutritional Assistance dropped by $8.5 billion, from $37.2 to $28.8 billion between 1992–2000 – a decline reflecting a large increase in the percentage of households who are not receiving food assistance even though their income level is low enough for them to qualify. Under Clinton's presidency, the decline in the number of people receiving food stamps – 9.8 million – was 17 percent greater than the decline in the number of people officially defined as impoverished, and was accompanied by a dramatic increase in the pressure on private soup kitchens and food pantries.

While the full explanation for the fall in public food assistance under Clinton is not entirely clear, it appears that a major factor was his campaign to "end welfare as we know it." The official attack on dependency led both to a greater stigma in receiving public assistance, and to greater difficulties in securing food stamps. When the pre-Clinton welfare system was still functioning, a high proportion of recipients took their food stamps and cash assistance at the same time.[11]

Clinton's defenders, of course, would reply that his administration had replaced a bad program – welfare – with a good one, because the EITC creates incentives for work and does not discourage parents from living as a family unit. And while the EITC does correct some of the failings of the old welfare system, it has created new, and equally serious problems. Moving poor and unskilled women from welfare onto the labor market exerts downward pressure on wages, and the national minimum wage itself is still too low to allow even a full-time worker to keep just herself and only one child above the official poverty line. In addition, a single woman in this position will receive EITC to supplement her wage income, but she will also now have to pay for child care and receive less support from food assistance programs. When operating in conjunction with a below-poverty minimum wage as under Clinton, the EITC thus becomes a means of allowing businesses to continue offering such destitution wages, while shifting onto taxpayers the costs of alleviating the poverty of even those holding full-time jobs.[12]

Macroeconomic and financial market regulatory policies

Shortly after Clinton won office in 1992, as Bob Woodward documented in *The Agenda*, the focus of fiscal and monetary policies became deficit reduction. Despite attaining a balanced budget in 1997, Clinton persisted with stringent fiscal policies, with the stated aim of reducing and even eliminating outstanding federal debt. The federal government then ran surpluses from 1998–2000. Such fiscal stringency is supposed to produce lower interest rates, through two mechanisms: a reduction in the demand for scarce credit by the public sector; and freeing the Federal Reserve to pursue a looser monetary policy. The lower interest rates, in turn, are intended to stimulate a private investment-led growth process.

Relative to the fiscal policy posture, monetary policy was relaxed in Alan Greenspan's tenure during the Clinton Presidency. The Fed was willing to see unemployment fall well below what inflation hawks had long advised was prudent. At the same time, as we discuss more below, Greenspan was vigilant in preventing workers' wage demands from gaining significant upward momentum. And despite the Fed's accommodative posture relative to the unemployment rate, interest rates still remained well above historical levels. At least in part, the Fed contributed to maintaining these high rates to discourage foreign asset holders from taking funds outside U.S. credit markets.

There were three other major components of macro, monetary and financial regulatory policy, all of them closely bound up with the treatment of speculative financial markets. The first was its lender of last resort bailout operations. These were led by Alan Greenspan, just as they were in the Bush-1 administration, notably during the Wall Street crash of 1987. But the Clinton Treasury team of Robert Rubin and Lawrence Summers contributed to executing bailouts during both the 1994–45 Mexico and 1997–98 East Asian financial crises. They also led the bailout in 1998 of Long-Term Capital Management, the huge hedge fund that crashed dramatically despite being directed by two Nobel Laureates in financial economics and other Wall Street luminaries. These interventions succeeded, both in the sense of having prevented a disastrous cascading collapse of private credit markets, but also, correspondingly, of having protected the material interests of wealthy investors operating in these markets. At the same time, these bailouts contributed to validating the speculative financial behavior characteristic of these markets, setting the stage for further speculative excess, which, as we now know, fostered the conditions for financial collapse under Bush.

The second major component of Clinton administration policy in this area was supporting the successful repeal of the Depression-era Glass-Steagall framework of financial regulation through the 1999 Financial Services Modernization Act, otherwise known as Gramm-Leach-Bliley.[13] Dismantlement of Glass-Steagall, *de facto* and *de jure*, had been long in the making. Innovative financial market players were easily circumventing this old regulatory apparatus, with its focus on creating firewalls between segments of the financial services industry, and preventing commercial banks from operating in more than one state. But the point is that an alternative to both Glass-Steagall and complete deregulation could have been devised, through some combination of policies such as taxing speculative financial transactions and establishing lower reserve requirements for loans that finance productive, as against speculative, investments.[14] But the Clinton administration never considered such an approach. Quite the contrary. The 2001 *Economic Report of the President*, the last one written under Clinton, was unequivocal in dismissing Glass-Steagall and touting the virtues of financial deregulation:

> Given the massive financial instability of the 1930s, narrowing the range of banks' activities was arguably important for that day and age. But those rules are not needed today, and the easing of interstate banking rules, along with the passage of the Financial Services Modernization Act of 1999 have removed them, while maintaining appropriate safeguards. These steps allow consolidation in the financial sector that will result in efficiency gains and provide new services for consumers (p. 47).

Moreover, Robert Rubin, a major Clinton administration force behind the Glass-Steagall repeal, was also among the first to benefit personally from it, in moving from his Treasury position to co-direct the newly merged investment/commercial banking conglomerate Citigroup. Under any reasonable interpretation of Glass-Steagall, the former commercial bank Citicorp and the former investment banking firm Travelers would not have been permitted to merge.

Finally, there were the actions not taken to slow financial speculation while even Alan Greenspan himself was clear as early as 1996 that a potentially dangerous bubble was forming in the U.S. stock market. In recently released minutes of the Federal Reserve's main policy-making committee's meeting on September 24, 1996, Greenspan acknowledges that he would be able to control what he himself had termed the market's "irrational exuberance" through imposing so-called "margin requirements" on borrowing used by market speculators. Through margin requirements, market speculators who borrow money to purchase stocks are forced to carry a percentage of this new debt as cash with their brokers. Greenspan could have therefore raised the cost of borrowing for stock market speculators if he had imposed margin requirements in 1996. Greenspan has no doubt that imposing significant margin requirements could succeed at cooling the market, stating at the meeting "I guarantee that if you want to get rid of the bubble...this will do it." But Greenspan, like Clinton, was not willing to confront Wall Street. Instead, the Clinton administration and the Fed presented a united front in advancing across-the-board financial deregulation in the name of market efficiency and modernization.[15]

Economic performance under Clinton

However the Clinton administration may have jiggered economic policy, economic performance in the United States under Clinton was widely hailed as an unqualified success.[16] But looking at some basic indicators in a comparative historical perspective, presented in Tables 2.3–2.8 below, we observe a much more mixed picture. There have been some significant departures from historic trends. But, given the center-right direction of policy under Clinton, it should not be surprising that their benefits were skewed toward the wealthy. Moreover, virtually all the economic achievements of the Clinton years were dependent on the historically unprecedented stock market bubble, whose subsequent collapse began almost immediately after Clinton left office.

Macro performance

Table 2.3 presents some basic macro statistics – GDP growth, productivity, un-employment and inflation. The data are grouped by presidential eras – I have combined Kennedy/Johnson, Nixon/Ford and Reagan/Bush, as well as show-ing the Carter and Clinton years separately. Separately, in Appendix 1, I group the same data according to NBER business cycles, as a check on the reliability of presidential eras as a measure of economic trends. As becomes clear, no signifi-cant differences emerge in any of the macro patterns, regardless of whether one groups periods by presidential terms or through the more formal categories of NBER cycles.

These indicators make it clear that the Clinton years were not unusually successful in historical terms. Most strikingly, the Clinton period did not ap-proach the macro performance of the Kennedy/Johnson era, when both GDP (4.8 vs. 3.7 percent) and productivity growth (3.4 vs. 1.9 percent) increased much more rapidly than under Clinton, while average unemployment (4.8 vs. 5.2 per-cent) was also lower. The rate of inflation under Clinton did fall to a level close to that of the Kennedy/Johnson years (2.0 for Kennedy/Johnson vs. 2.6 for Clinton). Inflation also declined over time under Clinton, whereas it took off towards the end of Johnson's Presidency. Of course, a decline in inflation in itself does not tell us much about who gains or loses from it. It might indicate slack labour markets of no benefit to wage-earners, a topic we take up in more detail below.

Judged by less rigorous standards than the 1960s, the macroeconomic record of the Clinton years does compare favorably with those of Nixon/Ford, Carter and Reagan/Bush. GDP growth was higher and both unemployment and inflation were lower. Productivity growth was still slow, even relative to the Nixon/Ford years. But the overall performance of the American economy was stronger, if not to a dramatic degree. Clinton's tenure, of course, was embel-lished by the circumstance that no recession occurred during his Presidency.[17] If, from the supplemental tables shown in Appendix 1, we consider the relative performance of the economy in the full business cycle of 1991–2000 against its predecessors, this most recent cycle does not stand out relative to either the 1970s or the 1980–90 cycle, and looks still worse relative to the 1960–69 cycle. In short, it is hard to make a serious case that the U.S. economy in the 1990s was unusually robust once we take account of the 1990–91 recession. Of course,

TABLE 2.3: Macroeconomic performance indicators *(percentages)*

	1961–68 Kennedy/ Johnson	1969–76 Nixon/ Ford	1977–80 Carter	1981–92 Reagan/ Bush	1993–2000 Clinton
GDP real growth (pct.)	4.8	2.7	3.4	2.9	3.7
Productivity growth (pct. for non-farm business sector)	3.4	2.1	0.5	1.7	1.9
Unemployment rate (pct.)	4.8	5.8	6.5	7.1	5.2
Inflation rate (pct. measured by CPI)	2.0	6.4	9.7	4.6	2.6

Source: National Income and Product Accounts (NIPA); Bureau of Labor Statistics

supporters of Clinton would claim that his ability to avoid a recession since 1993 was a major accomplishment in itself. But this claim loses force given that a recession began almost immediately after Clinton left office.

Clinton supporters also correctly point out that even if the overall eight-year record might not have been exceptional according to these indicators, the figures look far better when focusing on 1995–2000 alone, the last five years of the Clinton presidency. As Table 2.4 shows, GDP and productivity both grew substantially faster from 1995–2000 than the early Clinton years, while unemployment and inflation were both lower. Indeed, aside from the stock market boom, it is the performance over 1995–2000 for these macro indicators that formed the basis for claims that a New Economy emerged during Clinton's presidency.

Is there substance behind these New Economy claims? The year 2001 was obviously not kind to the New Economy contention that both the stock market and labor market had permanently transcended their Old Economy cyclical patterns, given that the stock market collapse and rise in unemployment were both prominent features of the 2001 cyclical downturn. But the question does still remain as to whether the remarkable advances in infor-

TABLE 2.4: Two phases of macroeconomic performance under Clinton

	1993–95	1996–2000
GDP real growth (pct.)	3.1	4.1
Productivity growth (pct. for non-farm business sector)	0.9	2.5
Unemployment rate (pct.)	6.2	4.6
Inflation rate (pct. measured by CPI)	2.8	2.5

Source: National Income and Product Accounts (NIPA); Bureau of Labor Statistics

mation technologies between 1995–2000 – especially the widespread commercialization of the Internet – had indeed created a sustainable upward ratcheting in productivity, and that this productivity advance would be the wellspring for long-term improvements in economic performance. Does this claim for the New Economy hold up better than the others?

As of the end of the Clinton administration, *The Economist* magazine reported that "a consensus emerged among most economists, including those at America's Federal Reserve...that America's structural rate of productivity growth had increased to around three percent." *The Economist* reported later that Alan Greenspan himself had endorsed the New Economy view that long-term productivity growth in the U.S. had risen to a three percent average annual rate.[18]

Between 1973–94 U.S. productivity growth averaged 1.5 percent. The difference between a 1.5 percent average productivity growth rate over a long period of time and a "New Economy" rate of 3 percent may seem small. However, due to the powers of compounding, the difference is actually formidably large. If an economy that produces $100 of goods and services in one year improves productivity by 1.5 percent per year for 10 years, that means that it will produce $116 by the tenth year. But if productivity grows by 3 percent per year, the economy will produce $134 ten years later. In other words, after only ten years, the economy improving its productivity by 3 percent per year becomes 17 percent richer than the economy whose productivity is growing by only 1.5 percent.

Indeed, if it is true that the U.S. has shifted to a new long-term productivity growth path of 3 percent per year resulting from the New Economy effects of information technology, this would mean that the impact of information technology on long-term productivity in the U.S. would substantially exceed all previous major technical innovations of the twentieth century, including the spread of electrical power and automobiles in the 1920s, which together brought the average rate of productivity growth to only 2.5 percent.[19] However, contrary to this position, Robert Gordon of Northwestern University has argued that virtually all of the increases in productivity between 1995–2000 occurred in the manufacturing of computer hardware. Gordon argues that "there has been no productivity acceleration in the 99 percent of the economy located outside the sector which manufacturers computer hardware."[20]

We certainly cannot resolve this debate here. But it is easy to be skeptical about the Clinton administration economists' own explanation as to the underlying sources of the 1995–2000 surge in productivity and what they regard as the factors needed to maintain a New Economy pattern of productivity growth. In the 2001 *Economic Report of the President*, the last such document authored by Clinton economists, the Clintonites argue that the productivity gains of 1995–2000 were not due solely to the introduction of the new information technologies itself, but that changes in business practices and government policies were also crucial contributors. Among the business practices, they single out the switch to compensating business executives with stock options rather than salaries as an efficiency-enhancing force driving firms to embrace new technologies. In the same vein, they cite the deregulation of financial markets as a factor promoting efficiency among private businesses. In fact, of course, both of these changes were prominent features of the stock market bubble – hardly solid foundations, in other words, for a long-term upward ratcheting of productivity growth.

But the Clintonites' arguments aside, some significant longer-term increases in productivity are likely to emerge as information technologies continue to be diffused through the economy. The 5/12/01 survey of recent research by *The Economist* magazine reaches the plausible conclusion that productivity is more likely to grow at an average rate of between 2.0 and 2.25 percent in the foreseeable future rather than the 1.5 percent rate that it experienced from 1973–94.

But even if such gains do emerge, the role of Clinton administration policies can hardly be cited as a major contributing force, especially if these contributions are indeed tied, as the 2001 *Economic Report of the President* claims, to such factors as the deregulation of financial markets.

Changing composition of GDP

Further perspective on the macroeconomic record of the Clinton years is offered by Table 2.5, showing the breakdown of GDP into component expenditure categories – consumption, government, investment, and net exports. Two sets of figures stand out here. The first we have already noted – the substantial contraction of government spending, which at 18.2 percent of GDP is far below that of any of the previous presidential periods we are considering. What we also see in Table 2.5 is that the slack created by the fall in public expenditure was taken up mainly by consumption, which, at 67.1 percent of GDP, is more than 5 percentage points higher than during the Kennedy/Johnson boom. It is clear from these figures that the rise in consumer spending was the primary driving force of aggregate demand under the full Clinton presidency, allowing government expenditures to fall without generating a slowdown in overall growth. The figures also show that private investment also grew relative to GDP under Clinton. The increase in private investment over the full Clinton period, to 16.4 percent of GDP, was only moderate relative to the 16.1 percent under Reagan/Bush-1. But this full-period figure does not capture an important factor, which, again, was the sharp rise in the investment share of GDP as the Clinton years proceeded. Thus, in 1993, the investment share was at 14.4 percent of GDP, but by 2000, the figure had risen to 17.9 percent. Overall then, the boom years under Clinton were fueled first by the sustained increase in private consumption, and second by a private investment boom. Both of these forces have broader ramifications for understanding both the boom and the bust.

Financial market behavior

The most dramatic economic change of the Clinton presidency has been the transformation of the country's financial structure by the stock market boom and shifts associated with it. Table 2.6 provides some indication of what has

TABLE 2.5: Components of GDP *(in percentages)*

	1961–68 Kennedy/ Johnson	1969–76 Nixon/ Ford	1977–80 Carter	1981–92 Reagan/ Bush	1993–2000 Clinton
Consumption	61.7	62.2	62.6	64.9	67.1
Government	22.4	21.9	20.0	20.6	18.2
Investment	15.5	15.9	18.2	16.1	16.4
Net exports	0.4	-0.05	-0.9	-1.6	-1.7

Source: National Income and Product Accounts (NIPA); Economagic web page

been involved. During the Kennedy/Johnson and Reagan/Bush periods, the Standard and Poor index of the stock prices of the top 500 companies in the economy (S&P 500) rose at a rapid annual rate (after controlling for inflation), 6.8 percent under Kennedy/Johnson and 9.4 percent under Reagan/Bush. During the Nixon/Ford and Carter years, the S&P 500 actually fell in real terms. Under Clinton, it registered an annual growth rate of 15.3 per cent that has no historical precedent.

The performance of the stock market under Clinton becomes even more astounding when measured against GDP during the various presidential eras. In theory, fluctuations in stock prices over a full business cycle are supposed to reflect the underlying performance of the real economy. Thus, by measuring the difference between growth of the S&P 500 and GDP, we can observe the extent to which the stock market is responding to real economic developments. Here again, the Clinton experience is without precedent. Since 1993 the rise in stock prices has been 11.6 percent above that of the real economy. Even in the Reagan and Bush years, during which economic policy overwhelmingly favored the prerogatives of capital, and financial capital in particular, stock prices rose only 6.5 percent faster than GDP.

Table 2.6 also presents some data on changes in household financial patterns during the Clinton boom. The third row of figures suggests the degree to which the consumption boom was debt financed. Household debt – including mortgage and consumer debt – ratcheted upward dramatically during Clinton's tenure, to reach 97.4 percent of disposable income. This compares with a ratio

TABLE 2.6: Financial market indicators

	1961–68 Kennedy/ Johnson	1969–76 Nixon/ Ford	1977–80 Carter	1981–92 Reagan/ Bush	1993–2000 Clinton
S&P 500 real average annual growth rate (pct.)	6.8	–5.1	–5.5	+9.4	+15.3
S&P 500 real growth minus GDP real growth (pct. gap)	+2.0	–7.9	–8.8	+6.5	+11.6
Total household debt/disposable personal income (pct.)	68.0	66.3	71.4	79.0	97.4
Total household debt/financial assets (pct.)	17.5	19.5	22.5	23.7	22.5
Household bank deposits plus govt. securities/total financial assets (pct.)	23.0	25.2	26.4	26.2	17.7
Corporations' internal funds/total debt (pct.)	16.9	12.7	11.7	10.5	9.8
Corporations' debt/equity (pct.)	57.5	97.1	165.7	159.2	83.1
Real interest rate (10-year Treasury bond minus CPI rate)	2.4	0.7	–0.5	5.3	3.6

Source: Economagic web site; Flow-of-Funds Accounts

of 79.0 percent during the Reagan/Bush years, itself an unprecedented level compared with previous periods. The next row, showing household debt relative to total financial assets, indicates how this expansion of debt was collateralized – by a rise in asset values rather than incomes. Thus, we see that the households' debt/financial asset ratio actually fell slightly during the Clinton presidency, even while the debt/income ratio was shooting up. But the composition of household assets also changed markedly. Traditionally, property-owners have maintained a steady share of their holdings in insured bank deposits and non-defaultable Treasury securities – prior to the Clinton period, somewhere between 23-26 percent. Under Clinton, this "safe asset" proportion fell to 17.7 percent, a sharp departure from previous patterns.[21]

Table 2.6 next shows some figures on corporate financial patterns. In row 6, we see that under Clinton, corporations internal funds – their flow of available new funds from after-tax profits and allowances for depreciation of operating equipment – fell to a low of 9.8 percent relative to corporation's total debt. In other words, as with households, corporations were carrying unprecedented levels of debt in this period relative to the income and depreciation allowances they were generating from selling products. But here again, parallel to the households' situation, the next row of data shows that corporate debt *fell* in this same period relative to the value of corporate equity – the debt/equity ratio was at 159.2 percent under Reagan/Bush but only 83.1 percent under Clinton. As we see, the Kennedy/Johnson era was the only one in which the corporate debt/equity ratio was lower. But this was also a time when corporate internal funds were at a peak relative to their debt burden. The overall point is that the heavy corporate debt load in the Clinton years, like that for households, was collateralized on the basis of the stock market boom.

Finally Table 2.6 reports figures on real interest rates for ten-year Treasury bonds. It shows that rates did fall in the Clinton period relative to Reagan/Bush years, from an average of 5.3 to 3.6 percent. But the 3.7 percent rate under Clinton is still far higher than the level of any previous presidential era. Indeed, for the 1961-80 period prior to Reagan, the average real Treasury rate was 1.1 percent, less than a third of its level in the Clinton period.[22] These figures make it difficult to argue that the sharp increase in household and corporate debt under Clinton was a response to low interest rates. The reality is that rates were low under Clinton only relative to the unprecedented peaks of the Reagan/Bush years: they were high by any other historical benchmark. Moreover, the basic justification of the Clinton administration for its drive to eliminate the federal deficit was that this alone could cut interest rates dramatically, by reducing total demand for credit and enabling the Federal Reserve to pursue a looser monetary policy. In practice, however, rates fell relative to the Reagan/Bush years, when federal deficits soared, but

TABLE 2.7: Real wage trends

	1961–68 Kennedy/ Johnson	1969–76 Nixon/ Ford	1977–80 Carter	1981–92 Reagan/ Bush	1993–2000 Clinton
Average wage for non-supervisory workers (in 2001 dollars)	$13.60	$15.14	$15.03	$13.91	$13.60
Average wage for 10th percent decile (in 2001 dollars)	—	$6.67 *(data begin in 1973)*	$6.86	$6.17	$6.11
Ratio of 90th/10th percent decile wages	—	3.7 *(data begin in 1973)*	3.6	4.2	4.4

Source: Bureau of Labor Statistics; Mishel, Bernstein, and Boushey (2002)
Note: Wage data for decile groupings begins in 1973.

remained historically high despite the attainment of fiscal surpluses for three years. The claim that government deficits alone were responsible for high real interest rates of the 1980s clearly needs to be rethought.

Conditions for workers and the poor

Tables 2.7 and 2.8 provide some summary measures of how working people and the poor fared during Clinton's presidency. Both the real wage and poverty trends are highly unfavourable to Clinton within the historical context we are considering.

Real wages

Despite the relatively strong macro performance driven by the stock market boom, both the average wages for non-supervisory workers and the earnings of those in the lowest 10 percent decile of the wage distribution not only remained well below those of the Nixon/Ford and Carter administrations,

FIGURE 2.1: Average real wages and productivity level in the United States, 1960-2000

(wages are average hourly earnings, in 2001 dollars, for nonsupervisory workers in private sector)

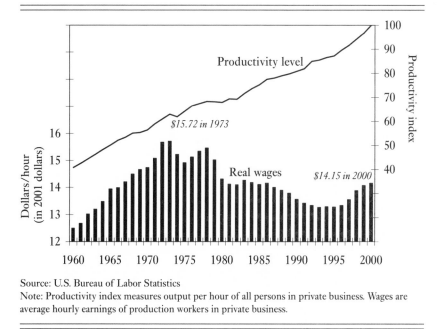

Source: U.S. Bureau of Labor Statistics

Note: Productivity index measures output per hour of all persons in private business. Wages are average hourly earnings of production workers in private business.

but were actually lower even than those of the Reagan/Bush years. We see this in Table 2.7. Moreover, wage inequality – as indicated in the table by the ratio of the 90th to 10th wage decile – increased sharply during Clinton's tenure in office, even relative to the Republican heyday of the eighties.

Still, as the table also shows, the pattern of real wage decline in the U.S. did not begin with Clinton. Where it did began and how the movement of real wages has proceeded becomes clearer in Figure 2.1, which gives the year-by-year data for both real wages and productivity between 1960–2000. As the figure shows, average real wages in the U.S. rose sharply, indeed faster than productivity, from 1960 to 1973, the year of the first oil crisis and the final breakup of the Bretton Woods system of international financial regulations.

From 1974 onward, real wages followed a long downtrend with only brief and shallow interruptions. Moreover, as the figure shows, this decline in wages from a peak of $15.70 in 1973 to a trough of $13.27 in 1993 was occurring while productivity in the economy was increasing year by year, virtually without interruption. Indeed, by 1993, the economy was 36 percent more productive than it was in 1973, even while the average real wage had fallen by 15 percent. It is true that the *rate of growth* of *productivity gains* did slow after 1973. But there still was positive productivity growth over this period of declining real wages. Paul Krugman, the well-known Princeton economist and *New York Times* columnist has asserted "Economic history offers no example of a country that experienced long-term productivity growth without a roughly equal rise in real wages." In fact, as Figure 2.1 makes evident, we need not search the dark recesses of economic history, but rather only the experience in the U.S. between 1973–93, to find one major violation of Krugman's claim.[23]

Thus, Clinton came into office in 1993 with real wages at a forty-year low and with the gap between the average real wage and the economy's productivity level at a peak. No further declines in real wages occurred from 1993–96, Clinton's first full term. But there was also almost no upward movement in wages from this forty-year low even while, again, productivity rose every year through 1996.

From 1997–99, real wages did rise sharply for three consecutive years, something that had not happened since the 1960s. The basic explanation for this is straightforward. In 1997, the unemployment rate fell below five percent for the first full year since 1969, then continued to fall further, to 4.2 percent, by 1999. Meanwhile, productivity growth was also accelerating in this period. Businesses thus needed more workers to keep up with the boom, and workers bargaining power finally began to rise as a result. However, the fact that the real wage increase was tied closely to the strong improvements in both unemployment and productivity means that the real wage gains were also, in turn, largely a result of the stock market bubble. As we have discussed, the stock market aside, the Clinton administration accomplished almost nothing in the way of labor laws or the broader policy environment to improve the bargaining situation for workers.

TABLE 2.8: Individual poverty rates *(in percentages of population)*

1961–68 Kennedy/ Johnson	1969–76 Nixon/ Ford	1977–80 Carter	1981–92 Reagan/ Bush	1993–2000 Clinton
17.6	11.9	11.9	14.0	13.2

Source: Current Population Survey

This does not mean that improvements in real wages cannot occur again without another stock market bubble. But it does suggest that some other path to achieving low unemployment will be central to breaking the thirty-year trend of low wages and a growing wage-producctivity gap. The Clinton economy of the late 1990s, whose successes were so heavily dependent on the stock market, offers little guidance as to what such an alternative path to sustained improvements in real wages might be.

Poverty
The performance of the Clinton economy in reducing poverty closely paralleled the experience with wages. As we see from Table 2.8, the individual poverty rate did fall under Clinton relative to Reagan/Bush. But the decline, from 14.0 to 13.2 percent was minimal, given that the government's anti-poverty efforts were sharply curtailed under Reagan and the Bush-1 administration. Moreover, conditions under Clinton worsened among those officially counted as poor. This is documented through data on the so-called "poverty-gap," which measures the amount of money needed to bring all poor people exactly up to the official poverty line. The poverty gap rose from $1,538 to $1,620 from 1993-99 (measured in 2001 dollars).

In addition, the official government's poverty measures are seriously flawed, in particular, in ways that tend to understate the extent of poverty in more recent years. The government's methodology is based on estimating a subsistence-level food basket for families of various sizes. It then assumes that food costs account for one-third of a poor family's overall budget. This approach has numerous problems.[24] But specifically for considering the experience under Clinton, the most significant is that child care costs rose sharply for a high percentage of poor households after Clinton slashed federal welfare support for single mothers. But because child care costs are obviously not counted as part of the subsistence food basket, these increased costs are not reflected at all in the official poverty statistics. It is therefore likely that even the small reduction in the official poverty rate that we observe for the full Clinton presidency relative to Reagan/Bush would disappear if this one factor alone were properly accounted for.

Nevertheless, it is also true that the proportion of people below the poverty line did decline from the beginning to the end of Clinton's presidency – according to the official statistics from 15.1 percent in 1993 to 11.3 percent in 2000. Even after recognizing the weaknesses in the poverty measures and the fact that conditions did worsen under Clinton for those officially counted as poor, this decline in the official poverty rate from 1993–2000 is at least one indicator of improvement – the one, of course, that Clinton and his close associates touted loudly. But even here, the nature of this improvement, genuine though it was, needs to be weighed in a broader context. First, the decline in the poverty rate to 11.3 percent by 2000, which was the lowest yearly rate since 1974, means that that prevalence of poverty is still at least as severe as it was 26 years ago. Meanwhile, per capita GDP in 2000 was 70 percent higher than it was in 1974, productivity was 61 percent higher, and the stock market was up by 603 percent.

Moreover, the reductions in the poverty rate under Clinton were heavily tied to conditions in the job market. This, of course, was a deliberate and aggressively pursued policy aim for Clinton, who pushed hard to slash support for poor people without jobs. But embracing such an approach also means that the reductions in poverty that did occur were a result of the surging economic conditions generated by the stock market bubble, in a manner similar to the rise in real wages.[25] We therefore will not be able to assess the full effects of Clinton's policies towards the poor until his approach has been evaluated in the aftermath of the stock market collapse and economic slowdown. As one initial indicator, it is not surprising that the individual poverty rate rose in 2001 to 11.7 percent, the first such rise in four years. Projecting into the next few years, it is almost certainly the case that Clinton's approach to poverty reduction – depending on the assumption of improving job market conditions for low-wage workers – will continue to produce worsened life circumstances for the most vulnerable members of society.

CHAPTER THREE

The Down Side of Fabulous

"Near full employment can be established by means of a government deficit, but if it goes on too long the captains of industry fear that the workers will get out of hand and will want to 'teach them a lesson.'"

— JOAN ROBINSON 1976

"No one can doubt that the American people remain susceptible to the speculative mood – to the conviction that enterprise can be attended with unlimited rewards in which they, individually, were meant to share."

— JOHN KENNETH GALBRAITH 1988

Professors Alan Blinder and Janet Yellen are two of the most distinguished economists to have worked in the Clinton administration. In 2001, they published a book on the 1990s economy titled *The Fabulous Decade.*[1] And what was so fabulous about this period, according to these insiders/experts? They rate two developments at the top of the list: first, the simultaneous decline of inflation and unemployment; and second, what they term "the amazing, vanishing budget deficit." Curiously, they barely mention the stock market boom in their book, as either another prodigious, or even less celebratory feature of the 1990s economic landscape. But surely any evaluation as to what was exceptional about the economy's performance in this period would have to give prominence to what we may term, in the spirit of Blinder and Yellen, "the amazing, levitating stock market."

Blinder and Yellen's reticence over the stock market may well reflect ambivalence as to whether its unprecedented ascent was an altogether positive development. Fair enough. But similar concerns may also be appropriate, if less obvious, in assessing the inflation/unemployment decline and the elimination of budget deficits as well. This is certainly the view I have already suggested in Chapter 2. But let us take up the question of these three developments in more depth now.

What happened to the inflation/unemployment trade-off?

Whatever else may be said of macroeconomic performance under the Clinton presidency, the simultaneous fall of unemployment and inflation clearly defied the expectations of virtually all orthodox economists. Between 1993–2000, the unemployment rate fell steadily from 7.5 to 4.0 percent. Meanwhile, the inflation rate also declined steadily, to a low point of 1.6 percent by 1998. Inflation did increase in 1999–2000, but only to 2.2 percent in 1999 and 3.4 percent by 2000. Most economists, adhering to the Natural Unemployment/ Non-Accelerating Inflation Rate of Unemployment (NAIRU) doctrines dominant since the early 1970s, had long predicted that unemployment in the region of 4 percent, or even 5 percent, must lead to headlong inflation. This is because with low unemployment rates, workers would gain increased bargaining power. They would demand higher wages and businesses, in turn, would pass on their higher labor costs to their customers through price increases. An inflationary wage-price spiral would ensue. Supporters of this position thus held that policy makers were obligated to maintain unemployment at or above its NAIRU rate – that is, above the unemployment rate at which inflation would take off. To this end, it was generally believed that unemployment needed to be perhaps as high as 6 percent.

What caused the dramatic shift in the trade-off between unemployment and inflation, and to what extent was the Clinton administration responsible for it? Some leading economists have conceded that the inflation-safe unemployment rate – that is, the threshold unemployment rate, or NAIRU, below which inflation would begin accelerating – is subject to change over time. Robert Gordon, for one, concludes from an extensive econometric analysis of the past two decades that inflation-safe unemployment rate varies over time – falling, for example, from 6.2 percent in 1990 to 5.6 by mid-1996.[2] Douglas Staiger, James Stock and Mark Watson concur, finding in a 1997 paper that the inflation-safe unemployment rate in that year was between 5.5 and 5.9 percent, a full percentage point below its level for the early 1980s. They also admit that "the most striking feature of these estimates is their lack of precision." Their 1997 estimate of the inflation-safe unemployment rate not only varies over time but also has the capacity to range widely at a given point in time. In an updated 2002 study, they conclude that the inflation-safe unemployment rate varies in close correspondence with the trend in the actual unemployment rate.[3]

The general thrust of these broad econometric findings appears solid enough. Indeed, they are difficult to dispute precisely because they are so broad. But in focusing exclusively on the details of how the inflation-safe unemployment rate varies over time, they miss the fundamental question that leaps out from these results – namely, what causes the inflation-safe unemployment rate to vary in the first place? It is remarkable that leading economists who have devoted so much time to estimating values for the inflation-safe unemployment rate have also largely neglected this question. Staiger, Stock and Watson do attempt to answer it in their 2002 paper but come up empty. After showing the close correspondence between the inflation-safe unemployment rate and the trend for the actual unemployment rate, they then acknowledge that their data "fail to isolate any economic or demographic determinants of the trend unemployment rate" (p. 7).

Slowly, however, some new modes of thinking are emerging. Almost as an aside in his 1997 paper, Gordon, for example, writes,

> The two especially large changes in the NAIRU [i.e. inflation-safe unemployment rate]...are the increase between the early and late 1960s and the decrease in the 1990s. The late 1960s were a time of labor militancy, relatively strong unions, a relatively high minimum wage and a marked increase in labor's share in national income. The 1990s have been a time of labor peace, relatively weak unions, a relatively low minimum wage and a slight decline in labor's income share. [4]

Gordon also casually refers to intensified world competition in product and labor markets, and increased flows of unskilled immigrant labor into
the United States, as factors contributing to a decline in the inflation-safe
unemployment rate. Though again these observations are mere asides in
Gordon's paper, the overall point is clear: it is changes in the balance of
forces between capital and labor, and the growing integration of the U.S.
into the global economy – which has increased the difficulty of U.S. firms
raising prices and U.S. workers getting wage increases – that have been the
main forces that have weakened the pressure for inflation to accelerate even
at low unemployment rates.

Gordon's general hunch is fully consistent with econometric models
of the unemployment/inflation relationship that – unlike Gordon's own
model – incorporates the effects of falling wages and benefits for workers
relative to productivity growth. I present the main results of such an exercise in Appendix 2, in which I include the effects of falling wages and
benefits for workers relative to productivity growth in a simple econometric model. The model shows that adding this one factor alone generates
predictions of the actual movements of the inflation rate of the 1990s
between 2-3 times more accurate than the typical model that ignores the
effects of low wages and benefits relative to productivity at low unemployment rates. The model does an even better job of predicting the movements of the actual inflation rate when, in line with Gordon's suggestions,
we also take account of intensified global competition, which led to lower
import prices.[5]

The central point is that, as we have seen, wage gains for average workers during the Clinton boom remained historically weak, especially in relationship to the ascent of productivity (see Figure 2.1 and Table 2.7). These
facts provide the basis for the poll findings reported in *Business Week* at the
end of 1999 that substantial majorities of U.S. citizens expressed acute dis-
satisfaction with various features of their economic situation. For example,
51 percent of American workers interviewed by the magazine declared that
they "felt cheated by their employer." When asked their view of what *Business Week* termed the "current productivity boom," 63 percent said that the
boom has not raised their earnings, and 62 percent that it had not improved

their job security.[6] Such negative popular reactions are striking, given the persistent portrayal by the media of the Clinton economy as a time of unparalleled prosperity.

But such attitudes were not lost on leading government policy makers at the time. Thus, Bob Woodward's paean to Alan Greenspan published in 2000, *Maestro: Greenspan's Fed and the American Boom*, includes the following revealing passage:

> The old belief held that with such a low unemployment rate workers would have the upper hand and demand higher wages. Yet the data showed that wages weren't rising that much. It was one of the central economic mysteries of the time. Greenspan hypothesized at one point to colleagues within the Fed about the "traumatized worker" – someone who felt job insecurity in the changing economy and so was accepting smaller wage increases. He had talked with business leaders who said their workers were not agitating and were fearful that their skills might not be marketable if they were forced to change jobs. (p. 168)

Greenspan openly acknowledged his "traumatized worker" explanation for the dampening of inflationary pressures in his regular semi-annual testimony to Congress in July 1997. Saluting the economy's performance that year as "extraordinary" and "exceptional," he remarked that a major factor contributing to its outstanding achievement was "a heightened sense of job insecurity and, as a consequence, subdued wages." During her stint as a Federal Reserve Governor, Janet Yellen, co-author of *The Fabulous Decade*, reached similar conclusions as to the sources of declining inflationary pressures at low unemployment, reporting to Fed's Open Market Committee on September 24, 1996 that "while the labor market is tight, job insecurity also seems alive and well. Real wage aspirations appear modest, and the bargaining power of workers is surprisingly low." As we have seen, these facts of declining bargaining power for workers did not deter Professor Yellen from nevertheless concluding that the overall economic performance in the 1990s was "fabulous."[7]

This "heightened sense of job insecurity" lies at the very foundation of the Clinton administration's economic legacy. But what lies behind the heightened sense of job insecurity itself, even as unemployment fell to a level unseen since the 1960s? It will be helpful here to return to what I described as the "Marx problem" in Chapter 1. Marx's explains in his theory of the reserve army of labor that workers have less bargaining power than employers in labor markets because they do not own their own means of production. But Marx also stressed that workers' bargaining power diminishes further when unemployment and underemployment are high, since that means that employed workers can be readily replaced by the reserve army outside the factory gates.

In terms of the contemporary global setting, the dynamics of the reserve army effect in the United States and other high-wage economies changes when firms operating in low-wage economies can produce export-competitive manufactured products. In this situation, the potential size of the reserve army necessarily expands to also include both the unemployed and, even more to the point, employed but low-paid workers in the developing economies. As such, U.S. capitalists gained an additional bargaining advantage in wage-setting negotiations. This is because firms can now *credibly claim* that their own relatively high labor costs will threaten their export markets and increase import competition from low-wage competitors. In addition, the firms whose operations are not tied to a specific location can credibly threaten to move to low-wage economies if costs in their current locations appear too high. The crucial issue here is not that firms actually leave their existing high-wage location but that they can brandish a *credible threat to exit.*

Moreover, what makes such threats credible is not the rise of low-wage countries' manufacturing capacity alone. Rather, it is that, given the rise in export competitiveness among low-wage countries, the Clinton administration did not act to counter the increased bargaining power accruing to capitalists. Quite the contrary as we have seen – by not advancing policies that would strengthen workers' bargaining position in any of the key areas of trade, labor market regulations or macroeconomic policies, the Clinton administration enabled business to consolidate its increased relative bargaining strength.

Kate Bronfenbrenner of Cornell University has conducted the most directly relevant study of how threats by employers have influenced labor negotiations.[8] Through a series of surveys of workers and union organizers throughout the 1990s, she has found that threats by employers have both inhibited organizing drives and held down wage demands. For example, in her 1993–95 survey, she found that 50 percent of all firms and 65 percent of manufacturing firms that were targets of union organizing campaigns threatened to close their shops and relocate if the workers voted to unionize. Though only 12 percent of those firms that ended up unionized did carry through on their threat to relocate, workers nevertheless found the threats credible. In particular, in cases where firms did make threats to shutdown or relocate, unions lost a significantly larger percentage of elections. Bronfenbrenner's general finding from her series of surveys is that

> Throughout the last decade, the increasingly rapid pace of global capital mobility, and the job dislocation and corporate restructuring that follows in its wake, has fostered a climate of intense economic insecurity among U.S. workers. This rising sense of economic insecurity has effectively served to hold down wage demands and wage increases even during a period of economic expansion, low unemployment and tight labor market. (2001, p. 2–3).

In a related study on this issue, Minsik Choi of the University of Massachusetts-Boston considers what happens to unionized workers employed by U.S. firms with a high proportion of their investments in foreign operations. Everything else equal, we would expect firms with a larger number of foreign plants would have greater capacity to make credible threats against their U.S.-based workers in wage negotiations. Choi has found this to be especially true in industries with the highest proportion of foreign plants operating in conjunction with their domestic activities. For example, in firms producing soap, cleaners and toilet goods, Choi finds that workers in the U.S. plants of these firms earn about 18 percent less than even non-unionized workers employed by firms with no foreign investment.[9]

Overall then, the absence of inflationary pressures as unemployment fell under Clinton should be no mystery. Class conflict has always been the spectre haunting the analysis of inflation and unemployment. With the Clinton administration providing virtually no support to workers as the bargaining strength of business increased, it is not surprising that workers felt "traumatized" – as Alan Greenspan put it – and therefore scaled back their wage claims even in a period of low unemployment.

The Wall Street levitation

What caused the bubble?

Given the historically unique character of the 1990s bubble, it will be some time before we have a definitive understanding of the experience. But it is certainly possible now to begin identifying both the central causal forces and the factors that have been highlighted in media accounts that were of less significance.

Corporate fraud

As the news about various corporate account frauds and embezzlement schemes spread in mid-2002, it became tempting to conclude that the stock market bubble was simply an outgrowth of widespread malfeasance. How could investors properly evaluate companies if the officers of these firms, in conspiracy with their accountants and bankers, were consistently reporting inflated profit figures?

There is truth to this view. The main point with all the various accounting schemes was to artificially pump up profits and thereby impress Wall Street. These tactics obviously succeeded much of the time. But there is also a more basic consideration here, which is that, even given the data on earnings that companies did report, investors were still bursting all historical patterns in bidding up stock prices, apparently unconcerned about historical patterns between stock prices and earnings. So even if investors did not have full knowledge as to what actual earnings were for many firms, it was still clear, based just on the publicly available information, that they were willing to pay more to buy stocks than at any previous historical period.

FIGURE 3.1: Price-earnings ratio for Standard & Poor's composite stock price index, 1880–2000

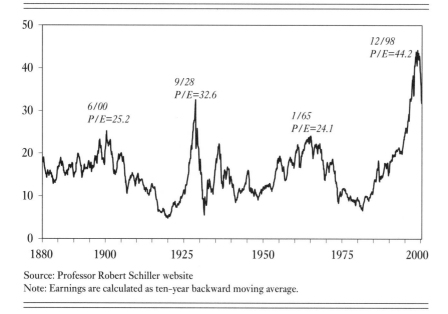

Source: Professor Robert Schiller website
Note: Earnings are calculated as ten-year backward moving average.

We can see this by examining the historical movements of the price-to-earnings ratio for the Standard & Poor's Composite Index in Figure 3.1. This series has been compiled as far back as 1880 by Professor Robert Schiller of Yale, and he presented this series in his prescient 2000 book *Irrational Exuberance*. [10] As we see from the figure, the price/earnings ratio for this Standard & Poor series bounds upward through the 1990s to the unprecedented peak of 44.2 in December 1998. This means that by the end of 1998, investors were willing to pay $44.20 for one dollar of reported earnings – receiving, in other words, an average return due to reported earnings of 2.3 percent. This figure contrasts with the average price/earnings ratio of 14.5 for the period 1880-1989, which meant that on average, stock market investors received a return of nearly 7 percent in purchasing equity shares. As the figure also shows, this December 1998 peak figure is also well in excess of all previous peaks, such as the June 1900 figure of 25.2, the September 1928 figure of 32.6 and the 24.1 figure for January, 1965. In short, it is clear from these figures that the main driving force behind the 1990s stock market bubble was not inflated earnings reports, but the willingness of investors to spend roughly 2 ½ times more for a dollar of reported earnings than, as an average, they had done over the previous 110 years.

The Internet as gold rush

Conventional explanations of the bubble had given pride of place to the dramatic advances in computer and Internet-related technology. But we have seen that productivity did not register exceptional growth through the full Clinton presidency, even after national accounts were revised upward to make special provision for computer-driven improvements. Still, we have also seen that productivity did accelerate between 1996–2000, to an average annual rate of 2.5 percent, relative to the dismal 0.9 percent figure for 1993–95, the first three years of Clinton's term. But such productivity figures are hardly a sufficient basis to underwrite the Clinton stock market boom. Even if we assume that the productivity figures represent a broad trend rather than, as Robert Gordon argues, an effect driven by the computer hardware industry alone, it is still the case that 2.5 percent productivity growth is well below the 3.4 percent rate in the Kennedy/Johnson period. Nothing close to the Clinton stock market boom ever occurred under Kennedy and Johnson.

But the Internet revolution was supposed to have been about far more than technical economic data on productivity. It was supposed to be about opening vast new vistas for corporate profits. This perspective was expressed most forcefully in one statistic that was repeated relentlessly as a fact in trade publications, general news reports and even an official U.S. government report – the statistic being that Internet traffic was doubling every three months. If this figure had been accurate, it would have meant that the Internet was growing at more than 1000 percent per year – vast new profit opportunities indeed! In the late 1990s, companies such as WorldCom and Global Crossing, both now bankrupted, invested exorbitant sums in laying millions of miles of fiber-optic cable lines beneath streets and across oceans driven by this promise of hugely expanding markets for Internet carrying capacity.

The trouble is there was never any evidence that this statistic was true, despite having been universally embraced as the foundation for hundreds of corporate plans.[11]

Of course, the promise of future Internet-led leaps in productivity and profit opportunities still remains. But even if we allow that possibility, it still does not explain the magnitude of the stock price inflation under Clinton. As the economic journalist Doug Henwood aptly noted in 1999, at the height of the boom:

> The Internet stocks that have headlined the mania over the last year are without known precedent in U.S. financial history. At its highs in early April, the market capitalization of Priceline.com, which sells airline tickets on the web and has microscopic revenues, was twice that of United Airlines and just a hair under American's. America Online was worth nearly as much as Disney and Time Warner combined, and more than GM and Ford combined. Yahoo was capitalized a third higher than Boeing, and eBay nearly as much as CBS. At its peak, AOL sported a price/earnings ratio of 720, Yahoo of 1468 and eBay of 9571 … . Oh yes, enthusiasts respond, but these are bets on a grand future. But previous world-transformative events have never been capitalized like this … . RCA peaked at a P/E of 73 in 1929. Xerox traded at a P/E of 123 in 1961. Apple maxed out at a P/E of 150 in 1980. And all these companies were pretty quick to turn a profit, and once they did, their growth rates were ripping. In the so-called Nifty Fifty era of the early 1970s, the half-hundred glamour stocks that led the market sported P/Es of forty to sixty … . And those evaluations were once legendary for their extravagance.[12]

Policy, inequality, supply and demand

While corporate fraud and the Internet obviously contributed substantially to the bubble, something else had to magnify the effects of these factors beyond all previous experiences with fraud and glamorous new technologies. In my view, three interconnected factors were crucial. They were:

1) Policy influences, including both financial deregulation and Federal Reserve actions; 2) The rise in inequality and corporate profitability – what mainstream financial economists call "the fundamentals"; and 3) Shifts in supply and demand in the stock market, specifically a contraction in the supply of shares and a corresponding increase in demand. This discussion draws much from the insightful and rigorous 2003 book by Dr. Lawrance Evans of the U.S. Government Accounting Office, *Why the Bubble Burst: U.S. Stock Market Performance Since 1982.*

Policy factors

Charles Kindleberger and others have amply documented the way in which speculative manias have historically recurred in financial markets.[13] After the Wall Street crash of 1929 and the slump of the 1930s, post-war governments in all major capitalist economies set in place far-reaching systems of financial regulation to prevent renewed bouts of destructive speculation. In consequence, for the first 25 years after the end of World War II, stock markets were relatively tranquil. This experience suggests one simple explanation for the bubble: that in the absence of effective regulation, speculative excess will inevitably occur in financial markets, though exactly how bubbles will emerge and develop can never be known in advance. In this sense, the Clinton era asset inflation reached unprecedented peaks because neither the administration nor Alan Greenspan offered adequate controls to inhibit its development. Rather, as we have seen, Greenspan explicitly chose in 1996 not to impose margin requirements on stock market speculators, even though he knew that such a measure would have broken the speculative momentum. Beyond this, had Greenspan and Treasury Secretary Robert Rubin not conducted successful bail-out operations when the sequence of Mexican, East Asian and Long-Term Capital Management crises broke out, the U.S. stock market would probably have dived as the cumulative effects of these shocks coursed through global financial markets.[14] By a "successful" bail-out, I mean an operation that not only prevented a chain-reaction of debt defaults, but also protected the wealth of U.S. investors – since substantial losses by American investors would almost certainly have burst the U.S. bubble.

Increased inequality and profitability

As we have seen, the rewards of economic growth under Clinton were claimed increasingly by the wealthy, with wages stagnating or declining for most workers over most of this period. According to Daniel Larkins of the U.S. Commerce Department, after-tax corporate profits reached a forty-year peak under Clinton in 1997 of 5.6 percent, before falling to 5.0 percent in 1998 and more sharply in succeeding years (a topic we consider in more detail in the next chapter). But the peak years under Clinton compare with peak figures under Nixon (1969) of 4.8 percent, Carter (1979) of 4.0 percent and even Reagan (1984) of 4.2 percent.[15] Larkin's calculations also make clear that *before they paid taxes*, the profits that U.S. corporations earned were not high by historical standards during the Clinton Presidency. Thus, the central factor through which corporations benefited during the Clinton period was not through the return on sales they achieved from their operations, but rather because the taxes they paid on their returns were at historically low levels.

Some share of this profitability increase through 1997 was no doubt due to the loose accounting standards of the Clinton boom. But it is not likely that this factor alone could dramatically change such a strong upward trajectory for profitability, especially given that accounting laxity was not something that had sprung to life *de novo* in the Clinton years. In any case, the rise in profitability that was real, along with the cooked-up figures, both fed expectations of further profit increases, especially in conditions where the political system clearly heavily favored the interests of the rich, regardless of whether Democrat or Republican incumbents held the White House.

Mainstream economists argue that financial markets are "efficient" in the sense that the markets are said to value companies strictly according to their "fundamentals," the most important such fundamental being a firm's current and expected profitability. It is now evident that the 1990s bubble was driven by speculative forces far beyond what the fundamentals would have suggested is appropriate. But it is also true that one major fundamental – high after-tax profits – translated into expectations of much more profitability coming in the future. In other words, the exuberance behind the market's dizzying ascent was certainly exaggerated to the point of irrationality, but it was also not without foundation in reality.

Shifts in supply of and demand for U.S. equity shares

Supply. Throughout the 1990s market boom, the biggest block of shares was actually purchased by the U.S. corporations themselves. From 1994–2000, corporations repurchased an average of $121 billion per year of their own stocks. These buy-backs amounted to 40 percent of firms' after-tax profits, and nearly 16 percent of their spending on new capital equipment. This pattern of corporate share repurchases stands in sharp contrast to the period 1960–79, during which corporations were net issuers of shares, at an average rate of 7.7 percent of their after-tax profits.

The 1994–2000 share repurchase movement was preceded by an earlier phase of intense buy-back activity between 1984–90, when corporations bought back an average of $92 billion per year of their own shares, which represented a remarkable 79 percent of corporate after-tax profits. But this earlier buy-back phase resulted primarily from the merger and leveraged buy-out activity of that period, including the repurchases firms undertook as a defensive strategy to prevent hostile takeovers. The 1994–2000 buy-back phase was much more concentrated on using repurchases as a tool for driving up stock prices.

According to mainstream economic theory, corporations cannot possibly increase the value of their company simply by buying back their own shares. If a corporation earns $100 in profits, why should it matter to the firm's market value whether the managers decide to distribute the $100 as dividends or use the money to buy back shares? Everything else about the firm would remain exactly the same – the employees, productive equipment, products and marketing capacity would be unchanged. Even shareholders should be basically just as well off regardless of whether the extra $100 came to them in the form of dividends or through being able to sell shares back to the company for a price mark-up reflecting the $100 in new profits.[16] To a certain extent, this logic is impeccable. Corporate buy-backs cannot possibly push up the value of firms indefinitely. Among other things, firms would eventually run out of shares to sell.

But the problem with the mainstream perspective is precisely that it attributes too much rationality to market participants, overlooking the considerable extent to which financial markets are driven by the imperatives of speculation – that is, on the basis of uncertain knowledge, rumors, whims and fads. If a firm's stock price goes up simply because the firm has bought back its own shares, the market may indeed see this maneuver as irrelevant to valuing the firm's long-term productive potential. But they could also interpret this as signaling that, for whatever reason, the firm's price is on an upswing, and therefore is a good purchase opportunity. Thus, if corporate executives can drive up share prices even for a brief period through buy-backs, they can then profit through selling while the speculative market psychology is still experiencing a cyclical up phase. There is no reason to expect corporate executives to overlook such opportunities. Keynes was emphatic on this point in his 1936 *General Theory*, explaining for example, that financial market investors:

> ...are largely concerned, not with making superior long-term forecasts of the probable yield of an investment over its whole life, but with foreseeing changes in the conventional basis of valuation a short time ahead of the general public. They are concerned, not with what an investment is really worth to a man who buys it "for keeps", but with what the market will value it at, under the influence of mass psychology, three months or a year hence. Moreover, this behavior is not the outcome of a wrong-headed propensity. It is the inevitable result of an investment market organized along the lines described (p. 155).

The importance of raising share prices through buy-backs became especially attractive to corporate managers during the 1990s market boom because, increasingly, they were receiving a large fraction of their pay through stock options rather than salary. The managers would therefore benefit personally through any strategy of pushing up share prices during the period in which they could exercise their option to sell shares.[17]

Demand. We should divide the changes in stock market demand according to the domestic and foreign segments of total U.S. equity owners. In terms of demand from the U.S., we have already seen the extent to which in the 1990s, American households moved their portfolios out of low-risk bank deposits and Treasury securities into riskier assets – above all equities. The rise of mutual funds, institutional investors and derivative markets, through which the risks associated with stock-ownership are spread, certainly contributed to this shift. But it was also clear at the time that U.S. property owners had come to believe that equities were less of a hazard than they had been at any prior point in history. The Clinton administration alone is obviously not responsible for creating this state of mind among investors. In part, such thinking stems from the rise in profitability and especially the positive feedback effects of favorable returns on investor expectations. Alan Greenspan did at times try to calm the markets through his warnings about "irrational exuberance." But the enthusiasm with which the Federal Reserve and the Clinton administration pushed for the deregulation of financial markets more than counterbalanced any downward jawboning efforts by Greenspan.[18]

In terms of foreign demand, from 1985 onwards, the U.S. has become a net debtor nation, as foreign-owned assets in the country have exceeded American-owned assets abroad. Through the 1990s, foreign wealth-holders have increasingly purchased dollar-denominated assets in U.S. financial markets. By the end of 2000, the magnitude of the foreign debt had reached $1.6 trillion, equal to 16 percent of GDP. By contrast, the foreign net asset position in 1992 was 7.1 percent of GDP – i.e. its magnitude relative to GDP more than doubled over the Clinton presidency. Considering new equity acquisitions alone by foreigners, total purchases between 1993–2000 was $1.2 trillion, making foreigners the largest source of new funds in the market over these years.[19]

This inflow of foreign savings is the other side of the persistent American trade deficit. Indeed, it has been the continued willingness of foreigners to accept payment in dollars and to invest in dollar-denominated assets that alone made the trade deficit sustainable. Here the instability of financial markets across the rest of the world was critical for making American assets so attractive. Independently of the Wall Street bubble, foreign investors prefer U.S. equities and other assets not because returns on them as such are always highest, but because the rest of the world is perceived – in most cases correctly – as offering too much risk relative to the potential rewards.[20]

The bubble and the real economy

From a perspective beyond that just of Wall Street itself, the 1990s bubble mattered because of its broader reverberations on the U.S. and world economy. Several channels of influence operated here. For one thing, the boom enabled firms to meet pension fund obligations through rising portfolio values rather than transferring revenues into retirement funds. This in turn released internal cash flow for distribution as dividends or investment in new capital. Rising share prices also fuelled the pace of corporate mergers, by enabling firms to buy other companies through stock transfers rather than having either to borrow or pay cash. The rising stock market also set off a debt-led investment boom, especially in the information technology sector.

But the single most important effect was through underwriting the debt-financed consumption boom, which, as we saw, was the primary engine of U.S. growth in the 1990s, as the government's share of total spending fell and the trade deficit persisted. The way this primary effect operated is through the so-called "wealth effect," in which households become willing to spend a higher fraction of their annual income because their net worth – the value of their stocks, bonds, real estate holdings and other assets minus their total debt – has increased. A 2001 Federal Reserve Board research paper by Dean Maki and Michael Palumbo confirms earlier studies that had found a substantial wealth effect – specifically, that households increase their spending by between 3 and 5 cents for every extra dollar of wealth that is recognized by them and sustained over time. [21] The rise in the stock market between 1995–1999, the high tide of the boom, was about $9 trillion greater than the figure that would have resulted through stock values just rising in step with GDP growth. This implies that the bubble, at its height, was injecting between $275–$460 billion, or roughly 2–4 percent more spending into the economy, which in turn stimulated further growth through its impact on investment and jobs.

We can see the link between the wealth effect and consumer spending more closely by considering the data presented in Figure 3.2. The top panel of Figure 3.2 presents macro-level figures – i.e. aggregate data for all households in the economy. Beginning in the early 1990s, we can see by the upper

FIGURE 3.2: The wealth effect from U.S. stock market bubble

A) Overall household net worth and consumption rise together

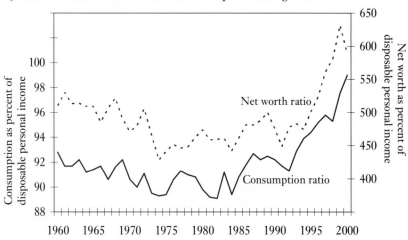

B) But consumption rise by richest 20% explains almost entire effect

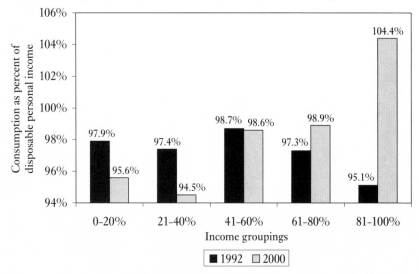

Source: U.S. Bureau of Economic Analysis, Flow of Funds Accounts, Maki and Palumbo (2001)

line the sharp rise in overall household net worth ratio – total household assets minus liabilities as a proportion of disposable income. The lower line in the panel then traces the household consumption ratio, this being the share of total disposable income that households are spending. The consumption ratio is clearly closely tracking the sharp ascent of the net worth ratio over this period.

But Maki and Palumbo's research on the question goes beyond examining the wealth effect from this macro perspective. The macro picture can be misleading, since most people did not hold significant amounts of wealth during the Clinton stock market boom, just as they never have previously. Thus, to understand the real force driving the macro-level wealth effect, we have to focus on the consumption patterns for just those households that do actually hold a significant amount of wealth. Maki and Palumbo's key findings on this question are shown in panel B of Figure 3.2. This panel shows consumption ratios for the years 1992 and 2000. These ratios are divided by income groupings, starting with the poorest 20 percent of households by income level, then those in the 21–40 percent income group, and so on. As the figure shows, the lower two income groups actually reduced their consumption ratios between 1992–2000 and the ratio for the middle grouping basically stayed constant between the two years. Those in the 61–80 percent income group did increase their consumption ratio, but by a relatively modest amount, from 97.3 to 98.9 percent. Virtually all of the action, as we see, is with the richest 20 percent of households, who increased their consumption ratio dramatically from 95.1 to 104.4 percent. For these households to spend more than 100 percent of their income, they would obviously have needed to draw on their savings or to borrow. Their rapidly growing wealth enabled them to do this.

The conclusion is clear: the overall rise in consumption spending in the Clinton years – which was itself central to the economy's overall growth in this period – was driven almost entirely by an enormous increase in consumption by the country's richest households, tied to the similarly formidable increase in wealth for these households.

The fiscal reversal

The reversal of the federal government's overall fiscal stance was certainly a major change over the course of the Clinton presidency. In 1992, the last year of the Bush-1 presidency, the federal deficit was $290 billion, or 4.7 percent of GDP. In 1993, Clinton's first year in office, the deficit fell to $255 billion, which was 3.7 percent of GDP, and continued falling every year thereafter. By 1998, the federal fiscal position moved into surplus for the first time since 1969. Surpluses continued through 1999 and 2000. This was the first time the federal government recorded three consecutive years of surplus since 1947–49.

The Clinton administration was unequivocal in citing the reversal of the government's fiscal stance, and in particular the achievement of fiscal surpluses, as its most important economic policy achievement. Clinton himself wrote that his administration's economic strategy

> ... has been based, first and foremost, on a commitment to fiscal discipline. By first cutting and then eliminating the deficit, we have helped create a virtuous cycle of lower interest rates, greater investment, more jobs, higher productivity, and higher wages. In the process we have gone from the largest deficits in history to the largest surpluses in history. (*Economic Report of the President*, 2001, p. 3)

Maintaining a fiscal surplus became so central to the Clinton economic vision that his administration began promoting the idea of maintaining surpluses permanently until the entire outstanding federal debt of $3.4 trillion was eliminated. Indeed, Vice President Gore emphasized this point in the 2000 Presidential campaign, promising unequivocally even in his final campaign debate with George W. Bush – the single most important platform of his campaign – that "I will pay down the debt every single year until it is eliminated, early in the next decade."

The Clinton administration was correct in recognizing the dangers of excessive government deficits. Deficits can be especially harmful to the economy if they result from policies to cut taxes for the rich. This is the story behind the Bush-2 policy agenda that we will discuss in the next chapter.

But the Clintonites were also seriously in error to have elevated fiscal stringency and the attainment of surpluses to the status of economic cure-all. In fact, federal surpluses are inherently neither good nor bad for the economy, just as there is nothing inherently detrimental about the government running deficits. In fact, under various circumstances, there are some very sound economic reasons for the federal government to run deficits, and these must not be forgotten.

The first reason for the government to run deficits – which was perhaps the single most important point established by the Keynesian revolution in economics during the 1930s – is that it is a powerful tool for counteracting recessions. During a recession, spending by households and businesses slump. Businesses then respond to the overall fall in sales by laying off workers and otherwise reducing the scale of their operations. This rise in unemployment leads to further cuts in household and business spending. Government deficit spending is able to reverse this self-reinforcing slide toward deepening recession. It does so by using its borrowed funds to increase its own spending and hiring of unemployed workers. This increased government spending then puts more money in the pockets of households and businesses. Households and businesses are therefore now able to increase their own spending. Hiring of workers by the private sector correspondingly rises. The recessionary forces are thereby reversed. Seen in this perspective, Al Gore's proposal to run government surpluses and pay down the federal debt every year, even in recessions, would mean that the government was not only relinquishing this tool for fighting recessions, but that it was actively contributing to making recessions more severe.

The other major positive reason for governments to go into deficit is to finance expensive, long-term capital investments, in areas such as education, environmental protection or public infrastructure, because these long-term investments will yield higher productivity and other long-term benefits. Opponents of federal deficit spending frequently argue that the government needs to learn to live within its means, just like private households and businesses. But, in fact, government borrowing to finance long-term productivity-enhancing projects is analogous to businesses borrowing on their capital account to invest in new machinery or to households taking out mortgages to purchase a home. To assume that the federal government should never go into debt to finance a new school building is analogous to saying that a household should never take out a mortgage to purchase a home.

But surpluses can also be the appropriate policy under some circumstances. The clearest example here is the building of the Social Security trust fund. This makes sense because it permits spreading out the costs of maintaining the program's long-term obligations. But beyond the needs of the Social Security system, the major benefit claimed by the Clinton administration flowing from the surpluses from 1998–2000 – as the earlier quotation from Clinton himself made clear – was that it brought lower interest rates for the private sector, which then set off a "virtuous cycle" of private economic expansion and better jobs.

There are two ways in which the Clinton government surpluses were supposed to have produced lower interest rates. The first is that, without a federal deficit, private sector borrowers did not have to compete for credit with the government. The overall demand for credit therefore fell while the supply of credit from private savers and financial institutions stayed approximately the same. Falling credit demand and stable credit supply should then combine to bring lower rates.

The second factor has to do with the relationship between federal deficits and how financial markets respond to inflationary pressures. When the government runs deficits, this also means that more government spending is being injected into the economy. The extra government purchases of products means that overall demand in the economy is likely to be growing faster than overall supply of products on the market. This then translates into increased inflationary pressures.

Here we come to the key point, which is that lenders on financial markets are adamant in their opposition to inflation. This is because when inflation goes up, the real return on loans goes down. For example, if one loans at 5 percent, but inflation also goes up by 5 percent over the course of the loan, the real return also falls by 5 percent, i.e. to a zero real return. Thus, lenders build in an "inflation premium" into the interest rates that they charge to protect their profits. Interest rates will therefore rise when the inflation premium rises. Correspondingly, if lenders think that a budget surplus will dampen down inflation, they will then also lower their inflation premium, thereby lowering interest rates.

There is some validity to these explanations as to how the Clinton surpluses contributed to lower interest rates, just as there is with virtually any simple supply-and-demand analysis of what makes prices – including interest rates, the price of credit – rise or fall in a given market. But simple supply-and-demand stories are also almost always insufficient for understanding real-world market situations, because, to be true, they require that everything else about the market situation that might also affect supply or demand be held constant.

In this case, to assume that lower interest rates will necessarily follow when the federal government reduces its demand for credit, one must also assume that other factors – including the deregulation of financial markets and the corresponding explosion in speculative financial activity, as well as the other factors influencing inflation – will not significantly influence interest rates.

We have already discussed how factors other than the decline in federal deficits – and in particular here the stagnation of real wages over the first five years of the Clinton presidency – were crucial in lowering the inflation rate over the 1990s. But we also need to return to the distinction between "real" interest rates and the "nominal" rates that are the rates written on contracts. The real rates, again, are simply the nominal rates minus the inflation premium – they are "real," in other words, because they measure the return to lenders after accounting for inflationary effects.

As we have already seen, the real interest rate on long-term Treasury bonds did fall, under Clinton, to an average of 4.3 percent relative to the average, under Reagan and Bush, of 5.8 percent. But the average under Clinton was still much higher than all previous presidential epochs that we examined. Indeed, from the beginning of the Kennedy/Johnson period through to the Carter presidency – 1961–80 – the average real Treasury rate was 1.6 percent, a bit more than one-third the average rate under Clinton, even though the federal government ran deficits for eighteen of the twenty years between 1961–80. The swing in private-sector interest rates was less wide over this full period. But still, considering the Corporate AAA rate, the average rate between 1961–80, at 7.0 percent, was comfortably below the 7.6 percent rate for the year 2000, a figure achieved in the midst of the government having produced three straight years of fiscal surpluses. Clearly, if the goal of the Clinton presidency was to lower interest rates, running fiscal surpluses was hardly an efficient tool for doing so.

But the more general conclusion to draw here is that circumstances are everything: whether a fiscal surplus or deficit will be beneficial depends first on timing – whether the economy is in an expansion or recession – and second, on how the costs and benefits of the fiscal stance are distributed. How do these issues play out with respect to the fiscal turnaround under Clinton?

From our earlier overview of the Clinton economy we can identify four factors that could have potentially contributed to eliminating the deficit and generating surpluses. The first would be the higher rates of economic growth attained under Clinton, since the higher incomes from growth will mean increased revenues, even if the rate of taxation stays the same. The second factor would be the tax increases of 1993 that, as we have seen, did raise the tax burden on the rich relative to the situation under Reagan and the first Bush presidency while also moderately lowering rates for the less well-off. One could certainly embrace a relatively benign view of the Clinton fiscal policy if these were the two primary factors responsible for the surplus.

But we need to still consider the two other potential contributing factors. One obviously would be the fall in government spending programs relative to GDP, from an average, as we saw, of 21.9 percent of GDP in the last year of the Bush-1 presidency to 18.1 percent by the end of the Clinton years. The second is the increase in capital gains tax revenues that were a byproduct of the stock market bubble. Our view of the fiscal surpluses would be considerably less favorable to the extent that they depended on the rampaging stock market or on allowing crucial spending needs to have languished.

To obtain some sense of the relative contributions of these four sources of the fiscal turnaround since the end of the Bush-1 presidency in 1992, I conducted the following statistical exercise: if any of these four factors were at their level for 1992 under Bush rather than at their actual levels under

FIGURE 3.3: Factors in the Clinton fiscal turnaround
(Estimates are for 1996–99, using 1992 as base year)

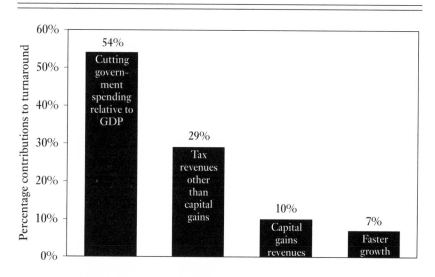

Source: See Appendix 3 for estimation procedures and data sources

Clinton, what difference would it have made for the government's fiscal situation? We consider this specifically for the years 1995–99 under Clinton. The results of the exercise are shown in Figure 3.3. A fuller discussion of the methodology for generating these results is presented in Appendix 3.

As we can see from the figure, the decline in government spending relative to GDP was, by far, the most important of our four factors in generating the fiscal turnaround, being responsible by itself for over half of the total change. An increase in government revenues from non–stock market sources was the next most important contributor, at 29 percent of the total change. The rise in capital gains tax revenues was responsible for 10 percent of the overall turnaround while economic growth is the least important of the four factors, contributing 7 percent to the turnaround.

Thus, the freezes in government spending programs and the rise in capital gains revenues together explain nearly two-thirds of the financial turnaround.

Put another way, if we allowed only for the government spending freezes and the capital gains tax revenue increases – and ignored the impact of non-capital gains tax revenues or economic growth – the government's fiscal stance would have still moved into surplus by 1998. By the same token, relying on just the rise in non-capital gains tax revenues and economic growth, the government would have remained in deficit throughout the Clinton presidency.

What then do we make of the overall costs and benefits of the fiscal turnaround under Clinton? Governments certainly cannot run persistent deficits at high interest rates, such that interest payments on the government debt absorb a large and increasing share of its budget. The Clinton administration does deserve credit for avoiding this type of debt trap, though the danger of this type of extreme situation occurring had already been sharply reduced under the Bush-1 presidency.

Beyond this, the commitment to fiscal stringency that was mainly responsible for the budget turnaround came with real costs. The end of the Cold War created the opportunity for large cuts in military spending and a redirection of public policy toward meeting social needs in areas such as education and research, environmental protection, public infrastructure and poverty reduction. As we saw above, the military budget did fall substantially under Clinton, from 4.7 to 3.0 percent of GDP. But even with these reductions, the military budget remained at a colossal $295 billion by 2000, which was more than the amounts spent by all the rest of NATO, plus Russia, plus all the countries in the Middle East and North Africa, including Israel, combined.

What if, as one extremely modest peace dividend initiative, federal spending in education had been permitted to remain at exactly its 1992 level relative to GDP rather than falling by nearly 24 percent over the Clinton presidency? This policy would have generated an additional $16.8 billion in educational spending in 2000 alone. It would have reduced the 2000 surplus by 7 percent, to $220 billion. But assume the additional funds were divided evenly between hiring new teachers, awarding $10,000 scholarships to college students, and building new averaged-sized high schools. This small peace dividend alone would have meant roughly 100,000 new teachers, 560,000 more scholarships, and 1,400 new high schools.

One could obviously spin out similar scenarios in other areas of vital public sector needs. But the more general point is that, by touting fiscal stringency and the attainment of surpluses as virtual policy totems, the Clinton administration pushed major costs onto the public – i.e. fewer teachers, a dirtier environment, far less capacity to fight poverty – that were difficult to notice because they took the form of foregone opportunities. Meanwhile, whatever the benefits attained by fiscal stringency in terms of lowering interest rates, they were also attainable via maintaining effective financial market regulations. But the Clintonites were unabashed in giving the financial markets what they wanted – and thus, financial regulation was always regarded as part of the problem, while fiscal stringency was the first-option solution.

Overall then, Clinton's economic program through his full term of office remained consistent with the center-right Eisenhower Republican policy stance that he adopted during the weeks in which he first formed his administration after his victory in November 1992 – that is after he shelved the "Putting People First" program that had been the centerpiece of his 1992 "it's the economy, stupid" campaign. The core of Clintonomics was down-the-line neoliberalism: global economic integration and fiscal austerity, with minimum interventions to promote equity in labor markets or stability in financial markets. Gestures to the least well-off were slight and back-handed, while wages for the majority remained below their level of the previous generation, even after the three years of raises that accompanied the stock market boom and productivity surge. Wealth at the top exploded of course. But the stratospheric rise in stock prices and the debt-financed consumption and investment booms produced a mortgaged legacy. The financial unraveling had begun even as Clinton was basking in praise for his economic stewardship.

CHAPTER FOUR

Money Grab and Recession: The Bush Economy

"A feast is made for laughter, and wine maketh merry; but money answereth all things."

— ECCLESIASTES 10:19

"The fact that our econometric models at the Fed, the best in the world, have been wrong for fourteen straight quarters does not mean they will not be right in the fifteenth quarter."

— ALAN GREENSPAN 1999

From new economy to recession

The 2000 Presidential election was conducted in what most observers considered a high noon of prosperity. The news media were filled with stories about the "New Economy," driven by the Internet and globalization, that would deliver an indefinite period of high productivity growth, low inflation and unemployment, and broadly-based income gains. The stock market was still booming then, with the Standard & Poor 500 index monthly close peaking in August at 1517, a figure nearly triple where the index closed only five years before. In its July 1, 2000 issue, *The Economist* reported that the consensus among their panel of economic forecasters was a GDP growth rate in 2001 of 3.2 percent – that is, more of the same unbroken New Economy prosperity. Even academic economists had joined the chorus, with leading figures such as Columbia's Edmund Phelps explaining in August 2000 that the U.S. economy's growth had become "structural" because "entrepreneurs could launch effectively 'new economy' ventures" through a highly developed stock market.[1]

The major economic policy debate between the candidates Al Gore and George Bush was how best to distribute the gains from the annual federal budget surpluses that the forecasting models were projecting deep into the future. The major Gore proposal, as we have seen, was to pay down the federal debt until it was completely eliminated. The Bush plan, by contrast, was to "return the surplus to the people" via massive tax cuts, flowing mostly to the wealthy.

Amid such talk of unending good times, it came as a jolt to most observers when the Republican Vice Presidential candidate Dick Cheney announced on a television talk show on December 3, 2000 that "we may well be on the front edge of a recession here. There is growing evidence that the economy is slowing down."[2] After Cheney's statement, George Bush also began interjecting gloomy economic prognostications into his public statements. This was the time when Bush and Cheney, along with Gore and the Democrats, were still fighting over who actually won the election. It would be another week before the Supreme Court threw the victory to Bush. The timing is important: Bush had some obvious political motives for turning negative on the economy at this point, after having been almost entirely upbeat throughout the election.

Bush, first of all, was seeking to inject a sense of urgency into the country's economic situation, and thereby exert new pressure on Al Gore to concede defeat (despite the fact that Gore had actually won the popular vote and would have almost definitely won the electoral college vote had all the votes in Florida been counted fairly). In the event that Bush was handed the election victory and the economy did turn sour early in his administration Bush also wanted to inoculate himself against being blamed for a recession, and to correspondingly foist responsibility onto Clinton. Finally, and most importantly, Bush saw an upcoming recession as an opportunity to advance his main campaign agenda item, which was to cut taxes for the rich. Bush claimed that the Congress would need to pass his program of tax cuts as the primary tool for fighting a recession. This was a curious position to take, since Bush had promoted his tax plan throughout the fall campaign without ever mentioning its anti-recession features. Moreover, in the original version of the plan Bush presented soon after taking office, it included no provisions at all that would take effect before 2002. It was therefore difficult to see how such measures would be capable of fighting a recession occurring in 2001.

But there is one final twist to the scenario: despite the obvious political motives behind Bush's and Cheney's recession forebodings, their pronouncements turned out to have been accurate. A recession was indeed on its way, and well before the September 11 attacks. In fact, the first signs of a downturn had already begun even during the election season. The growth of GDP fell to less than one percent over the second half of 2000, after having grown by nearly 4 percent over the first half of the year. The overall stock market, as measured by the S&P 500 index, had fallen 24 percent by December 2000 relative to its August peak. Unemployment also began inching up, from 3.9 to 4.0 percent in November 2000, then to 4.2 percent in January 2001.

These trends continued over 2001. As we can see in Figure 4.1, GDP growth turned negative in the first quarter of 2001, falling by 0.6 percent. The decline sharpened to 1.6 percent in the second quarter. This was all before the September 11 attacks. In the third quarter of 2001, which included the September 11 attacks, GDP fell again, by another 0.3 percent, before beginning to rise by 2.7 percent in the fourth quarter of the year. For 2001 as a whole, GDP rose at an anemic 0.3 percent rate, in sharp contrast with the 3.8 percent rate for 2000.

A recession is commonly characterized as two consecutive quarters of negative GDP growth. By that standard, a full recession had occurred in the first six months of 2001, i.e. well before the terrorist attacks, then continued through the end of September before recovering in the last quarter. But beyond this pattern for GDP growth, we need to also consider the perspective of the National Bureau of Economic Research (NBER) the most widely recognized authority on dating recessions in the United States. The NBER defines recessions more broadly, as "a significant decline in activity spread across the economy, lasting more than a few months, visible in industrial production, employment, real income and wholesale-retail sales." The National Bureau concluded that a recession began in March 2001 – six months before the terrorist attacks.

FIGURE 4.1: The onset of recession

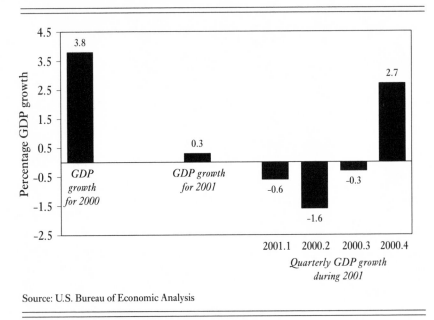

Source: U.S. Bureau of Economic Analysis

It is also significant that, even into early 2003, the NBER had not de-termined whether the recession had in fact ended. Initially, most econo-mists and forecasters were upbeat about the prospects for a full and rapid recovery. They were supported in this view by the positive growth figures for the fourth quarter of 2001, and even more so, by the economy's perfor-mance in the first quarter of 2002, when growth rose to a buoyant 5.0 per-cent rate. The well-known Yale University economist William Nordhaus captured the prevailing sentiment when he wrote,

> As of April 2002, the signs of economic recovery are sprouting like
> spring flowers. The United States has emerged from the short but
> painful winter that followed the burst of the asset bubble in early
> 2000 and the anxiety caused by the events of September 11 and the
> anthrax scare in the fall of 2001.[3]

But contrary to these expectations, the economy never did reach anything close to a full bloom over 2002. It rather proceeded fitfully, growing strong, then falling back. For the fourth quarter 2002, GDP growth was a paltry 0.7 percent.

If we consider a range of indicators besides just GDP, it becomes clear that a significant decline in economic activity occurred during 2001 and that there had been no full recovery by the end of 2002. First, unemployment rose significantly, as it always does in recessions. It increased to a 5.5 percent average for the fourth quarter of 2001, relative to the 4.2 percent figure for the similar period in 2000. This 5.5 percent figure is low by historical standards for recessions, and, in fact, is roughly in line with the average U.S. unemployment rate over the past forty years, including all expansions and recessions. Still, starting from the low 4.2 percent base, the rise to 5.5 percent unemployment meant that an additional 2 million people – more than the combined populations of Boston, Milwaukee, and San Francisco – were out of work in the fourth quarter of 2001 relative to the same period in 2000. The unemployment rate then rose still further in 2002. At 5.8 percent for the full year, unemployment was actually worse in 2002 than 2001, and indeed, was higher than any year since 1994.

Productivity growth characteristically falls in recessions because firms cut back on their investments in new productivity-enhancing equipment. Especially early in a recession, they also frequently find themselves losing sales, and thus cutting back on production, faster than they can lay off workers. New Economy doctrine had suggested that the Internet had shifted the economy into a significantly higher productivity growth path that would be largely impervious to old economy problems like recessions. But the old economy patterns did indeed assert themselves, albeit with some innovative twists.

After having surged to 3.4 percent in 2000, the rate of productivity growth turned negative for the first six months of 2001 and barely recovered into the third quarter. However, productivity growth did then accelerate in a stop-and-go pattern similar to what we saw with GDP. But even the periods of surging growth seem to have been largely tied to an "old economy" pattern – i.e. pushing workers on the job harder without providing extra pay, through intensifying the work process and lengthening the working day. In May 2002, *Business Week* reported that white collar workers felt that the productivity gains "have come on their backs....They complain about managing the orphaned workloads of downsized colleagues, scouring new avenues for business, and fighting for high-profile posts so that if the axe falls, it won't hit them." The same *Business Week* story described how major corporations, including Wal-Mart, Taco Bell, Starbucks and U-Haul, were forcing their production-level employees to work extra hours without receiving overtime pay (and being hit with class-action lawsuits as a result). This tactic obviously enables firms to increase their productivity per employee, since they rely on the extra hours from their existing workforce rather than hiring new workers as the way to maintain the firm's level of operations. Indeed, it may well be that the official government figures on working hours are significantly below the real number of hours workers were clocking during the recession. If so, this would mean that the hourly productivity growth figures have been overstated.[4]

Real wages also typically fall during recessions. But in 2001, the average real wage for non-supervisory workers did continue to rise following the increases from 1997–2000, even if by a modest 1 percent relative to their 2000 figure. But even this small 2001 gain has to be measured in the context of the speed-ups and stretch-outs that businesses imposed on both their managerial and production-level employees in 2001. Indeed, if it is correct that average hours are being understated in the government data, this would then mean that hourly earnings did not rise at all in 2001, but may well have fallen, in line with a typical recession pattern. Over 2002, the average wages at best stagnated.

Other indicators point to a serious downturn. Given that the stock market bubble so heavily drove the expansion, it should not be a surprise that overall household wealth dropped sharply in 2001, by 5 percent relative to 2000 and more than 9 percent relative to 1999. Moreover, this decline in overall household wealth takes account not only of the stock market collapse, but the countervailing rise in home prices as well (more on this below). Of course, the stock market drop was felt mainly by the wealthy. But the recession also hit people hard at the other end of the spectrum. The U.S. Conference of Mayors reported that requests for food aid rose 23 percent in 2001 relative to 2000 while requests for emergency shelter increased 13 percent. These figures continued to worsen further in 2002.[5]

Overall then, it is clear that the 2001 downturn marked a turning point for the U.S. economy, with the single greatest casualty being the sense that the economic growth engine under Clinton – whether it came from the stock market, the fiscal surpluses, Alan Greenspan, the Internet or elsewhere – had become a spent force. The economy's performance over 2002 only validated that prognosis, despite the relentless cheerleading of a wide swath of forecasters, journalists and economists, who managed to convince each other that the Clinton-era party simply could not end. What were the causes of the recession and its unfolding? Why couldn't the Maestro Greenspan work his magic to have prevented it or, at least once it started, to quickly revive the growth engine? What are the longer-term prospects emerging out of the current economic mix, with the stock market bubble having collapsed; corporate America awash in accounting scandals; Bush demanding more tax cuts for the rich on top of those he already delivered; the military-industrial complex restored as the unquestioned preeminent federal spending priority; and the projections for unending fiscal surpluses having vanished into thin air? These are the questions to which we now turn.

Stock market bust

It is difficult to resurrect the mindset around which, in the 1990s, economists conducted spirited debates as to whether the stock market run-up that we were observing was a bubble, in the mode of the 1920s and similar historical experiences, or the leading edge of a new epoch in financial history, in which stock prices had become uncoupled from the underlying profitability of firms. Reality, of course, has intervened to conclude this debate. Even purveyors of such new-era manifestos as *Dow 36,000* (this particular representative work having been authored by James Glassman and Kevin Hassert of the American Enterprise Institute) were forced to beat a retreat from their bubble-inspired claims.[6]

In fact, the demise of the stock market bubble coincided almost exactly with the winding down of the Clinton era. As we can see in Figure 4.2, the Standard & Poor's 500 monthly index reached its peak of 1517.7 in August 2000, but its sharp descent begins in November – the election month – when the average fell by 8 percent. That drop then continues through September 2001, to a trough of 1090.9, a decline of 40 percent from the peak. But virtually all of the decline occurs before September 11. Moreover, the index rose for the next three months after September 11, even after the markets completely shut down for a week after the terrorist attacks. As the figure also shows, the market started falling again in April 2002, after the post-9/11 recovery, reaching a new trough of 815.3 in September 2002, 46 percent below the August 2000 peak. Though 9/11 and the subsequent military engagements did of course influence the market, these factors clearly have not been decisive in pushing stock prices downward.

Nor was there any other single event which transformed market psychology from bull to bear mode – which is to say, injected some modicum of sanity amid the rampaging herds. It was certainly not the various corporate embezzlement and accounting scandals that brought the market down. The news about Enron, Global Crossing, Tyco, Merrill Lynch, WorldCom, Xerox and Vice President Cheney's old firm Halliburton, among others, all surfaced after the bubble burst. This is the normal pattern. John Kenneth Galbraith emphasized this point in his study of the 1929 stock market crash:

> At any given time there exists an inventory of undiscovered embezzlement. This inventory – it should perhaps be called the bezzle – amounts at any moment to many millions of dollars...In good times people are relaxed, trusting and money is plentiful. But even though money is plentiful, there are always people who need more. Under these circumstances the rate of embezzlement grows, the rate of discovery falls off, and bezzle increases rapidly. In depression all of this is reversed.[7]

As the market was approaching its peak, a fairly steady trickle of stories did begin creeping into the business press suggesting that perhaps the dot.com start-ups should be expected to produce profits rather than simply business

FIGURE 4.2: Standard & Poor's 500 monthly stock market index
(January 2000–December 2002)

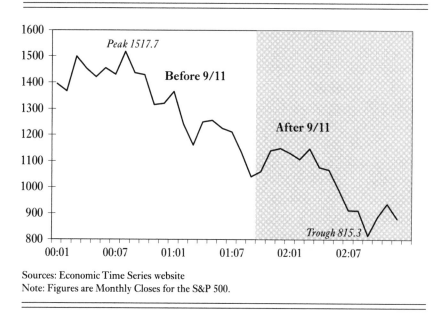

Sources: Economic Time Series website
Note: Figures are Monthly Closes for the S&P 500.

plans and expenses. But one could not have known when the force of such reasoning might attain majority assent. As the one-time boy-wonder stock analyst for Merrill Lynch Henry Blodget said a few months after the downturn had taken hold, "The market went from saying, 'We like companies that are growing quickly but are losing lots of money' to saying 'We want to see earnings.' It's very hard to predict a 180-degree turn like that." In short, the bubble collapsed because it was bound to do so, sooner or later. The late economist Herbert Stein explained such phenomena thusly: "If something cannot go on forever, it will stop."[8]

But the collapse of the bubble was not simply a matter of greedy speculators getting foreclosed on their vacation homes, or even this plus trusting grandmothers losing their retirement accounts. Rather, the impact of the market collapse has reverberated, and will continue to do so, well beyond its impact on the immediate market players themselves. As I have argued in the previous discussion on the Clinton experience, the stock market was the primary force pushing the U.S. economy forward during the 1990s. Correspondingly, the market collapse was the primary force pushing it down over 2001–02. In particular, as we have seen, the stock market boom produced first a debt-financed consumption boom for the wealthy then a debt-financed investment boom for corporations. It also created a highly attractive investment location for foreigners, whose inflow of funds into the U.S. market provided a major demand force pushing up stock prices.

But the collapse of the bubble meant that businesses were now saddled with excess productive capacity from their bubble-induced spending excesses. We can see this from Figure 4.3, which shows the monthly movements in the rate of industrial capacity utilization between January 2000 and December 2002. As we see, the upper flat line in the figure shows the average rate of capacity utilization over the full Clinton presidency, 1993–2000, which was 82.4 percent, a figure that basically accords with the average rate of 82.0 percent between 1967–92. But the rate of capacity utilization fell sharply beginning in July 2000, which was around the peak period for the stock market. Almost all of the descent in capacity utilization occurs before September 11. By the end of September 2001, the rate had fallen to 75.5 percent, and would fall still further to 74.4 percent by the end of 2001. This monthly rate was the lowest figure recorded since early 1983 under Reagan, when the country was just coming out of the severe 1982 recession. As the figure also shows, capacity utilization remained low throughout 2002, with the December 2002 figure, at 75.4 percent, being still seven full percentage points below the 82.4 percent average rate under Clinton. It is no surprise then that new investment spending also stalled over this period, falling by nearly 11 percent between 2000 and 2001, and with virtually no improvement in 2002.[9]

It was also not surprising that foreign investors began losing their enthusiasm for U.S. investment opportunities in this same period. Between 2000 and 2001, new equity purchases by foreigners fell by 20 percent, from $482 to $287 million, a decline that was more than double the 16 percent decline in the S&P 500 between 2000 and 2001.[10] The decline in foreign purchases of bonds and other U.S. assets was less sharp in 2001, but began gathering force in the first quarter of 2002, with overall foreign asset pur-

FIGURE 4.3: Capacity utilization rate for all U.S. industry
(2000.1–2002.12, monthly figures)

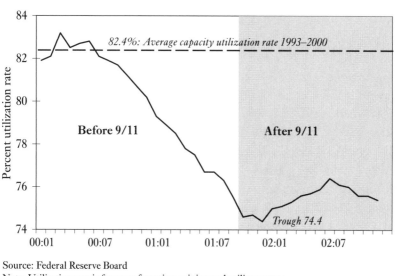

Source: Federal Reserve Board
Note: Utilization rate is for manufacturing, mining and utility sectors.

chases declining by more than 60 percent in the first quarter of 2002 relative to the first quarter of 2001.

During 2002, these forces also brought a weakening of the dollar in global currency markets, with the dollar falling by about 14 percent against the euro and 10 percent against the yen over the course of the year. With investors having become less enthusiastic about holding stocks and bonds in the U.S., it follows that they would be similarly less eager to hold dollars against alternative currencies.

The overall effects of such a dollar decline, if it is sustained, would be complicated. At one level, it would be good news both for U.S. firms trying to export and the domestic firms facing foreign competition within U.S. markets, since the cheaper dollar makes U.S. exports more competitive and imports into the U.S. more expensive. On the other hand, the rest of the world is highly dependent on sales in the U.S. market, so that the fall of the dollar would increase the difficulties of other countries emerging from their own recessions and slow growth trends. In terms of financial markets, the fall of the dollar would make the U.S. still less desirable as a safe haven for investors, worsening the problems caused by the stock market collapse. This would certainly be bad news for U.S. financial markets. But it would be only mixed news – not an unalloyed gain – for other countries trying to attract foreign investors. Of course, a declining dollar makes holding savings in other assets relatively more desirable. But it also means that global investors would be simply less rich than they had been. By the end of 2001, foreigners were holding nearly $7 trillion worth of financial assets in the United States. All of this wealth would be vulnerable to the decline in the value of U.S. financial markets and the dollar.

As a net effect then, the shift by foreigners out of U.S. markets and the corresponding fall of the dollar becomes one more important factor contributing to the overall sense of uncertainty following the stock market decline and recession. This is obviously not a climate in which one would expect private investors to themselves return the economy to high-growth path.

Greenspan to the rescue?

The collapse of the stock market bubble and the onset of recession began at almost precisely the point at which the cult of Alan Greenspan was also reaching its peak. Bob Woodward concluded *Maestro*, his 2000 Washington-insider paean to Greenspan by writing, "With Greenspan, we find comfort. He helps breathe life into the vision of America as strong, the best, invincible," (p. 228). President Clinton expressed this same sentiment when he reappointed Greenspan to a fourth term as Chair of the Federal Reserve in January 2000, quipping in the midst of the Internet frenzy "I've been thinking about taking 'Alan.com' public; then we could pay the debt off even before 2015." Not to be outdone, Senator John McCain went so far during his presidential campaign as to declare, "I would not only reappoint Mr. Greenspan, but if Mr. Greenspan should die, God forbid...I would prop him up and put a pair of dark glasses on him."[11]

If Greenspan had been anywhere near as capable as his extravagant reputation suggested, why couldn't he prevent the recession? In fact, Greenspan did act aggressively to counteract the recession, but it was hardly a virtuoso performance. Greenspan's most basic failure occurred well before the recession began, through allowing the stock market bubble and accompanying excesses of corporate and household indebtedness to proceed, and, more generally, through giving his enthusiastic blessing to the deregulation of U.S. financial markets. The U.S. financial structure thus became highly unstable under Greenspan's approving gaze. Under such circumstances, Greenspan had only limited tools for fighting the recession once it had begun to gather force.

What are the Fed's tools?

Greenspan deliberately maintains an aura of mystery about his job. But the reality is that the Fed has limited tools for counteracting a recession, especially, again, given an increasingly deregulated and, consequently, more speculation-driven financial market. The primary policy instrument that Greenspan controls for counteracting recessions is one short-term interest rate known as the Federal Funds rate. Almost all the worldwide news reports about Fed policy meetings are really about decisions by the Fed to move this single rate, which they control, up or down.

Granted, the Federal Funds rate is highly influential. It is the rate at which private U.S. banks borrow and lend among themselves on a short-term basis, when borrowing banks need to cover their own short-term debts and lending banks have extra cash on hand. The expectation is that because the Federal Funds rate affects the borrowing costs for the entire U.S. banking system, changes in this rate will then ripple through the rest of the economy.

But how forcefully these ripple effects operate depends on other factors in the economy. For one thing, it is never a given that other interest rates, especially those that directly affect businesses and households, will decline in step with a decline in the Federal Funds rate. In addition, even if the other rates do indeed fall, we don't know in advance how businesses and households will respond to the lower rates. Moreover, in a situation like that prevailing at the end of the Clinton bubble economy, when corporations and households were already overextended with debt, it was not necessarily desirable to encourage them to be borrowing even more. This was especially true since the value of their financial assets were falling with the end of the stock market bubble.

Finally, throughout the boom, Greenspan had been trying to keep interest rates high enough so as to maintain the value of the dollar in currency markets and, thereby, continue to attract foreign investors into the U.S. The recession made him abandon this effort. As we saw, both foreign investment and the value of the dollar had gone into sharp decline through the end of 2002. This would clearly complicate the effects of any cuts in the Federal Funds rate – creating, as we discussed, beneficial effects for U.S. exporters and domestic firms competing with foreigners in the U.S. market, but negative effects on the U.S. financial markets and for the growth prospects of the main trading partners of the U.S.

Interest rate ripple effects

Greenspan's immediate problem with his primary policy tool begins with the ripple effects from the Federal Funds rate to the other rates in the economy. As we can see in Figure 4.4, these ripple effects turned out to be substantially weaker than one would expect from an all-powerful *maestro*.

The three lines in the figure show the movements in the Federal Funds rates and two other representative rates from January 2000 to December 2002. The Baa corporate bond rate is the rate at which average corporations – neither the least nor most risky firms – are able to borrow on a long-term basis. The thirty-year mortgage rate is the standard rate homebuyers face when purchasing a home or taking out a home equity loan.

We first see Greenspan's aggressive measures at countering the recession through rate cuts, beginning when he lowered the monthly average for the Federal Funds rate in January 2001, from 6.4 to 6 percent. This was the first of a series of eleven cuts in the Federal Funds rate over the next year, through which the rate fell to a 40 year low of 1.73 by January 2002. Greenspan maintained the Federal Funds rate between 1.73–1.75 percent until November, at which point he cut the rate again, this time to 1.25 percent, which he

FIGURE 4.4: Monetary policy and market interest rates
(Federal Funds, Baa Bond, and 30-year mortgage rates, 2001.1–2002.12)

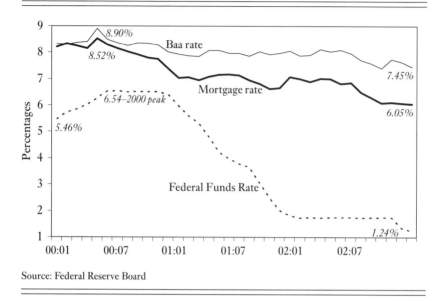

Source: Federal Reserve Board

then maintained into 2003. For the full year of 2002, the Federal Funds rate averaged 1.67 percent, the lowest annual average in forty-four years, and the second lowest annual figure recorded altogether for this rate.

However, despite these highly aggressive moves by Greenspan, we see that the bond and mortgage rates shown in Figure 4.4 do not follow the Federal Funds rate in the pattern of steep descent. The other rates do fall, but much more moderately. The mortgage rate falls at a deliberate pace over the two-year period, from a peak of 8.52 in May 2000 to 6.05 by December 2002. The Baa bond rate declines are more moderate still, from a peak of 8.90 percent in May 2000 to 7.45 by December 2002.

Divergent corporate and consumer responses

We have already seen that corporations came out of the 1990s boom with too much productive equipment and debt. It is not surprising then that the relatively modest interest rate cuts that were available to them, as reflected in the slowly sequenced 1.5 percentage point fall in the Baa rate between May 2001 and December 2002, did not energize them into a new burst of borrowing and spending. The corporations raised only half as much money on credit markets in 2001 relative to 2000, despite the lower rates, and the level of corporate borrowing continued to fall further over 2002. Corporate investment expenditures fell as well, exerting downward pressure on overall economic growth throughout 2001–02.

The response by households was another matter. Despite the moderate pace of the 2.4 percentage point decline in the mortgage-lending rate between May 2001–December 2002, households did increase their mortgage borrowing by $181 billion in 2001, a rise of nearly 30 percent over the 2000 level. The increase for the first three quarters of 2002 was still sharper. These loans financed, in roughly equal shares, both new housing purchases and refinancings (that is, taking out a new mortgage on a house that one already owns). This injection of credit kept the housing market buoyant even during the downturn, and also gave households extra cash to pay off some of their other debts and increase their consumption spending.

But the other side of this is that the median home price was pushed up by nearly 11 percent between 1999 and 2001. As the upward price momentum continued through the middle of 2002, the *Wall Street Journal*, among other observers, began warning of the dangers of a housing "market bubble" in which "stretched buyers push mortgages to the limit."[12]

As Dean Baker of the Center for Economic and Policy Research makes clear, the sharp rise in housing prices actually began in 1995, somewhat prior to the period in which the stock market ascent had shifted from high gear into overdrive.[13] But the upward movement of housing prices was actually strengthened when the stock market bubble burst, since the stock market collapse moved investors into real estate holdings as an alternative to equities. At the same time, the housing bubble and corresponding explosion in household debt was also triggered by major changes in mortgage underwriting standards, "with lenders doing everything possible to keep the boom alive," according to the *Wall Street Journal*. This included allowing "some well-to-do borrowers to apply up to 50 percent of their income to their regular mortgage payment. A decade ago, the norm was 28–32 percent of income."

Market analysts were also confused in interpreting the decline in mortgage rates. The drop that we observed from 8.5 to 6.0 percent over the course of nearly two years was significant, but hardly extraordinary amid the recession and Greenspan's dramatic lowering of the Federal Funds rate. Nevertheless, the business press at the time, including the same *Wall Street Journal* articles that warned of the dangerous build-up of mortgage debt, also refer to these mortgage rates as being lower than at any time in nearly three decades. But such references to historically low rates are misleading, since they neglect the distinction between nominal market rates and the real rates that adjust for the effects of inflation. When the nominal mortgage rate fell to a low of 6 percent by the end of 2002, this was at a time when inflationary pressures in the economy were virtually non-existent. This meant that the real rate – which is the rate that better reflects the true debt burdens borrowers will face – was also in the range of 6 percent. In fact, a real rate of 6 percent is substantially higher than the average real rate of 4.8 percent that prevailed from 1972-2001. Homeowners that chose to refinance their houses in this period also faced additional costs, including the closing costs of their old loans, which, on average, amounts to more than 4 percent of the total amount of the old loan – for example, $4,000 or more in costs to close out a $100,000 mortgage.[14]

Households had already gone into the recession carrying extremely heavy debt loads. Given the changes in the housing market during the recession, it is not surprising that, for the first three quarters of 2002, both household mortgage payments, at 6.2 percent of total disposable income, and overall debt servicing payments, at 14 percent of disposable income, were approaching historic highs. The average household's total outstanding debt was at an unprecedented level in the first three quarters of 2002, reaching 107 percent of disposable income.

What are the implications of this? At the least, such household debt burdens should act as a drag on economic growth in the coming years. Even if growth did take hold, there would still be a limit as to how much additional debt households can assume over the next growth phase. This is precisely because the 2001-02 recession departed from the pattern of previous recessions, during which household debt burdens fell. Beyond this, if a sharp decline in housing prices were to occur amid the ongoing decline in stock prices, the destabilizing tremors will reverberate widely. First, new housing construction would fall, along with consumer purchases of furniture and other housing accessories. The negative wealth effect would also reduce overall consumption by households. According to the most careful recent estimate, households would reduce their overall spending by 6 percent due to a fall in the value of their home – that is, if the home value falls by $100, then household spending would fall by $6.[15]

Overall then, we see that Greenspan had only limited success in using highly aggressive Federal Funds interest rate cuts to fight off recession. This became a major cause for concern by the time of the November 2002 cut to 1.25 percent. Given that the rate cuts started in January 2001 with the Federal Funds rate at 6.5 percent, it became clear with the cut to 1.25 percent that Greenspan was running out of maneuvering room before the Federal Funds rate hit zero. Greenspan acknowledged this problem, but also argued that, if pressed, the Fed could pull out new weapons to counteract continuing stagnation or even a double-dip recession. He said that the most important such weapon was one that the Fed last used more than fifty years ago – to purchase long-term government bonds in an more direct effort at lowering long-term private market rates such as the Baa corporate bond rate than was possible through cuts in the short-term Federal Funds rate.

Greenspan is certainly correct that the Fed could pursue a wider array of policies to push the economy onto a new growth path. But the fact that he was forced to acknowledge that his interventions through 2002 may well have been inadequate to the task only underscores the severity of the situation at that time—a situation created, in no small measure, by Greenspan's own acquiescence in enabling deregulated, speculative financial markets to determine the prospects for prosperity in the U.S.[16]

The Bush tax-cutting agenda

From its introduction as the centerpiece of Bush's presidential campaign platform onward, the Bush tax proposals always had only one primary purpose, which was to deliver a sumptuous tax bonanza to the rich. What is remarkable is how firmly Bush has hewed to this overarching purpose, de-

TABLE 4.1: Effects of Bush tax policies on different income groups

Income group	Average income (dollars)	Bush February 2001 proposal		Tax law passed June 2001			
				2001 Cuts		Post-2001 Cuts	
		Average total tax cut (dollars)	Percent of total tax cut	Average total tax cut (dollars)	Percent of total tax cut	Average total tax cut (dollars)	Percent of total tax cut
Lowest 20%	$9,300	$45	0.8%	$56	2.5%	$10	0.2%
Second 20%	20,600	212	3.5	269	12.1	107	2.2
Middle 20%	34,400	509	8.4	405	18.3	194	4.1
Fourth 20%	56,400	951	15.7	575	25.9	449	9.4
Top 20%	170,900	4,174	64.7	912	42.2	4,059	84.1
Top 1%	1,117,000	54,480	45.0	3,120	7.0	50,003	52.2

Source: Citizens for Tax Justice

spite the recession, September 11, the wars in Afghanistan and Iraq, and despite receiving widespread criticism, even from the likes of Bill Gates's father and David Rockefeller. It should therefore not be surprising that none of the Bush tax initiatives have been effective in either countering the recession or promoting a healthy expansion.

Tax cuts, round one

The effects of the Bush-led tax programs become clear through the figures presented in Table 4.1, based on research by the outstanding Washington D.C. research institute, Citizens for Tax Justice. The table first shows the impact on income distribution of Bush's proposal which he made in February 2001, i.e. only one month after taking office. The most extensive feature of this proposal was across-the-board cuts in income tax rates. At the time, rates ranged between 15 and 39.6 percent. Under Bush's initial plan, a new bottom rate of 10 percent would be created for the first $12,000 of taxable income, while the top rate would be cut to 33 percent. There were several additional features in the proposal, the best known being a phased reduction and then complete elimination of the estate tax – what the Republicans had taken to calling the "death tax," since it is a tax on a portion of the estates passed on to heirs by the wealthy.

As Table 4.1 shows, the richest 20 percent of households would receive nearly 65 percent of the overall benefits from the initial Bush proposal once it had been fully phased in – that is, including all the income tax cuts and the estate tax elimination and the other measures. The top 1 percent would themselves receive 45 percent of the benefits, amounting to an average of more than $54,000 in reduced tax liabilities per year. By contrast, families in the lower 40 percent of the income distribution would receive only 4.3 percent of the total tax reductions. And again, with this initial Bush proposal, none of the cuts would have been implemented during 2001, and almost all of them were to be gradually phased in over a decade. Thus, despite the Bush and Cheney claims that this would be an anti-recession insurance policy, it was difficult to see how it would have any serious impact at all on the actual recession that was occurring in 2001.

But the real purpose of this initial Bush proposal was to set the terms of subsequent negotiations – i.e. to place on the table a measure that was un-equivocally a brazen giveaway to the rich. Bush could then appear as embrac-ing the high road of compromise through accepting an amended proposal that was only slightly less skewed in its effects. Indeed, the Democrats in Congress did manage to get this initial Bush proposal amended, even while, in the final measure that became law in June 2001, Bush conceded nothing of significance.

The most significant change in the June law was its inclusion of a mild stimulus measure, which was a tax rebate of $300 for individual taxpayers and $600 for married couples. The law also provided that the rebate checks start getting sent almost immediately to taxpayers, thereby encouraging house-holds to increase their spending while the economy was still in recession. In total, roughly $50 billion in rebate checks were sent to 96 million taxpayers. If households spent all $50 billion immediately, that would directly increase spending in the economy by about 0.5 percent. In other words, at most, the impact of this stimulus measure would be about 10–20 percent the size of what the wealth effects from the stock market bubble had provided in terms of increased consumer spending, which is why it is appropriate to describe this measure as, at most, a *mild* stimulus initiative.[17]

At the same time, the June 2001 tax still also included across-the-board income tax cuts and a reduction, leading to a complete repeal, of the estate tax. Once again, none of these features of the new law would have any discernable effect on the recession, while they would have a major long-term impact on the distribution of income. Thus, returning to Table 4.1, the Citizens for Tax Justice estimates that the longer-term distributive effects of the June law are even more skewed to the rich than Bush's February proposal. As the table shows, with rebate checks getting sent in the second half of 2001, the overall effects of the cuts in 2001 are somewhat more evenly distributed, with, for example, the richest 20 percent of families receiving "only" 42.2 percent of the overall gains. But after 2001, the richest 20 percent get 84.1 percent of the overall benefits and the top 1 percent alone getting more than half of the overall benefits. Meanwhile, the least wealthy 40 percent of families in total receive only 2.4 percent of the benefits after 2001.

Tax cuts, round two

In the aftermath of the September 11 attacks, if not before then, it had become evident that the $300–600 tax rebates, along with Greenspan's interest rate cuts, had not been successful at preventing a recession. This brought new calls for further government stimulus measures. But here again, Bush and the Republicans in Congress saw this situation as, primarily, yet another opportunity to deliver more tax breaks for the rich.

The new round of Bush tax proposals began in October 2001, only three weeks after the terrorist attacks. It was a plan targeted exclusively to provide major tax breaks for big corporations. This included repeal of the so-called Alternative Minimum Tax on corporate profits. The Alternative Minimum Tax had been established in 1986 as a device for prohibiting total tax avoidance by big corporations and the wealthy, even after allowing for the usual legions of clever corporate attorneys and accountants successfully exploiting every possible loophole in the existing tax codes.

But the Republicans in the House of Representatives apparently concluded that even this Bush measure did not go far enough in showering benefits onto the corporations. The Republican-controlled House thus passed a bill in December 2001 that not only repealed the Alternative Minimum Tax, but would also send out a new round of rebate checks – only this time the checks would not be limited to $600 and would not be going to average households. These rebates were reserved for corporations, who would receive checks from the government based on how much they had paid as their Alternative Minimum Tax obligation at any time since the law had taken effect fifteen years previously. Among the beneficiaries of this feature of the House measure would be IBM, who were in line for a $1.4 billion rebate check, Ford (a $1 billion rebate), GM ($833 million) and GE ($671 million). Enron itself would have received a $254 million rebate.[18]

This proposal did not survive in the Democratic-controlled Senate. But Bush's bargaining strategy nevertheless held up – that is, starting negotiations with audacious giveaways to the rich, then "compromising" by accepting a measure only slightly less brazen. The measure that finally passed in March 2002 did include $14 billion in additional insurance money for unemployed workers to accompany $114 billion in tax breaks for corporations, though the main vehicle for assisting the corporations was to allow them to more quickly write off the costs of their new equipment purchases. The Alternative Minimum Tax did remain intact.

But the overall effect, as we see in Figure 4.5, was a stimulus program at a time of national emergency in which the $114 billion in benefits to corporations was more than eight times greater than the funds going to assist laid-off workers. On top of this, the benefits for the corporations were not offered as a one-time emergency inducement, but rather were to remain available for three years (with a good chance that they could become permanent). This, again, undermines any sense of the policy as a means of stimulating immediate spending by corporations. Indeed, because of this feature of the law, the corporations could now postpone new equipment purchases for three years, and thereby still receive the benefits of the new law long after the recession should have ended.

FIGURE 4.5: Who gained from March 2002 anti-recession stimulus program?

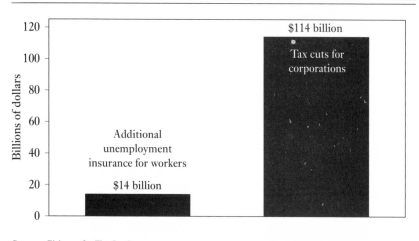

Source: Citizens for Tax Justice

Tax cuts, round three

With the economy still sputtering by the end of 2002, Bush introduced a new set of proposals in January 2003, aimed at lowering taxes on the rich still further. The main feature of the 2003 initiative was to totally exempt from taxation the dividend payments that shareholders receive from corporations. This proposal, in other words, was as audacious as the 2001 Bush plan to eliminate the estate tax. It advanced the idea that while working people must pay taxes on the wages they earn, corporate shareholders shouldn't face a tax burden on what the even government itself officially classifies as *unearned* income from dividends.

There were seven other elements to Bush's 2003 proposal, including an increase in child care credits from $600 to $1000 for eligible families and moving forward to 2003 the lowering of tax rates on wages and salaries that, according to the 2001 Bush measure, were supposed to take effect in 2004 and 2006. But according to the Bush Treasury Department's own estimates, the benefits over a ten-year period for corporate shareholders of the elimination of dividend taxes would be greater than all the other seven proposals combined.

There was little disputing who the winners and losers would be from this proposal, at least in the short term. For the year 2003, the Citizens for Tax Justice estimated that the average amount of extra after-tax income for the less well-off 60 percent of households would be $131, while the richest 10 percent of households would receive an extra $5578 in after-tax income – that is, the richest 10 percent of households would receive 43 times more additional after-tax income from this measure than the less well off 60 percent. The Citizens for Tax Justice also estimates that the richest 1 percent of households would end up with $30,127 more in their pockets due to the Bush proposal, about 300 times more than the lower 60 percent.[19]

These disparities were so extreme that in announcing the proposal, Bush felt compelled to launch a preemptive attack on potential critics – asserting that anyone who suggested that the proposal had a class bias was engaging in class warfare. With Bush having thus invoked the spectre of Marxism in support of his plan, his advisors followed suit. Perhaps most prominently, Glenn Hubbard, Bush's Chair of the Council of Economic Advisors at the time, defended the Bush proposal in an article that explicitly analyzes its effects with respect to "capitalists" and "workers," hardly the normal jargon of the aggressively class-blind U.S. economics literature. But aside from his choice of terms, Hubbard offered up little more than standard trickle down theory in support of the proposal. In particular, Hubbard tried to show how workers as well as capitalists would benefit, even if the workers never received a penny of the tax relief themselves. The way the workers would gain would be through the capitalists getting more money, which they would then use to invest in new productive equipment. The increase in investment would then spur productivity growth, and the rise in productivity would produce a bigger income pie for workers and capitalists to share. *Business Week* advanced the same basic position in a cover story that posed the question "Is It Class Warfare?" *Business Week's* answer was that the Bush plan would certainly make the rich richer and increase inequality, but that it would still promote productivity and economic growth, which in turn would benefit workers.[20]

In response to Hubbard and *Business Week*, one can first of all raise justifiable doubts as to whether increases in productivity necessarily translate into higher wages. After all, we saw in Chapter 2 how, between 1973–93, the productivity of the U.S. economy rose (albeit at a relatively slow rate) while the average real wage for nonsupervisory workers fell. But let's put aside for now the issue of how the overall income pie gets sliced up, and consider the initial premise of the plan: how confident should we be that Bush's proposal would really make the income pie bigger?

The main channel through which the proposal is supposed to operate is through increasing the attractiveness of corporate equity ownership, and thus reinvigorating the stock market from its post-bubble and post-Enron swoon. But there is no reason to expect that this measure would be any more successful than Bush's 2002 tax giveaways to corporations at stimulating investment in new plants and machinery. The most basic problem is that, despite the collapse of the stock market bubble and the continued slump through 2002, stock prices were still too high by the end of 2002 relative to the earnings of firms, if long historical patterns of price-to-earnings ratios offer any guide for understanding the future.

Thus, for the third quarter of 2002, the price-to-earnings ratio for the 500 firms in the Standard & Poor's index was 27.2, which means that stock purchasers were paying $27.20 for one dollar of corporations' reported earnings.[21] This translates into a return of 3.7 cents on a dollar invested in buying stocks. A 3.7 percent return amounts to little more than half the historical average return on stock purchases of about 7 percent – and the market arrived at this 3.7 percent figure, again, two full years after the 1990s bubble burst. In other words, for stock prices to return to something approximating their historical relationship with earnings, either corporate profits will have to explode or, far more likely, stock prices will have to continue falling to roughly half of where they stood at the end of the third quarter of 2002.

Granted, if taxes on dividends are eliminated, every penny of corporations' earnings will be substantially more valuable to shareholders. However, this factor is not likely to compensate shareholders adequately against the continued downward pressure on stock prices exerted through the collapse of the 1990s bubble. But this then raises another question: after the huge imbalances generated by the bubble, do we really want to rely on the stock market *again* as the primary engine driving the economy forward? Certainly, if there was one lesson to be learned amid the wreckage of the collapsed bubble, it is that the stock market is "a whirlwind of speculation," as John Maynard Keynes explained in reflecting on the 1929 stock market collapse and 1930s Depression. As Keynes said then, perhaps self-evidently at the time, "when the capital development of a country becomes the by-product of the activities of a casino, the job is likely to be ill-done."[22]

In fact, there are only two certain things about the Bush fiscal tax program, circa 2003. First of all, it would widen the inequalities that have grown relentlessly in the United States for a generation. Second, it will unambiguously produce a sharp drop in government revenue. Bush did not explain what government programs he intended to cut or eliminate altogether to make up for the revenues lost through giving additional tax breaks to the rich. We know he certainly didn't have the military in mind. As we will discuss in detail below, that means that, if Bush does indeed succeed in releasing corporate shareholders from the obligation to pay dividend taxes, the real losers from this measure would have to be all the other programs on which the government spends money, including education, health, income security and poverty alleviation.

Government spending and state fiscal crises

While the Bush tax policies contributed almost nothing toward countering the recession and promoting a new growth upswing, the overall tax and spending policies of the government through 2001 were quite significant in this regard. Indeed, government policies – including here state and local as well as the federal government – were a crucial counterforce to the stock market collapse and corresponding decline in corporate investment spending, preventing an even sharper downturn.

Recall that overall economic growth fell from 3.8 percent in 2000 to 0.3 percent for the full year of 2001. In Table 4.2, we see how the expenditure patterns of various sectors of the economy contributed to this growth decline. These overall growth contribution figures do not measure the growth rate of a sector itself, but rather how significant any given sector's increases

TABLE 4.2: Government spending and GDP growth in 2001 recession
(in percentages)

Negative contributors to growth	
Private investment spending	-1.90
Exports less imports	-0.18
Positive contributors to growth	
Household consumption spending	+1.67
Government spending	+0.65
TOTAL GDP GROWTH	+0.24 (rounded in NIPA aggregate tables to 0.30)

Source: U.S. National Income and Product Accounts, Table 8.2

(or declines) in spending had been as a factor contributing to the economy's overall meager 0.3 percent growth.

To begin with, the table shows what we have already discussed, that the collapse of private investment was the primary force pulling down overall growth in 2001, making a contribution to overall growth of -1.9 percent. The U.S. position in world trade – i.e. our sale of exports minus our purchases of imports – also made a negative contribution to overall growth of -0.12 percent. The U.S. has imported more than it has exported every year since 1976. In 2001, in fact, the negative effects on growth of this pattern were less than is normally the case. This is because, during the recession, purchases of imports by U.S. consumers and businesses became less buoyant than during the boom years. But the other side of this situation is that the U.S. slowdown was felt throughout the rest of the world, which counts heavily on sales within the U.S. as a significant source of their own growth.

Table 4.2 then lists the two positive contributors to growth, these being overall household and government spending. Of these two sources of growth, we see that household spending was a substantially larger factor – contributing +1.67 percent to overall growth in 2001 as opposed to +0.65 percent for the government sector. But the relative size of these two contributions can be misleading, both toward understanding the economy's overall performance in 2001 and the prospects for avoiding sluggish growth over the next several years.

The first way in which these figures might mislead concerns the growth contribution by the household sector. We have already discussed how important ever-increasing levels of household debt were in preventing a deeper recession over 2001, even while also producing highly fragile financial conditions for a large share of households. It is unlikely that further increases in debt-financed household spending will be sustainable, unless job opportunities and household incomes also start growing more rapidly.

And what about jobs and incomes themselves? The central point here is that the household sector of the economy, unlike private businesses and the government, does not, for the most part, hire people into jobs. It is rather where people come home from work after having been on the job, either with a private business or the government. With private businesses having cut back on their investment spending in 2001, this meant that the government sector was the most stable source of jobs as well. Thus, between the fourth quarters of 2000 and 2001, the private sector lost 1.3 million jobs, while the government sector gained 463,000. The government sector's positive contributions to the job market, in turn, provided firmer footing for consumers to increase their borrowing and spending. Thus, along with the increases of household debt itself, it is not an exaggeration to say that the growth of government spending was the major counterweight to the recession in 2001, preventing an even sharper downturn.

Government spending and growth

How did the government sector make its contribution to the economy's overall growth in 2001? We will need to consider both spending patterns and the government's budgetary stance to answer this question.

Of course, the major new spending sources in 2001 were all related to the September 11 terrorist attacks and war in Afghanistan. But direct spending by the military, though important, was not the primary factor. As we can see from Table 4.3, increased military spending did account for most of the contribution to overall growth by the *federal* government, with the military contribution to growth being 35 percent of the federal government's 45 per-

TABLE 4.3: Breakdown of government contributions to overall GDP growth

	Share of government growth contribution
Federal government spending	+45 percent
Military spending	+30 percent
Non-military spending	+15 percent
State and local government spending	+55 percent

Source: National Income and Product Accounts Table 8.2

cent total contribution. But a full 55 percent of the government's contribution to growth came rather from state and local governments.

The overall spending increases by state and local governments resulted from increased funding for domestic security measures – for police, firefighters and emergency medical assistance – while also maintaining or even increasing funds within the main additional budgetary areas of health, education and infrastructure. A large share of the overall increases resulted from spending programs that go up automatically in a recession when people's incomes go down, Medicaid being the major case in point here.

The problem is that, by the end of 2001, state and local governments could not continue to increase their spending until they got more revenues, either from a growing economy, raising taxes, or through receiving more funds from the federal government. This is because, unlike the federal government, almost all state and local governments are prohibited by law from financing their activities through running budget deficits. Many states were able to increase their spending over 2001 because they had built up "rainy day funds" during the 1990s boom years. But 2001 was the rainy day for these governments.

By the 2002 fiscal year (typically July 1 2001–June 30 2002), most states were forced to impose major cutbacks in their budgets, including across-the-board program cuts, layoffs, early retirements, and reorganizations. Cutbacks were particularly severe among programs serving low-income residents. As of January 2002, Kevin Carey and Iris J. Lav of the Center on

Budget and Policy Priorities reported that "More than two-thirds of the states have already taken steps to cut spending on programs that serve low-income residents. Among these states, 17 have cut health care programs, ten have cut income support or employment support programs such as childcare and job training, and 17 have cut other social service programs." By October 2002, the human costs of such cuts were evident. The *Wall Street Journal* surveyed the situation thusly:

> In Massachusetts, cuts to the public health budget have left a Boston group that provides free flu shots at senior centers and homeless shelters with only 2,500 flu vaccines, half as many as two years ago. In California, children will spend longer in foster care because of cuts in adoption services. In New Jersey, the working poor will lose access to state-funded health care. In Louisiana, there will be fewer hospital beds available for low-income adults.[23]

Of course, public programs that serve low-income people are generally easier to cut since the direct beneficiaries of such measures tend to have little political power. The fact that the poor lack political power then translates into governments maintaining greater flexibility in the ways they fund these programs than is the case with other budgetary items.

But the post-recession fiscal crisis also hit more rigidly administered budgetary areas, like education. A January 23, 2002 story in *Education Week* titled "City Schools Feel the Pain of Fiscal Bites," reports on how cutbacks were being forced on school districts throughout the country. Detroit, for example, announced in January 2002 more than 650 layoffs, including 165 teachers, 129 custodians, 46 social workers and 67 clerical workers. The district also cut funding for summer school programs, significantly reduced the purchase of services and equipment, and cut maintenance costs by 10 percent.

Conditions deteriorated further in fiscal year 2003, with fourteen states cutting spending on secondary education and twenty states cutting budgets for colleges and universities. The situation in Portland, Oregon – one of the most affluent large cities in the country – became dire after Oregon voters rejected tax increases to prevent budget cuts for education. As a result, the Portland school district announced in February 2003 that it would cut fifteen days from the school year, and was considering raising that figure to twenty-four days.[24]

As of early 2003, the general outlook for fiscal year 2004 appeared equally grim. According to a survey of state officials by the Center on Budget and Policy Priorities, state budget deficits in fiscal 2004 will total between $60 billion and $85 billion, which amounts to between 13–18 percent of total state expenditures.

On top of this, the Bush administration's fiscal policies were only deepening the crisis. In 2001, the federal government contributed $274 billion to state and local governments, which amounted to 21 percent of the total spending by state and local governments. The squeeze from the state and local governments' own revenue sources would suggest that these federal contributions should be substantially increased. Overall Federal spending on so-called "grants in aid" to state and local governments did increase in the 2002 and 2003 fiscal years. But all of these increases were due entirely to two programs: mandated spending on Medicaid and homeland security.

But beyond Medicaid and homeland security, the Bush policies are producing sharp cuts in state and local government budgets through two channels. Considering only the non-mandated or "discretionary" programs, the Bush administration proposed cuts of 4 percent for the 2003 fiscal year (assuming no inflation at all for 2002–03, and thus no additional cuts in spending levels due to inflation). Some of the major areas Bush targeted for cuts in 2003 were Community Development (-37 percent), Low Income Energy Assistance (-18 percent), Drug-Free Schools and Communities (-17 percent), and the Labor Department's Youth Activities Program (-11 percent).[25] In addition, the federal government tax cuts enacted in 2001 and those proposed in 2003 will themselves reduce the revenues received by state and local governments. This will occur because state and local governments depend on the federal government to establish what constitutes taxable income. If the federal government narrows the tax base through enacting new deductions or eliminating altogether taxes on estates or dividends, revenues to state and local governments correspondingly fall.

Max Sawicky of the Economic Policy Institute estimated that overall spending cuts in state and local budgets for the fiscal year 2003 amount to roughly $100 billion.[26] Cuts of this magnitude drag down overall economic growth by nearly 1 percent, i.e. substantially more than the state and local governments' positive contribution to growth in 2001. In other words, in addition to the damages inflicted on vital social programs and services, it is clear that, from an overall economic standpoint, state and local governments obviously will not continue as an engine of growth over the coming years as it was in 2001. They have rather become a major burden inhibiting the prospects for a viable recovery out of recession.

The return of federal deficits

Moving the country out of recession and a slow-growth trend will therefore depend heavily on the ways in which the federal government intervenes in the economy. For one thing, the federal government is the only source of funds for the short-term – i.e. 2003 and 2004 – that can prevent even more severe contractions in state and local government spending. But more generally we are confronted with the issue of deficit spending by the federal government. This, of course, was the topic that, as recently as the 2001 budget forecasts of both the federal Office of Management and Budget and the Congressional Budget Office, to say nothing of the 2000 Presidential campaigns of both George Bush and Al Gore, had been dismissed as a *passé* relic of earlier economic times. The new era was supposed to have been about managing permanent surpluses, and specifically the speed at which every penny of the federal government's $5.8 trillion in outstanding debt would be paid off. Both Bush and Gore claimed it could be done within a decade. We now see that all such projections were constructed on sand. At least the ground is now cleared to return to a serious discussion about both the virtues and dangers with federal deficits.

For 2001 the surplus contracted $127 billion relative to the 2000 surplus of $236 billion. The initial forecast of the Office of Management and Budget for 2002 was a deficit of $106 billion. But by June the OMB estimate had risen to $150 billion. As OMB Director Mitchell Daniels Jr. acknowledged at the time, the reason he had to revise his deficit estimate upward by 50 percent by the middle of 2002 was that his initial forecast was based on the obviously precarious assumption that the stock market would be returning in 2002 to something approximating its dizzying growth pace of the 1990s. This, in turn, was to have generated an upsurge in capital gains tax revenues as well.[27] In the end, the federal deficit for 2002 was $158 billion.

We now need to decide where to pile the OMB model amid the trash heap of forecasting failures. But a much more important issue is also at stake. This is the question of whether the shrinking of the federal surplus in 2001 and the subsequent return to deficits is good or bad for the economy. The debate among economists, politicians and the press on this issue had reached a bizarre turn by the end of 2002, as the return of fiscal deficits supplanted the mirage of unending surpluses, and with the Bush tax program promising still more red ink into the long-term future. Democrats and their supporters in academia and the press – the champions, in an earlier era, of deficit spending as a tool to stimulate sagging economies – had become increasingly strenuous in arguing that deficits could only do harm almost all of the time. Republicans, meanwhile, had invented a new term of derision – "Rubinomics" – for this Democratic position. The term, of course, referred to Bill Clinton's chief economic advisor and Treasury Secretary Robert Rubin who, as we saw in Chapter 2, sold Clinton on what Clinton himself termed an "Eisenhower Republican" stance regarding the need to eliminate deficits.

In fact, dismissive labels aside, understanding whether federal deficits are good or bad for the economy is actually a complex question without an obvious answer. It requires us to distinguish short- and long-term effects of deficits as we come out of the recession. It also entails that we examine the tax and spending priorities of the Bush administration rather than whether, simply, spending exceeds revenues (generating a deficit) or revenues exceed spending (creating a surplus).

Deficits in the short term

If we are considering the impact of government spending on economic growth during and immediately after the 2001 recession, the answer is straightforward: if the federal government had maintained a surplus at its 2000 rather than its 2001 level, this would have eliminated the government's positive contribution to economic growth in 2001. The recession would have been far more severe.

But deficit hawks raise another point beyond simply looking at the government's level of direct spending. From this perspective, eliminating the surplus prevented long-term interest rates from falling more sharply in response to Alan Greenspan's aggressive cuts in the short-term Federal Funds rate. As we saw, the Baa corporate bond rate fell only from 8.9 to 7.5 percent over the eighteen-month period in which Greenspan cut the Federal Funds rate from 6.4 to 1.25 percent. The most important reason this happened was that lenders in financial markets feared that the evaporation of the surplus and return to deficits would bring higher inflation rates.[28] Of course, such presumptions of higher inflation are, yet again, based on forecasts whose credibility by this point should be nonexistent. Regardless, the lenders managed to protect themselves against potential future inflation by maintaining relatively high long-term interest rates. Here, then, is the crux of the deficit hawk position: allowing the surplus to evaporate is a self-defeating proposition, since, while it may have produced a stimulus to the economy through increased government spending, it simultaneously generated the depressant of higher interest rates for business borrowers.

The debate, in other words, boils down to whether or not the stimulus of increased government spending has a stronger effect on the economy in the short term than the depressant of higher interest rates. This is an issue on which, over the years, conflicting economic models have generated enough computer print-outs to wallpaper any five major research institutes. And we would not be particularly interested in plunging into the debate, except that resolving it, at least in terms of the current situation, matters a great deal for very concrete things, like, for instance, whether state and local government programs for education, job training and community development will face even more severe cuts over the next few years.[29]

Fortunately, there is a straightforward way of sorting out the merits of the alternative perspectives as they apply to the current situation, without having to sift through all the twists and turns in the economists' debates. The basic point is this: the increased government spending in 2001 and 2002, funded by drawing down the surplus and moving into deficits, injected a *direct, certain, and significant increase of spending into the economy.* If the government had instead insisted on maintaining a large surplus, even during the recession and its immediate aftermath, this would have correspondingly produced direct, certain and significant *cuts* in government spending and vital public services.

If, alternatively, government policy was committed to maintaining a large surplus even in recession, the mechanism for fighting the recession would be far more tenuous. The effectiveness of the strategy would depend entirely on 1) the private financial markets – still, as always, in the grip of their forecasting newsletters – deciding that long-term interest rates might indeed be ready to fall significantly; and 2) corporations deciding to borrow at these lowered rates to finance increases in their investment spending. These uncertainties would then be compounded because the corporations were already carrying too much debt as well as too much productive capacity relative to the demand for their products. Even at low interest rates, why would corporations choose to increase their productive capacity when they weren't making full use of the equipment they already had? Moreover, since the strategy of lowering interest rates also meant imposing cuts in government spending, that would also bring even weaker overall demand for the products that the corporations produce and, therefore, still less use by the corporations of their existing productive capacity.

In short, the effects of the federal budget on long-term interest rates, and, in turn, of interest rates on investment, are all fraught with uncertainty. Moreover, such uncertainty is magnified when financial markets operate in a virtually unregulated fashion, as they have under both Clinton and Bush.

Deficits in the long term

The necessity of running federal deficits to move the economy out of the 2001 recession and ongoing slow growth path does not mean that Bush, or his successors, should be granted a Reagan-style carte blanche on deficits. The federal government should move toward closing its deficit at the time when the economy reaches a new upswing of growth, with the exception of borrowings to finance long-term capital projects as opposed to year-to-year operating budget items. But the Bush administration has abandoned the idea of reaching a balanced budget even after it projects the economy moving into a renewed period of growth: even for 2008, when they expect the economy to be growing at 3.2 percent, the Bush economists still project a fiscal deficit of $190 billion. The renewed deficits under Bush are, first of all, the result of the tax bonanzas he has showered on the rich. But these deficits will no doubt serve another important political purpose for Bush: they will generate new pressures for cuts in social spending, just as occurred during the Clinton years of eliminating "big government."[30]

Such longer-term considerations become clearer through examining Table 4.4, which shows the Bush spending priorities into the year 2008, as presented in his 2004 budget proposal.[31] Of course, these spending projections are based on forecasting exercises and are therefore, without doubt, riddled with errors. Still, these figures are useful in providing some sense of Bush's longer-term strategy – both with respect to the budget itself and his broader political aims.

The Bush administration projects total federal spending in 2008 at 19.7 percent of GDP. This is actually an increase from the 18.1 percent figure during Clinton's last year in office, though still below the "big government" days of his father, when federal spending was around 22 percent of GDP. So as a general proposition, we see that the Bush-2 administration has no particular commitment to shrinking the size of government per se. The real question, again, is how Bush intends to mobilize the government's resources – including its capacity to run fiscal deficits – to advance his political agenda.

The data in Table 4.4 are illuminating on this question, both through the figures presented themselves as well as through its deceptions. We see first, not surprisingly, that the biggest jump in spending would be for the military. The administration's own figures show military spending rising from $295 in 2000 to $461 by 2008. This means the military would absorb 17 percent of the projected 2008 budget, as opposed to 16.5 percent in 2000.

However, these figures are misleading. At the same time that the Bush administration released these budgetary figures in early 2003, it was also loudly proclaiming its intention to invade Iraq. Despite this, the budgetary

TABLE 4.4: Federal expenditures by function under Bush and Clinton

	(1) 2000: Last Clinton budget	(2) 2008: Projected Bush budget	(3) Percentage point change between 2000–08 (2) – (1)
Total expenditures as a pct. of GDP	18.1	19.7	+1.6
Share of overall budget (%)			
Social Security	22.9	21.8	-1.1
Defense	16.5	17.0	+0.5
Income security	14.2	13.6	+0.1
Interest	12.5	9.4	-3.1
Medicaid	11.0	12.9	+1.9
Health	8.6	12.3	+3.7
Education	3.0	3.3	+0.3
Veterans	2.6	2.6	0
Transportation	2.6	2.5	-0.1
Agriculture	2.0	0.8	-1.2
Justice	1.6	1.4	-0.2
Natural resources	1.4	1.2	-0.2
Science	1.0	1.0	0
International	1.0	1.1	+0.1

Source: U.S. Office of Management and Budget
Note: Totals do not add to 100 percent due to rounding.

allocation for the military incorporated absolutely no funding at all for the war or for the longer-term costs of post-war occupation and reconstruction. Once the war began in March 2003, President Bush requested $75 billion to finance the operation. Funding at this level alone would entail an increase in the overall military budget by roughly 20 percent. Beyond this, the occupation and post-war reconstruction would certainly run well into 2008 if it were to at all reflect Bush's stated commitment to remake Iraqi and Middle East society in the war's aftermath. We consider the overall costs of an Iraq war in more detail below. For now, the point to stress is that the publicly stated budgetary allocations for the military, for 2003 and 2004 and through 2008, are too low, almost certainly by a large amount.

The other large stated increase in the Bush 2008 budget would be for health expenditures. The Bush administration projects this to rise from $154 billion in 2000 to $335 by 2008. This would mean a jump in the share of the federal budget devoted to health from 8.6 to 12.3 percent. Spending on Medicare, which is separate from the overall health budget, and education are also projected to increase substantially by 2008.

How then are these spending increases – the stated ones in addition to the unstated costs arising from an Iraq war – to be financed, especially given the major tax cuts that Bush has already pushed through and his plans for additional cuts? The Bush administration does, again, acknowledge that they would have to run deficits every year through 2008. But they are still deceptive in calculating how large such a deficit is likely to be. This becomes apparent from the official figures themselves presented in Table 4.4. As we see there, the Bush administration has targeted only one item in its budget to be cut sharply as of 2008, which is interest payments on the government debt. According to the Bush projections, interest payments are supposed to fall from 12.5 percent of the federal budget in Clinton's last year in office to 9.4 percent as of 2008. For the year 2008, a cut in the government interest payments of this magnitude amounts to $84 billion in savings – an amount roughly equal to the entire 2008 federal allocation for education spending. But the Bush economists do not explain how interest payments would be falling sharply even as the federal debt would be growing every year from 2002–2008. In fact, the federal government's interest payments will almost certainly rise as a share of the government's budget as long as the federal debt is also expanding.

In other words, the Bush spending projections are based on yet another forecasting charade. The stated Bush agenda is as follows: to dramatically expand the military, to provide additional funds for health and education spending as well, to deliver continued tax cuts for the rich, while making no major cuts in any other government spending programs, yet still managing to drive down the government's interest payments even while running deficits every year. Obviously, not all of these things will happen.

Rather, what will most likely happen as long as Bush is President is that he will fight hard for his real priorities, which are the tax cuts for the rich and increased military spending, including the war in Iraq and perhaps follow-up attacks on other countries that he views as within what he terms the global "axis of evil." Increased spending on health and education will then either be jettisoned or the projected federal deficits will expand dramatically. Such deficits – to finance the military and more take-home pay for the rich – are hardly to be celebrated in the spirit of John Maynard Keynes. They will rather represent a return to Reaganomics. But there will be one major departure even from the Reagan period. We have already seen how the federal government's share of the economy shrank significantly under Clinton. To therefore push a Reagan-style agenda onto a government sector that has already experienced "the end of the big government era" under Clinton will mean that any further contractions in social spending will cut even deeper to the bone.

Overall then, in the short term, the U.S. economy under Bush most certainly needs deficit spending, in particular, to finance a large increase in assistance to state and local governments. To use "big government" spending in this way would be the most equitable and effective means of stimulating a renewed period of growth and thereby, to retrieve the economy from the quicksand of the stock market collapse. But this sort of big government solution to the growth dilemma cannot be made legitimate under Bush, given his obvious commitment to use government policy as fundamentally a means of handing out favors to the already rich and privileged. Still, Bush possesses one possible escape hatch, courtesy of Al Queda and Iraq. This is the possibility that he can transform the "war on terrorism," the war in Iraq, and any other possible pre-emptive attacks on "axis of evil" governments into a new big government-led growth engine. Under Bush therefore, the central debates around the effects of government deficit spending on the economy are anything but mere technical matters in economic theory. Fundamentally, they are rather about two highly contentious political issues – the issue of war and the issue of income distribution.

War and occupation of Iraq as government stimulus policy?
Could the war on Iraq in March and April 2003 and subsequent U.S. occupation of the country serve as the "big government" engine to drive the U.S. economy forward?

There have been important cases where war mobilization and spending produced a tremendous boost to the economy. The classic case is World War II, which indisputably brought the U.S., and then the rest of the world, out of the 1930s Depression. Government deficit spending, which gained political legitimacy at that time because it was the means to finance the U.S. military effort, created a powerful surge in demand to hire – both in the military and throughout the economy – the 17 percent of the workforce that was still unemployed by 1939, a full decade after the Depression had begun. The Vietnam war was a second such case. The war was a horribly destructive imperialist venture. But, in combination with the conscious expansionary policies pursued by Kennedy and Johnson, deficit spending to finance the war also created a near fully employed labor market.[32]

Keep in mind that in both of these cases, as well as any case in which war spending produced positive economic effects, comparable positive benefits could have been achieved through large-scale government deficit spending programs targeted at peaceful activities, such as education, health, housing, or environmental protection. The positive gains came not through spending on war itself, but from the fact that the government was able to attain political support for large-scale deficit spending at a time when there were great numbers of unemployed people ready to take the jobs generated by the increased government spending. The issue therefore is not war spending per se, but that the government could not achieve the same degree of political support for deficits on behalf of education, healthcare, or environmental protection.

Could the war in Iraq have generated similar positive effects on jobs and incomes in the U.S., even while simultaneously having brought death to a minimum of thousands of innocent civilians, destruction of property, the looting of Iraq's national museum, and of course, enhanced legitimacy among some for the claims of anti-U.S. terrorists? I write less than two weeks after the fall of Baghdad, so considerable uncertainly prevails on such questions. However, even at present we do have sufficient evidence from which to conclude that, on balance, the Iraqi war is unlikely to have induced significant short-term gains for the U.S. economy, and could well bring heavy long-term costs.

The positive boost to the economy would have to come through the increased federal deficit spending to execute the war. But given that Saddam Hussein was defeated in a matter of weeks, this increased spending, when it is all totaled, will not likely amount to more than the $75 billion requested by President Bush to execute the war. If most of this extra government spending was focused on purchases of military equipment and material produced by domestic U.S. military suppliers, this could produce an economic boost within the United States itself. However this stimulus of increased deficit spending on war will have been also counterbalanced by two factors. The first is the general condition of tension and uncertainty that had already become palpable even before the first bomb was dropped from a U.S. warplane. This sense of uncertainty is not conducive to businesses forming positive expectations about the future, and therefore served to dampen investment spending both in the build-up to war and once invasion began in March. The second counterbalancing force is oil prices. Even between January–February 2003, again, with war rumblings ubiquitous but before any shots had been fired, crude oil prices rose more than 20 percent – their highest level since the 1991 Persian Gulf war.

What about longer-term effects? Even given the rapid U.S. victory, the U.S. economy still faces the longer-term costs of maintaining a military occupation in Iraq. Estimates of these costs inevitably vary extremely widely, given that we cannot know in advance the extent of destruction resulting from the war nor the amount of money the U.S. government will actually commit to spend for reconstruction. Professor William Nordhaus of Yale offers a range of between $100–$600 billion over the course of a decade.[33] Whatever the exact level, expenditures on post-war reconstruction of this magnitude will certainly bring benefits to what is now a ravaged Iraqi society. But the main point for our purposes is that these funds will not be available to promote investment and jobs in the United States itself. They will therefore constitute a drain, rather than a boost, for the U.S. economy.

One final consideration requires attention here. Over the longer term, there is no doubt that U.S. oil companies and oil service firms will reap huge benefits through gaining control over Iraq's oil reserves, the second largest in the world, and through obtaining contracts to reconstruct the decimated infrastructure of Iraq's oil industry. Indeed, immediately after the war, the U.S. government awarded the oil servicing firm Bechtel a $680 million contract to begin bringing the Iraqi oil fields back into operation. Bechtel obtained this contract through a competiton that was restricted to a handful of U.S. firms. But such boosts to U.S. oil companies' profits will provide only modest benefits within the U.S. economy itself, and those will be highly concentrated among those, such as President Bush and Vice President Cheney, who have strong ties to the U.S. oil industry.[34]

Regulation of finance, labor and trade

How much will these prospects under Bush be affected by its agenda on regulatory issues? The central point is that Bush's actions on trade, labor and financial regulation will do nothing to alter the fundamental trajectory of his administration with respect to economic growth and jobs, the stability of the financial system, or the redistribution of income in favor of the rich. This becomes clear through considering Bush's regulatory policy initiatives through 2002.

Financial regulations

Even in the wake of the stock market swoon and rampant financial scandals, Bush initially resisted any efforts to even think about a new regulatory structure for the financial system. But Bush's intentions notwithstanding, public outrage over the stock market collapse and accounting scandals emboldened Congress in the summer of 2002 to rapidly push through at great speed the Sarbanes-Oxley Act, a measure aimed at significantly increasing the regulation of accounting practices by public corporations. In particular, Sarbanes-Oxley substantially increases penalties for defrauding shareholders and creates a new agency and new regulations to police the accounting industry. Bush had no choice but to sign the Act into law at the end of July.

Of course, as with all such measures, its effectiveness will depend on the ways in which it is interpreted, implemented and enforced by the appropriate regulatory agency. With Sarbanes-Oxley, the Securities and Exchange

Commission (SEC) is the regulatory agency responsible for its implementation. It is therefore not surprising that, at the same time that Bush signed the measure into law, he also proposed setting the SEC's budget at a level 27 percent below that which was proposed in the legislation. The Bush administration then appointed William Webster as the first head of the new auditing oversight board established by Sarbanes-Oxley. Webster's qualifications for this appointment were hardly stellar. True, he had previously been Director of both the FBI and CIA. But more recently, and more directly pertinent for the job as chief of the new auditing board, he was a board member of a company under investigation for securities fraud.

Bush was forced to reverse course and back down on both the SEC budget and the William Webster appointment. He then appointed William Donaldson as the Chair of the now strengthened SEC. Donaldson is an old-school Wall Street blueblood and longtime Bush family friend. He has a reputation for integrity, though hardly as a critic of Wall Street's extravagances. Donaldson's most recent high-level position was as Chairman of the New York Stock Exchange from 1990-95, during which period the bubble mentality and accounting excesses were in full bloom.

At the time that Donaldson took office in February 2003, *The Economist* was reporting that the SEC had already begun to "pull its punches on corporate governance rules" in implementing Sarbanes-Oxley.[35] This is not surprising, of course, especially given that, since the fall of 2002, the Bush administration skillfully managed to use the war build-up with Iraq as a means of diffusing public anger over the Wall Street scandals. Generally then, it is clear that the Bush administration has no intention of challenging the prerogatives of the financial markets, but rather, as much as possible, is committed to minimizing the impact of Sarbanes-Oxley, the one major federal regulatory initiative that did result from the scandals.

Labor market regulations

Bush began his Presidency with a series of aggressive assaults on labor. These included eliminating restrictions on awarding government contracts to anti-union firms, reducing the ability of unions to use members' dues to support political campaigns, and prohibiting strikes in the airline industry. He also supported the repeal by Congressional Republicans of workplace rules on ergonomics designed to combat repetitive stress injuries. These early Bush actions moved even *Time* magazine to describe Bush as a "classic old-school Republican with an unwaveringly pro-business, anti-labor agenda."[36]

Business representatives themselves had a different explanation for the Bush approach, which was that Bush was only aiming to restore balance after Clinton had, in their view, advocated too ardently on behalf of workers.[37] The only problem with this business view was that Clinton never consistently supported workers' interests, either in terms of labor laws and regulations, or, more generally, through the overall impact of his policies on working people and the poor. The starting point for Bush, rather, was an already strongly pro-business environment. As such, labor leaders correctly viewed with alarm the efforts by Bush to push an anti-labor agenda even further. Steve Rosenthal, political director of the AFL-CIO, described the situation by saying "Put it together, and it's probably as anti-union a package as we've seen from anybody in the past 50 years."

Bush actually stepped up these attacks even after September 11, despite his regular calls to national unity. He blocked still more airline industry strikes, began phasing out the Labor Department's Women's Bureau, and, in the name of national security, prohibited workers at several agencies in the Department of Justice from joining unions. He even held up formation of the Department of Homeland Security until Democrats would agree that employees in this new department would not have the right to join unions – this, despite the fact that the new agency was being formed primarily through merging existing government offices, and that roughly 45,000 of the 170,000 government employees who would transfer to the new department were already union members. In the compromise measure that passed on this issue, unions were not directly banned, but the Secretary of Homeland Security is granted the unilateral authority to determine hiring, firing and promotion, and the President holds the authority to ban unions from the Department if this is deemed necessary to national security.

Bush also became the first president in twenty-five years to invoke the 1947 Taft-Hartley Act in response to the October 2002 labor dispute between dock workers and management at twenty-nine West Coast ports, and the first *ever* to deploy this tactic when management had locked out workers. Under Taft-Hartley, if the president deems that a strike or management lockout "imperils national health or safety," he can ask a federal court to order parties to the dispute to resume business, and impose an eighty-day cooling off period. Harry Truman had called Taft-Hartley "a slave labor bill" when Congress passed it over his presidential veto, and Truman's stance was a major factor contributing to his 1948 re-election. Fifty-five years later, in the post September 11 environment, George Bush clearly felt no similar constraints in imposing this measure on U.S. workers.[38]

And yet, even amid these attacks, Bush has concurrently made some gestures aimed at softening his anti-labor stance. The Bush strategy is to work cooperatively with labor representatives – most especially the most right-wing unionists such as the Teamster's President James Hoffa – in areas where the administration's own pro-business agenda can be construed as also responsive to labor's interests.

Thus, Hoffa was recruited to support the Bush energy plan which later gained notoriety as having been drafted by the Dick Cheney-led task force loaded with representatives of Enron and other energy firms. Hoffa lobbied Congress on behalf of the energy plan after embracing Chaney's claim that it would create 25,000 new jobs for Teamsters. Hoffa was then rewarded for his support with White House insider status, receiving regular invitations to White House briefings and being chosen for membership on an administration task force on workplace issues.[39]

Trade policy
Bush has utilized trade policy in a similar fashion. Of course, from Bush himself on down, everyone in the administration swears fealty to free trade doctrine. Following the practice under Clinton, the 2002 *Economic Report of the President* written by the Bush Council of Economic Advisors, provides a long discussion on the universal benefits that accrue from free trade.[40] In the spirit of these pronouncements, Bush has also pursued some trade measures that had also been priorities under Clinton. These include obtaining for himself so-called "trade-promotion" authority, (what used to be termed "fast-track" powers) whereby Congress agrees to restrict itself to up-or-down

votes on Bush's trade proposals, forfeiting its right, in other words, to amend any proposal advanced by Bush. Bush has also attempted to extend the terms of NAFTA more broadly throughout Latin America.

But Bush has by no means been consistent in promoting free trade, opting instead for trade restrictions when restrictions better serve his political agenda. Restrictive trade measures under Bush have included imposing substantial new tariffs on imported steel and lumber and supporting legislation that would substantially increase subsidies to U.S. agribusiness. The decision on steel tariffs in particular drew support from labor representatives as a job-saving measure. It was also predictably denounced by the usual wide swath of free traders among academics and the mainstream media.

How do such trade measures fit within the broader Bush agenda? In fact, some complications and contradictions are at play with trade policy, just as is the case with labor regulations. The Bush administration is clearly trying to exploit these contradictions to increase his standing among working people, all on behalf of his administration's overall purpose of rewarding business and the wealthy.

What are the main issues? The first basic question is whether such tariff measures do actually save jobs. At one level, they certainly do, if we are referring to the jobs of steelworkers employed by firms that were about to be eliminated by foreign competitors. Of course, there is a reflexive counterargument to this consideration, which is that, in the name of free market principles, U.S. firms that are uncompetitive on the world market should be permitted to fail. But even if one accepts such a position in principle, applying it in this specific situation ignores the fact that U.S. manufacturers in steel and other trade-sensitive industries had been placed at a severe disadvantage in the world market due to the high value of the dollar. From October 1999 to January 2002 the dollar's value rose by 18 percent relative to other major currencies. This was equivalent to foreign firms receiving a subsidy of as much as 18 percent when attempting to compete in the U.S. market.[41] As such, one way to evaluate the steel tariffs is to regard them as compensation to both the business owners and workers in the industry against the costs they had to bear due to high dollar. On the other hand, as we discussed earlier in this chapter, the dollar did fall through 2002 by about 14 percent against both the euro and yen, thereby virtually eliminating this effective subsidy for foreign firms.

Additional considerations on the effects of the steel tariffs also complicate the picture further. One is that the tariffs enable domestic steel producers to sell at higher prices. This raises prices for consumers, but also for firms that use steel for their own production needs. It is hard to know in advance whether the U.S. firms buying steel would have to cut back on their own hiring of workers when they are forced to purchase steel at higher prices. But that is certainly a possibility if the ensuing increase in steel prices is high enough. It is also obviously the case that workers in foreign countries are hurt by tariffs in the same way that U.S. workers are assisted – that is, jobs in foreign countries become less plentiful if the foreign firms producing steel are unable to compete effectively in the huge U.S. market. In this sense, it is fair to consider the imposition of tariffs as a "beggar-thy-neighbor" policy. This factor is especially troubling when the neighbor being beggared is less well off than the one doing the beggaring. The Bush steel tariffs did exempt some developing countries, but Brazil was among the countries not exempted.

How to evaluate these contradictory factors? As is always the case when issues are not clear-cut, we need to weigh the relative size of the various effects. It could well be the case that, considered on its own, the benefits to U.S. steelworkers of the tariffs are greater than the losses to other workers and consumers, after taking full account of the impact of the job losses and shuttering of companies on families and communities. But even if this were the case, the net gains to the steelworkers will accomplish little in countering the overall effects of Bush's fundamental program of redistributing income to the wealthy. Nor can the tariff policies serve as a substitute for a government-directed job stimulus program that is needed to counteract the contractionary forces generated by the financial market collapse. Finally, of course, the primary beneficiaries of the steel tariffs are the owners of the less competitive steel firms in the U.S., not the workers. The steel companies lobbied hard for the tariffs, and they also happened to give more than $2 million to Republicans in the 2000 election cycle. Bush would never have supported the tariffs if the primary beneficiaries were the steel workers, any more than he would support drilling for oil in Alaska as a means of creating more jobs for Teamsters. He can support such measures precisely because they do not threaten his overall posture, as *Time* put it, as a traditional anti-labor, pro-business Republican.

Perhaps we can obtain a broader perspective on the complexities surrounding trade policy through focusing on what I consider a useful distinction between *social protection* and *trade protection*. From our discussions of the Marx, Keynes and Polanyi problems, it is clear that public policies are always necessary in any sort of capitalist economy if the public has gained the political power to implement an even minimally decent program of social protections, a centerpiece of which would be sustaining full employment at decent wages. But such social protections can be most effectively accomplished through macroeconomic policies along with financial and labor market regulations. When these policy interventions are effectively deployed, the need for trade protectionist measures should be greatly diminished. This is because, with public policies producing full employment at decent wages, the livelihoods of working people would not be threatened by competition from foreign producers, or, more generally, by the need to perhaps occasionally move jobs from a less to a more competitive firm.[42]

It is therefore the absence of decent social protections – which is to say the absence of effective jobs-targeted macroeconomic policies as well as labor and financial market regulations – that creates a defensible case for trade protection as a means of supporting working people in the U.S. Thus, the Bush gesture to U.S. workers through trade protectionism is, fundamentally, a measure of how far U.S. policy has retreated over the past generation from a commitment to sustaining full employment, decent wages and a basic social safety net.

CHAPTER FIVE

The Landscape of Global Austerity

"The decadent international but individualistic capitalism, in the hands of which we found ourselves after the War, is not a success. It is not intelligent, it is not beautiful, it is not just, it is not virtuous – and it doesn't deliver the goods. In short, we dislike it and are beginning to despise it."

— JOHN MAYNARD KEYNES 1933

"When I give food to the poor they call me a saint. When I ask why the poor have no food, they call me a Communist."

— BRAZILIAN ARCHBISHOP DOM HELDER CAMARA

From developmental state to neoliberalism

Why speak about a landscape of global austerity in the year 2003? For most people today, including those living in developing countries, living standards are well above what would have seemed possible a hundred years ago. For example, as of 1900, the average life span of someone living in Great Britain, the wealthiest of the imperialist powers at that time, was 50 years. Today in India – which had been Britain's largest colony and remains at present among the world's poor countries – the average life span is 60 years, a full decade beyond the British standard from the colonialist epoch.

But since the period beginning around 1980, the eclipse of state-directed development policies and the ascendancy of neoliberalism have produced dramatic upheavals in the world's poor and middle-income countries.

This chapter describes a fundamental link in this transformation: the ways in which the rise of neoliberalism is responsible for the spread of global austerity. But who is responsible for neoliberalism in less developed countries? As we discussed briefly in Chapter 1, neoliberalism is advanced aggressively throughout the less developed countries by the "Washington Consensus" of the U.S. government, the International Monetary Fund and the World Bank. But governments in less developed countries do also support neoliberal policies. We therefore will need to consider the processes through which the priorities of the Washington Consensus institutions ideas get transmitted into political platforms and policies throughout the less developed world.

We begin with an overview of the transition from developmental planning to neoliberal policies in developing countries, and the impact of this transition on overall growth, inequality and poverty. We then consider three case studies for observing the effects of neoliberal policies – its effects on small-scale farmers in a region of India; the reasons for the financial collapse of Argentina in 2001; and the emergence throughout the developing world of sweatshop labor conditions in manufacturing industries. We close by considering what the impact would be of two widely discussed policy approaches for reversing the rise of global austerity – increasing development aid contributions from the wealthy countries and raising the economic growth rates in the developing countries themselves.

The rise of the developmental state

The first thirty years after World War II, from roughly the late 1940s to the late 1970s, was the epoch of both decolonization and the Cold War. Correspondingly, it was also the period in developing countries in which governments pursued active interventionist policies to promote economic growth and, in many cases, increasing equality.

The specific forms that these policies took varied widely by region and country. Given that this was the Cold War era, it is certainly the case that state socialism was both the most influential, as well as most bitterly contested, alternative development model. It dominated economic thinking in China and much of Southeast Asia, as well as, of course, the Soviet Union,

Eastern Europe and Cuba. It also had strong adherents in parts of Africa, following the model of "ujamma" (collective self-sufficiency) advanced by Julius Nyerere in Tanzania. The government in these countries owned virtually all productive assets and economic activity was directed through a government-established comprehensive plan. State socialist governments were committed to maintaining high employment and relative equality in the distribution of income, health care, housing and educational opportunities.

A second approach was the "import-substituting industrialization" model practiced most actively throughout most of Latin America. The fundamental idea behind import substitution industrialization was that developing economies should take active measures to strengthen national capacity to produce manufactured goods for their domestic markets. This meant protecting domestic manufacturers from foreign competition while also providing them with cheap credit to finance their investments in new productive plants and equipment. The import-substituting industrialization model would also benefit from a buoyant domestic market, since the domestic producers of manufactured goods would need local buyers for these goods. The import substitution model was therefore compatible with the idea of rising living standards for Latin America's workers and poor. At the same time, in contrast to the state socialist model, it presented no challenge to the privileged economic positions of domestic capitalists and landed elite.

The East Asian economies – initially Japan, then the "tigers" including South Korea, Taiwan, Malaysia, Singapore and Thailand – created their own, third variant of state-directed development. The great myth about the achievements of the Asian tigers was that they were paragons of free market virtue. Thus, with typical hyperbole, Ronald Reagan said in his 1985 State of the Union Message, "Many countries in East Asia and the Pacific have few resources other than the enterprise of their own people. But through... free markets they've soared ahead of the centralized economies." In fact, the government's authority in the East Asian economies in terms of overall planning and strategic financing had always been at least as extensive as in the Latin import-substituting countries, and was, in many ways, more closely comparable to that of the centrally planned state socialist countries. The major distinction between the East Asian and Latin American models was that the East Asian approach was focused on promoting firms that could succeed as exporters. This alternative Asian approach had its historical roots in the fact that the governments in this region were able to discipline the corporations they protected and subsidised. In particular, the private firms would only continue to receive protections and subsidies from the government if they could meet product and quality standards necessary to penetrate export markets. The government's authority, in turn, resulted from the U.S.-backed land reforms in these countries after World War II, which weakened the power of landed elites and their big business allies to an extent that never occurred in Latin America.[1]

The great U-turn

Each of these state-directed developmental approaches did also include major failings, and these weaknesses became increasingly apparent with time. The fundamental problem with state socialism was not simply that it was brutally repressive, but that this repressive apparatus was necessary as a means of maintaining the government's prohibition of virtually all forms of market transactions and private enterprise. Under the import substitution model, many companies grew jealous in guarding their protectionist privileges, even to the extent of lobbying the government against domestic competitors seeking similar protection. The large government bureaucracies that formed under these policies also encouraged pervasive corruption. The Latin governments were particularly vulnerable to this precisely because, unlike in East Asia, the nationalist governments never broke the power of the landed elite who had traditionally relied on special favors, as opposed to productive activity, as a means of expanding their wealth. Finally, the East Asian economies, like the Latin import substitution policies, did also fall back onto "crony capitalism" in handing out subsidised credit and protection from competitors. It also relied on repression of labor movements for keeping production costs down, and thus, maintaining international competitiveness.

These and other problems with the three main developmental models certainly created an imperative for adjustments, renovations, and, in many cases, fundamental restructuring. But it never followed that there should be only one approach to rethinking development policy – that being to abandon outright the very idea of a significant state presence to promote growth and equality, and replace this approach with neoliberalism. But this is what in fact occurred. Beginning in the 1980s and continuing through the 1990s, governments throughout Latin America, Africa and Asia, came to accept the position expressed in the triumphal pronouncement of former British Prime Minister Margaret Thatcher, that "there is no alternative" to neoliberalism, either in Britain or anywhere else.

Yet this transformation of economic thinking throughout the world was not simply a matter of ideological persuasion. The influence of coercion needs also to be recognized. Governments in developing countries believed that they could not restructure successfully without substantial aid, credit and foreign investment. This could come only from the advanced capitalist countries and international lending institutions, and such support in turn depends on receiving a seal of approval from the Washington Consensus, and specifically the IMF and World Bank. The only way to qualify for such support was through demonstrating a commitment to the neoliberal model.

As such, by the late 1980s, even such previously committed social democrats as Jamaica's then Prime Minister Michael Manley pronounced that "we are making a radical change in direction" that will "among other things, involve the free play of market forces in the determination of prices." These same pressures remain in force up to the present. This has been most apparent with the election in October 2002 of Luiz Inácio Lula da Silva – Lula – as President of Brazil, the ninth largest economy in the world. A former steelworker and militant union–organizer, Lula was the candidate of the leftist Workers Party, and won the election with a landslide 61 percent majority. Nevertheless, immediately upon celebrating his victory, Lula "sent a message to uneasy financial markets, reiterating his pledge to respect Brazil's international agreements and stick to anti-inflationary policies." He then quickly nominated well-known orthodox financial market figures as both finance minister and central bank president. The *New York Times* reported that these choices were attempts by Lula "to demonstrate that his Workers'

Party is dumping leftist polices and shifting to the political center." What will actually transpire during Lula's presidency remains to be seen, but the forces pushing him away from the program on which he was overwhelming elected are obvious.[2]

There has been one major counterexample to the pattern of neoliberal ascendancy in the developing world. This is the case of China, which, given that it constitutes 20 percent of the world's population, obviously renders it as an extremely important exception. As with East Asia, there is considerable irony in the mainstream interpretation of the Chinese experience. After the death of Mao Zedong in 1976, the still Communist Party-led government of Deng Xiaoping did indeed take dramatic steps away from a rigid state socialist model in the late 1970s. It has been hailed ever since for achieving remarkable economic success through embracing a free market economy, even while maintaining a repressive political system. But in fact, in sharp contrast with the rest of the former state socialist countries, China undertook virtually no privatization of either industry or land and other agricultural assets until the early 1990s, and even over the past decade has proceeded cautiously with these measures. By the late 1990s, state owned enterprises continued to produce about 30 percent of total industrial output. Individual farms did replace agricultural communes in the rural sector. But land, agricultural equipment, and rural enterprises have all remained under collective ownership. It is also true that since the late 1990s, the Chinese government has substantially accelerated the pace of privatization and liberalization, and as well as more fervently espousing the rhetoric of neoliberalism. Still, the record for the 1980s and most of the 1990s stands in sharp contrast to the neoliberal transformations that occurred throughout most of the rest of the developing world.[3]

Figures of descent

What has been the impact of this transition from big government to the neoliberal framework? To provide an initial overall perspective, it will be useful to examine some general statistics on economic growth, inequality and poverty.

TABLE 5.1: Two eras of economic growth in developing countries
(figures are average annual growth rates, in percentages)

	Developmental state era 1961–80	Neoliberal era 1981–99
Low and middle income Countries, excluding China		
Overall growth rate	5.5	2.6
Per capita growth rate	3.2	0.7
China		
Overall growth rate	4.5	9.8
Per capita growth rate	2.5	8.4

Source: World Bank, *World Development Indicators*, 2001 CD-ROM

Growth

Table 5.1 shows figures on economic growth in both the developmental state and neoliberal eras for the low and middle income countries of the world – i.e. the average annual rate of gross domestic product – both in terms of overall GDP data and measuring growth on a per capita basis. Following previous discussions, I have set 1980 as the most appropriate point to mark the transition out of the post World War II era of developmental state policies and the ascendancy of neoliberalism. I have also included China separately since it had not pursued a neoliberal policy path by the end of the 1990s. Otherwise, these figures are calculated by adding up the overall GDP figures for all low and middle-income countries. This way, the patterns for large countries, like India, Brazil or Egypt, will carry more weight in the calculations than those for small countries like Bolivia, Uganda or Singapore.[4]

The overall growth pattern is unambiguous: there has been a sharp decline in growth in the neoliberal era relative to the developmental state period, from 5.5 to 2.6 percent, measured on average annual basis. Measured per capita – that is, the average increase in GDP relative to the growth in population – the downward growth trend is even more dramatic, with the growth rate in the neoliberal era at only 0.7 percent. This means that the average increase in overall income in the poor and middle-income countries just barely stayed ahead of population growth, after having increased 3.2 percent faster than population growth during the developmental state period.

Growth patterns do vary significantly by region, with various parts of Asia, including India (as we discuss more below), performing much better than Latin America or Africa prior to the Asian financial crisis of 1997–98. The table also shows the unique experience of China, where the average growth rate more than doubled during the 1981–98 period relative to 1961–80. It would not be possible, nor, for the most part even desirable, for the Chinese experience to be lifted out of its particular context and replicated elsewhere. Still, this performance should offer other developing economies some sense of the possibilities achievable through maintaining a strong public sector presence along with encouraging the spread of a vibrant private sector.[5]

Distribution

There are two ways of measuring changes in income distribution throughout the world – changes that occur between countries and those that occur within each country. Both of these are relevant for our discussion.

Even though neoliberal policies have generated a decline in the developing countries' average growth rate, this does not mean that these countries have necessarily become worse off relative to the wealthier countries. This would obviously depend on the growth experience in the wealthy countries as well. In fact, however, as we see in the upper panel of Table 5.2, growth in the developing countries has indeed been slower than in the wealthy countries during the neoliberal era, despite the declining growth in the wealthy countries themselves. The table reports the same growth rates on a per capita basis for developing countries, excluding China, that we saw in Table 5.1, now alongside the comparable per capita growth figures for what the World Bank calls the "high income OECD countries," which basically includes North America, Western Europe, Japan and Australia. As the table shows, the difference in the per capita growth rates between the wealthy OECD and developing countries was, on average, only 0.3 percent per year during 1961-80. But this annual differential rises to 1.3 percent during the neoliberal

TABLE 5.2: Global income distribution trends

Average annual per capita income growth in wealthy and developing countries

	Developmental state era 1961–80	Neoliberal era 1981–99
1) Wealthy OECD economies	3.5	2.0
2) Developing economies, excluding China	3.2	0.7
3) Growth differential between regions (row 1 - 2)	0.3	1.3

Percent change in growth differential between eras = 333 percent
[(1.3% differential − 0.3% differential)/0.3]

Source: World Bank, *World Development Indicators* 2001 CD-ROM

. . . .

Change in global distribution of income between 1980–98

	Including China	Excluding China
Income of richest 50% as share of poorest 50%	14% more equal	4% more unequal
Income of richest 20% as share of poorest 20%	30% more equal	8% more unequal
Income of richest 10% as share of poorest 10%	5% more unequal	19% more unequal
Income of richest 1% as share of poorest 1%	68% more unequal	77% more unequal

Source: Bob Sutcliffe, "A More or Less Unequal World," full citation in Chapter 5 note 7

era – that is, an increase in the average growth differential between the wealthy and developing regions of *more than 300 percent* between the two periods.

As for inequalities within countries, most features of the neoliberal model should encourage these to rise as well. Cutting tax rates for the wealthy will obviously increase inequality, while liberalizing financial markets and selling off state assets means more opportunities for wealthy investors to reap huge gains on buying and selling publicly traded companies. Weakening labor market regulations will tend to reduce wages for workers in the lower half of the income distribution. Cutbacks in government spending will produce greater disparities in public funds spent on health and education. Other features of a neoliberal policy environment can promote greater equality – for example, if successful manufacturing exporters in poor countries raise wages for their workers in line with the firm's growth in sales. But such factors are not likely to outweigh those encouraging greater inequality.[6]

One faces a range of difficult technical problems when trying to measure within country inequalities, or even more extensively, total income distribution throughout the world – in other words, considering overall distribution in terms of a single, borderless world economy. A large number of studies have been produced on this topic in recent years, and they have reached sharply divergent conclusions – that is, some studies find inequality increasing and others show it decreasing. However, in his extremely careful recent survey of this literature, Professor Bob Sutcliffe of the University of the Basque Country shows the ways through which these divergent conclusions are driven by different ways of organizing the statistical evidence.[7] Sutcliffe also shows that cross-currents are operating within the overall global economy – in particular, that there are more people clustering close to the 1998 world average income level of around $2,350, while, at the same time, there are growing disparities between those with very high incomes and those living in poverty (the richest 1 percent earned an average of $62,212 in 1998 while the poorest 1 percent earned $193).[8] Sutcliffe's review also makes clear that, by far, the single greatest equalizing force in the neoliberal era has been the rapid income growth of China. When one separates out the Chinese experience, as we have done above with the statistics on economic growth, it becomes unambiguous that inequality has been growing over the neoliberal era.

All of this becomes clear in the lower panel of Table 5.2 (see page 133), which presents a summary of representative figures from Professor Sutcliffe's review of the literature. The table presents figures on the change in the global distribution of income between 1980 and 1998, with 1998 being the last date on which reliable figures are available. I present the figures in two ways – both through including and excluding China from the overall sample of the world's population. I then report changes in global income distribution according to four separate distributional categories:

- The richest 50 percent of the world's population relative to the poorest 50 percent
- The richest 20 percent relative to the poorest 20 percent
- The richest 10 percent relative to the poorest 10 percent; and
- The richest one percent relative to the poorest one percent.

Considering first the figures that include China, we see that income distribution has become 14 percent more equal between 1980–98 if we compare the richest half to the poorest half of the world's population, and 30 percent more equal if we compare the richest 20 percent to the poorest 20 percent. At the same time, if we compare the richest to the poorest 10 percent, inequality rose over this period, though only by a modest 5 percent. However, in comparing the richest to the poorest 1 percent, we observe a sharp 68 percent increase in inequality, i.e. even when we keep China in the overall sample.

Considering now these same categories exclusive of China, we observe that inequality is growing according to each of the categories. Not surprisingly, the rise in inequality is more modest in the broader income categories and sharpens when the income categories become more differentiated. Thus, in considering the richest and poorest 50 percent of the world's population exclusive of China, inequality grew by 4 percent between 1980–98. But inequality grew by 19 percent in considering the difference between the richest and poorest 10 percent over this same period, and by a full 77 percent with respect to the richest and poorest 1 percent.

In short, there is no ambiguity that the world has experienced increasing disparities between the very rich and poor – that is, the top and bottom 1 percent of the world's population – over the neoliberal era. The only real debate is whether one should consider China in a separate category because they did not practice neoliberal policies during the neoliberal era. When we do include China in our measures, we see that its rapid economic growth has pulled a large share of the world's population out of deep poverty, and has moved them increasingly toward the middle of global income distribution. On the other hand, when we consider the neoliberal era exclusive of the Chinese experience, there is, again, no ambiguity that rising global inequality has accompanied the ascendancy of neoliberalism.

Poverty reduction

If, as we have seen, economic growth in most developing countries outside China has slowed substantially while income distribution has become more unequal, then it would follow that poverty in the developing world has either worsened or, at best, that the rate of poverty reduction has slowed. The logic is simple: if we imagine a total income pie for a country, the trend for increasing inequality means that the *share of the pie* going to the least well off will be getting smaller. Whether the *total amount of pie* going to the poor is also shrinking depends on how fast the whole pie is growing. Countries that have been the hardest hit by the slow growth in the neoliberal era would therefore be the countries where we would expect poverty trends to be worsening. China and a few other fast-growing developing countries should have experienced some poverty reduction.

I introduce this simple logical exercise into the discussion because, even more than with the data on income distribution, matters can become murky once one gets into actual measurement issues of poverty trends. There is, first, the issue of simply defining poverty in an appropriate way. Do we measure it as an absolute standard of basic minimum needs to stay alive, or as a standard of relative deprivation in any given society? There are legitimate considerations on behalf of each standard. The poverty figures discussed earlier for the United States combines both factors.

Focusing on absolute minimum needs poverty for developing countries, the World Bank in recent years has established a threshold at $1.08 per day per person. But their technique in deriving this threshold has been widely criticized by other experts. For example, Sanjay Reddy of Barnard College and Thomas Pogge of Columbia University argue that the $1.08 threshold is arbitrary, and that this threshold "may have led to a substantial understatement in the extent of world poverty."[9] According to Reddy and Pogge's own estimates, the percentage of people in poverty in a representative set of developing countries in the mid-1990s is probably in the range of 50 percent as opposed to the World Bank's estimate of about 35 percent.

Despite these controversies, what is surprisingly not in dispute is the basic conclusion of relevance to our present discussion: that little to no progress in reducing poverty has been made over the neoliberal period. Even the World Bank's own experts Shaohua Chen and Martin Ravallion acknowledge that "in the aggregate, and for some large regions, all our measures suggest that the 1990s did not see much progress against consumption poverty in the developing world." In explaining the pattern they observe, Chen and Ravallion write,

> We point to two main proximate causes of the disappointing rate of poverty reduction: too little economic growth in many of the poorest countries and persistent inequalities that inhibited the poor from participating in the growth that did occur (p. 1).

In other words, referring back to our simple exercise above, Chen and Ravallion observe that both the overall income pie was growing too slowly and that the share of the pie going to the least well off was shrinking. The IMF also recognized this basic pattern in their May 2000 *World Economic Outlook*, reporting that "progress in raising real incomes and alleviating poverty has been disappointingly slow in many developing countries, and the relative gap between the richest and poorest countries has continued to widen." [10] Beyond this, Reddy and Pogge believe that the negative poverty trends in developing countries may be significantly more severe than the World Bank and IMF authorities conclude.

These are broad overviews of trends that will apply to very different degrees, if at all, in any given country, region, or industry setting. How do these broad trends actually play out on the ground? We examine this question now, with our three case studies.

Peasant suicides in India

In November 1997, reports began appearing that hundreds of cotton-farming peasants in the Telengana region of Andhra Pradesh, a state in the Southern Central part of India, had committed suicide because of their inability to repay their debts to moneylenders and traders. The suicide pattern then spread, first to other agricultural areas in India, then to both handloom and powerloom weavers in the textile industry, whose economic circumstances had also deteriorated badly in this same period. Poor farmers have also undergone operations in recent years to remove kidneys and other organs, which they then sell to help cover their debts. Official estimates of the number of suicides in Andrhra Pradesh alone are about 1000. Other credible reports set this figure significantly higher.[11]

What is the connection between the ascendancy of neoliberal economic policies and this wave of desperate actions by individuals in India? At one level, of course, any decision to commit suicide is a personal act that cannot be generalized in broad political terms. Most people do not commit suicide even when economic circumstances become hopeless. Still, given that the suicides (and organ sales) have taken place in waves among people in similar economic circumstances, and that these circumstances were heavily affected by dramatic shifts in economic policy, it is certainly reasonable to inquire as to broad connections between neoliberalism in India and the suicide wave.

Neoliberalism in India

Structural adjustment policies were introduced in India in 1991. Prabhat Patnaik and C.P. Chandrashakar of Jawaharlal Nehru University report that the main features of this new policy regime included:

> a regime of "liberal imports," a progressive removal of administrative controls, including a move to "free markets" in foodgrains and a whittling down of food subsidies, a strictly limited role for public investment, the privatization of publicly owned assets over a wide field, an invitation to multinational corporations to undertake investment in infrastructure under a guaranteed rate of return, and finan-

cial liberalization that would do away with all priority sector lending and subsidized credit.[12]

From the time of India achieving independence in 1948 until 1991, the country had pursued a state-directed economic development strategy, with a highly interventionist state, and a large public sector, especially in areas of infrastructure and basic industry. The switch to a much more free-market oriented economy was therefore a major transition for India, akin to the economic policy reversals away from central planning that occurred in Eastern Europe and China.

India's transformation to a neoliberal regime is widely recognized as having stimulated a new era of faster economic growth. In fact, India's economic growth did accelerate after the 1970s, but this mostly occurred in the 1980s, the decade *before* the country embarked on its neoliberal restructuring program. Moreover, as C.P. Chandrasekhar and Jayati Ghosh of Nehru University have recently documented, the primary factors stimulating growth in the 1980s were a growing fiscal deficit and increased borrowing from foreigners – neither of these were sustainable engines of growth on their own. Growth did then slow substantially in the 1990s, especially in the second half of the decade. This is precisely when the longer-term benefits of the country's neoliberal reforms were supposed to have taken hold.[13]

In terms of agriculture specifically, the major effects of structural adjustment have been to eliminate tariff protections; reduce subsidies on fertilizers, irrigation, seeds, electricity and procurement; cut infrastructure investments in irrigation and agricultural extension services; promote investments in commercial and high technology agriculture such as horticulture, floriculture and agro-processing with a view of expanding export markets; and cut credit subsidies to small-scale, domestic farmers while increasing them for exports.

Effects of neoliberal agricultural policies on peasant farmers
Declining grain prices and non-agricultural job opportunities
The impact of this shift in policy hit India's small farmers from several angles. First, prices of dryland staple products in India, including rice, wheat, and

coarse cereals, fell sharply from the mid-1990s onward. For example, the price of rice fell by 28 percent between 1995–99, and the price of wheat fell by 54 percent between 1996-2000. These price declines in India were due to three factors – corresponding drops in the world prices of staples, sharp cuts in price supports for India's agricultural products, and the opening of India's agricultural-goods market to low-priced imports. While sharp price declines rendered the cultivation of staple crops less viable, the government cuts in developmental spending led concurrently to a collapse of non-agricultural job opportunities. As documented by Professor Utsa Patnaik of Jawaharlal Nehru University, the growth of overall rural employment in India fell from an average annual rate of 2.0 percent in the 1980s to 0.6 percent in the 1990s.

Shift to commercial crops

All the farmers in Andhra Pradesh who committed suicide were growing cotton or other commercial crops. By foregoing the cultivation of staple food crops, they made themselves and their families more vulnerable to experiencing food shortages if their earnings from growing cotton were insufficient. And in fact, along with the prices of the staple crops, cotton prices in India did also fall sharply over this period, by 47 percent between 1994–2000.

At the same time, cultivation of cotton required more expenditure on seeds, fertilizer, pesticides and electricity than was the case with staple crops. But the costs of these agricultural inputs rose sharply because of the reductions in government subsidies. Thus, the peasants were forced to borrow heavily from private moneylenders to maintain their supply of inputs. They also had to borrow to lease land. In addition, since the cultivation of cotton entailed more time for spraying fertilizer and pesticides, both male and female farmers were forced to lengthen their working day.

The reduction of the government's infrastructural investments also then meant less public investments for irrigation and less control of crop-damaging pests. This had severe consequences. A survey of the Andhra Pradesh suicide cases showed that 83 percent of their land holdings were not irrigated. As for pest control, many peasants cultivated cotton continuously in order to generate sufficient cash to pay back their debts. But once cotton was cultivated continuously, rather than in rotation with other crops, the pests survived from one planting cycle to the next.

This situation then led the peasants to apply excessive amounts of pesticides, which they obtained by borrowing more money. But even here, many of the pesticides were spurious, so much so that there were numerous cases of peasants who attempted suicide by drinking pesticide, but still survived. Such widespread fraud in pesticide sales became possible only by the sharp cuts in agricultural services and staff, an important part of whose job had been to check the quality of agricultural inputs being used by peasants. By the mid-1990s, agricultural extension services in Andhra Pradesh provided only thirty-nine field officers to cover 1,100 villages.

The cuts in government support for credit, seeds, fertilizer and pesticides created a large gap in the supply of needed provisions that was then filled by private businesses – i.e. the private landlords, money lenders and merchants selling fertilizers, pesticides and seeds. The private business people in agriculture in turn were able to increase their market power by bundling the various products they supplied into larger packages. The same people, in other words, were the seed and pesticide dealers, landlords and money lenders. As such, as Vamsicharan Vakulabharanam of the University of Massachusetts-Amherst argues, even if cotton prices were to rise, the revenues from these higher prices would be claimed almost entirely by intermediaries rather than the cotton farmers themselves. Vakulabharanam refers to this situation as "poverty-inducing growth."

Overall then, it is not difficult to see how this combination of circumstances had created situations of desperate indebtedness for large numbers of poor farmers. But the tragedy of the situation becomes much more vivid through considering some individual accounts. The following stories were compiled from the Indian press by the Radical Union for Political Economy in Bombay and published in the 1998 pamphlet, "What the Peasant Suicides Tell Us."

Thirty-five-year-old Chittadi Madhav Reddy was once a worker in a sports goods manufacturing company in Hyderabad. Three years ago, the company declared a lock-out, and Madhav Reddy was forced to shift to his village, Pathipaka ... with his wife and children. He was desperate to earn, but he had too little land – just one acre. So he took another two acres on lease and borrowed heavily. Unfortunately, like so many others in Telangana, he found his entire crop wiped out by pests. He attempted to commit suicide on December 18, 1997. His neighbors quickly detected the attempt and rushed him to the hospital. He survived to his regret.

Shayamala Mallaiah, 35, was an agricultural laborer who owned just one acre. He took on lease (for 6,000 Rupies) an additional two acres of fallow land – without an irrigation well. Mallaiah borrowed 70,000 Rupies at a monthly interest rate of 3 percent for purchasing a pair of bullocks, a cart, pesticides, fertilizers, and payment of the lease amount. However, 90 percent of his crop was lost. After his suicide, the children ... were separated from their destitute mother and sent to the social welfare hostel as part of the Government's "relief" package.

A. Narsoji, 45 ... owned moneylenders [an amount] equal to two-and-a-half-years' earnings in good harvests. But his crop had failed, he had already sold his two oxen to repay one loan and had nothing more to offer moneylenders who were hounding him. Larger and larger doses of pesticide failed to kill the pests that ravaged his cotton crop. Finally, Marsoji himself consumed the pesticide on January 25, 1998 and killed himself.

The Argentinian economic collapse

In 1991, Argentina initiated an economic program that followed to an unprecedented extent the precepts of neoliberal restructuring. There were four major features to the program: selling off state-owned assets; opening the country to foreign investors and imports; establishing a fixed relationship between the country's currency, the peso, and the U.S. dollar; and tying any increases in the supplying of credit to Argentine households and businesses to the country's ability to attract dollars. The interrelated aims of this policy were to dramatically reduce the influence of government interventions in the economy, control inflation, and, above all, create an attractive investment climate for foreign investors. Indeed, under the new program, even the requirement that foreign investors in Argentina register with the national government became optional.

At the time of its implementation and throughout most of the 1990s, the Argentine program was widely hailed. In 1991, the *New York Times* called the program "the envy of other Latin governments," and proclaimed Argentina "the next emerging economy." Declaring "a new discipline in economics" that was bringing dramatic changes throughout Latin America, the *Times* further noted in 1991 that "The free market open economies and deregulation are now part of the vocabulary of taxi drivers and laborers."[14]

Not surprisingly, the IMF also praised Argentina's neoliberal policies. As recently as its 1999 review of the country, the IMF highlighted the country's "strong investment-led growth," commended "the authorities for their prudent economic management," and noted "the substantial progress made by Argentina in recent years in structural reforms, particularly in privatization, deregulation, and pension reform." The IMF also singled out the country's policies of fixing the peso to the dollar and tying the growth of domestic credit to the inflow of dollars, observing that this plan "has served Argentina well and continues to be an adequate framework for stable growth."[15]

Such plaudits are remarkable indeed, given the course of events in Argentina since the 1991 launching of the new policies. Unemployment and inequality began rising sharply almost immediately after the plan was implemented, and the country began sinking into a depression by 1997. By December 2001, the model completely disintegrated amid massive food riots, a general strike, a state of emergency, twenty-seven deaths in the streets, and the flight from the country of both President Fernando de la Rua and Finance Minister Domingo Carvallo. Carvallo had been the principal architect of the plan, and had been regularly hailed as an economic wizard by global opinion leaders.

The immediate spark that set off the riots and fall of the government was the government's announcement that it was limiting the amount of money individuals could withdraw from their bank accounts. This was a hard blow to Argentina's middle class, preventing them from even proceeding with their Christmas holiday plans. It was also one further assault on the country's working class and poor, after years in which government austerity policies had, predictably, produced increasing poverty, unemployment and resistance. President de la Rua and Finance Minister Carvallo knew that freezing bank accounts was an extreme measure. But they also understood that, by this point in the unraveling of their free market program, the country's banking system was on the verge of collapse.

How could Argentina's neoliberal program have failed so spectacularly, even while receiving acclaim from the mainstream press and IMF virtually until the day the food riots began? It is crucial to recognize that the 1991 policies were only the most recent in a series of dramatic free market policy initiatives in Argentina over the past quarter century. Each of these earlier free market programs was also announced amid great promises for success and each also collapsed in failure.

Dismantling import substitution policies[16]

The powerful counter-tradition in economic policy confronting all of Argentina's recent free market experiences has been the import substitution industrialization economic development model that gradually took shape throughout Latin America during the first half of the twentieth century, and came to dominate economic policymaking in the region in the 1950s and 1960s.

As I discussed above, the fundamental idea behind import substitution industrialization was that developing economies such as Argentina should take active measures to build up the country's capacity to produce manufactured goods for its domestic market. The key policy tools for advancing this approach in Argentina included protective tariffs for domestic producers; controls on the movements of short-term financial flows; cheap loans for domestic producers by government development banks; and direct government participation in strategic industries such as steel. Clearly, each of these measures contradicted the tenets of free-market capitalism.

At the same time, the import substitution model never threatened the dominant position of domestic capitalists in Argentina's economy, while foreign capitalists also continued to exercise substantial influence. Thus, over the period 1949–65, the heyday of Argentina's import substitution era, the share of national income going to labor actually fell from 49 to 43 percent. Moreover, Argentina continued to purchase imported capital equipment and luxury goods during these years. The persistence of this strong demand for imported capital and luxury goods then also created persistent deficits in the country's trade balance. This, along with the other problems mentioned earlier that were pervasive under import substitution policies throughout Latin America – i.e. excessive government protection for selected firms and the corresponding culture of corruption – rendered the model unsustainable in the long run.

Despite these serious weaknesses, import substitution policies did still succeed on several levels. First, the Argentine economy did grow relatively quickly over these years – at an average rate of 3.6 percent between 1950–70. This in contrast to the average growth rate between 1971–2001 of 2.0. The model also attained its most immediate goal of generating a vibrant manufacturing base, initially for producing consumer goods, but also for machinery and equipment by the 1970s.

Nevertheless, because the model also placed some limits on the prerogatives of domestic and especially foreign capitalists, it faced persistent challenges from the 1950s onward. An especially aggressive attack came in 1976, when a junta of generals seized political power during a bout with hyperinflation and general economic breakdown. The generals did not aim simply to restore economic stability, but rather to dismantle the entire import-substitution apparatus and replace it with a free market "monetarist" model similar to that imposed in neighboring Chile by the fascist general Augusto Pinochet. This meant dramatically shifting the role of government in the economy to support the market power of business, weakening the union movement so as to further cut the share of national income going to wages as against profits, and opening the economy to multinational corporations and financial investors.[17]

This monetarist medicine yielded, predictably, rapid cuts in living standards and massive opposition. But the generals gained a quick reprieve from the full consequences of their program, when Argentina, as with the rest of Latin America, became the recipient of huge new inflows of foreign lending in the mid-1970s. This credit tap opened when the international banks found themselves with windfalls of deposits coming from oil exporting countries, after the oil exporters managed to raise the world price of oil fourfold in 1973–74.

However, the period of easy credit for Argentina also ended abruptly in August 1982, when Mexico announced its inability to cover interest payments on $90 billion in outstanding debt unless it received further new loans. The same private creditors who had been zealous loan merchants throughout Latin America in the late 1970s now considered the entire region too risky. Argentina, along with the rest of Latin America, was thus plunged into a debt crisis and the "lost decade" of depression, instability and a series of failed restructuring measures sponsored by the IMF and U.S. government.

The IMF imposed the first program for "solving" the debt crisis. This was its standard austerity package guided by free-market gospel, and was therefore a first sequel to the junta's attempt at dismantling the country's import-substitution development framework. The IMF held that excessive government intervention was the fundamental cause of the debt crisis. Their plan therefore involved eliminating public enterprises, sharply reducing government subsidies and deficit spending, weakening cost-of-living allowances, and decontrolling prices and exchange rates.

This program did succeed in generating a trade surplus, and thus increased the ability of Argentina to service its debt. But the main factor producing the trade surplus was the collapse of mass purchasing power and living standards. The logic here could not be simpler. Step one is to just slash the incomes of ordinary people and thereby ensure they will spend less. Then comes step two: with less money to spend, people will buy fewer imports. This eliminates the trade deficit. But people will also purchase fewer domestic goods under these austerity conditions. As such, the policy of deliberately forcing down mass buying power also predictably produced a collapse of domestic investment. Indeed, throughout the debt crisis years, large numbers of Argentina's capitalists were actively spiriting their money out of the country in search of safer and higher-yielding havens. Thus, the IMF austerity program failed on its own terms of generating the stability it claimed it could produce, even while it *intentionally* imposed huge costs on most Argentine people.

This failure then led to the third version of free market restructuring in Argentina since the 1976 military coup. The new program was designed by Ronald Reagan's Treasury Secretary James Baker in October 1985.[18] The Baker plan was advertised as distinct from IMF policies, because it purported to not entail wringing more austerity out of the Argentine people. To the contrary, it claimed that it could resolve the debt crisis by promoting accelerated long-term economic growth.

And what were to be the new "pro-growth" engines under the Baker plan? The plan emphasized two points. The first was that that the Reagan administration was prepared to lobby the private international banks to soften their credit terms with Argentina and other heavily indebted developing countries. But, second, in order for the countries to be eligible for this generosity, they had to agree to carry out comprehensive "structural adjustments" to promote free-market capitalism. Such adjustments were to include lowering taxes, especially for business and the wealthy; eliminating subsidies for consumer goods and export-oriented industries; opening domestic markets to free trade; encouraging foreign investment through tax incentives and other inducements; and allowing market forces to determine exchange rates, interest rates and wage levels. This was the period in which a "pro-growth" economic policy became by definition one which dismantles state intervention and delivers the economy, via the "free market," to private business. The fact that Argentina and other Latin economies had in fact grown at a reasonable rate during the import substitution era did not seem to matter.

This third round of enforced free market policies was, again, predictably, no more successful than its predecessors. The human costs were enormous, with Argentina's official poverty rate rising from 8 to 40 percent between 1980 and 1990. But, yet again, this latest program also failed on its own terms. Rather than stimulating private investment, the country's stock of machinery and equipment actually shrank by nearly 35 percent between 1981–89. This was in stark contrast to the rapid growth of investment in the previous three decades.

Moreover, even the country's debt burdens failed to lighten over the lost decade. Thus, the country's interest payments on foreign debt were 6 percent of total exports in 1978 and 37 percent during the height of the debt crisis. In other words, if Argentina succeeded in selling $100 in exported products, they had to devote $6 dollars to covering their foreign interest payments in 1978, but $37 during the debt crisis. By 1991, current interest obligations had retreated to 25 percent of exports, but when arrears payments were included, the ratio of interest payments to exports rose to a crushing 82 percent – that is, fully $82 of every $100 in export earnings now went to service debt. And it is important to again emphasize the role of capital flight by Argentina's wealthy in deepening the country's debt burden. By the middle of the decade, the amount of assets in foreign countries held by Argentinians was approximately equal to the total value of the country's debt. So one immediately available solution to the debt crisis would have been to restrict the outflow of capital from the country.[19] But such an initiative would obviously run contrary to the precepts of free-market restructuring, and was therefore never seriously entertained.

Neoliberalism circa 1991 and the path to collapse[20]

The initial impetus for the 1991 installment of Argentina's free market restructuring agenda was two bouts with hyperinflation in 1989 and early 1990, with prices rising by nearly 200 percent in July 1989 alone. But the hyperinflation itself resulted primarily from the collapse of the previous free market restructuring plan, as capital outflows led to a sharp currency devaluation. The devaluation meant that the price of imports rose dramatically, which in turn created the environment under which previously controlled domestic prices could also readily increase.

Given this clear connection between capital outflows, devaluation and hyperinflation, policymakers might reasonably have concluded from the 1989-90 hyperinflation experiences that allowing international capital to freely flow in and out of the country was hazardous. But this was not the conclusion reached by President Carlos Menem, who had taken office in July 1989, replacing Raul Alfonsin. Menem had defeated Alfonsin in part because of Alfonsin's failure to control hyperinflation but more generally due to the austerity policies that Alfonsin's government administered under the auspices of the U.S. government and IMF. Though elected as the candidate of the pro-labor Peronist party, Menem became persuaded of the merits of neo-liberalism soon after assuming office five months ahead of schedule when Alfonsin resigned due to the crises induced by hyperinflation. In particular, the Menem government interpreted the bouts with hyperinflation as evidence of the need for still another, more emphatic version of free market restructuring.

The only major innovation of the 1991 program was its so-called "monetary convertibility" plan. This locked the Argentine financial system into a complete reliance on the U.S. dollar and the capacity of Argentina to attract foreign investors. If foreign investment into Argentina were to fall, this would mean that the country's reserve holdings of dollars would decline, which would in turn produce an overall shortage in the supply of credit throughout the country. This was designed to eliminate inflationary pressures, since domestic credit in pesos would grow only at the rate at which dollars were brought into the country.

The other pieces of the 1991 free-market restructuring plan were supposed to fall into place once the convertibility plan defeated the country's inflationary dragon. Multinational firms and finance capitalists would understand that they could now do business in a stable currency – effectively, indeed, they could operate in dollars rather than pesos. The privatization feature of the program meant that a large supply of state assets were available for foreign investors to purchase at distress-sale prices. This included approximately 400-state owned firms, including airlines, oil companies, steel, petrochemicals, insurance, banks, telecommunications and postal services. These firms produced about 7 percent of the country's annual product. The revenues the government would receive from selling these state assets would also help in eliminating fiscal deficits, which in turn would assist in dampening any lingering inflationary pressures. Finally, deregulation of financial markets would assure foreign investors that they could move their money in and out of Argentina as they wished.

The monetary convertibility plan, along with the government's intention to eliminate fiscal deficits, did mean that Argentina was abrogating authority over its monetary and fiscal policy, and thus on any measures that might promote increases in the country's level of investment or employment. It should not be surprising that Finance Minister Carvallo, the architect of the policy, made quite clear his position that "there is no relation between unemployment and economic policy."[21]

Initially, this new restructuring plan was deemed a winner both on Wall Street and with the IMF. Inflation did fall dramatically, from 84 percent in 1991 to 1.6 percent by 1995. United States and European investors poured into the country to purchase the wide array of public assets on offer. But even as the supply of available public asset offerings became depleted, financial capitalists kept bringing funds into the country, primarily to purchase dollar-denominated Argentine government bonds yielding returns in dollars higher than what they would receive elsewhere.

This strategy first experienced major stresses during the 1995–96 financial crisis in Mexico, which frightened off international financial investors from all of Latin America, just as it had after the 1982 Mexican default. However, this time Argentina was already following free-market precepts to an unprecedented extent. The IMF was therefore eager to supply Argentina with the emergency credits needed to prevent it from following Mexico into crisis. But the IMF also insisted on government expenditure cuts as a condition for its bailout loans. This rendered Argentina's economy even more dependent on the whims of foreign creditors to bring investment and spending into the economy, even though the country had just become severely destabilized due to a decline in the inflows of foreign capital.

While this IMF bailout was therefore able to prevent an immediate crisis in 1995, it was also becoming increasingly clear that this latest free market model was also not sustainable. With the U.S. Federal Reserve raising interest rates after 1995, the value of the dollar also rose relative to the currencies of Argentina's chief trading partners – Europe and its Latin American neighbors, notably Brazil. The value of the peso then rose in lockstep with the dollar. This meant that the price for foreigners of Argentina's exports also rose, rendering them less competitive. It also meant that Argentine consumers could buy imports more cheaply, thereby cutting still further into the market for products made in Argentina.

The government initially kept the economy afloat through increased borrowing. But the interest rates that Argentina had to pay to obtain loans were rising, as the country again became an increasingly risky venture for international financial investors. By 1997, with the high value of the peso thus holding down exports while opening the country to increased imports, and with dollar-denominated debts at high interest rates building up, Argentina was proceeding toward another debt trap. The severity of this debt trap would be made still worse given that most of the debt was denominated in dollars. Because of this, even if Argentina were to abandon its convertibility plan and reduce the value of the peso relative to the dollar, that would only mean that the country would now need *more pesos* to repay a *given amount* of dollar-denominated debt.

The country had thus fallen into a deepening crisis from 1997 onward, with both foreign and domestic investors increasingly pulling their funds out of the country. This was the basis for the government's desperate attempt in December 2001 to stanch the outflow of funds and save its financial system through limiting withdrawals from personal bank accounts. But the general strike, food riots and state of siege immediately demonstrated the futility of this plan.

Are more rounds of IMF medicine the only option?

In the short-term, the government of President Eduardo Duhalde that assumed office in December 2001 took the only steps that had a chance of producing a measure of calm in the wake of the food riots, state of siege and deaths in the streets. These were: 1) suspend payments on dollar-denominated debts to relieve the country of its punishing austerity; 2) increase government spending to generate jobs and more private spending in the economy; and 3) repeal the dollar/peso convertibility law and devalue the peso to make the country more competitive on international markets.

Naturally, free-market critics viewed these measures as no solution at all, but rather the actions of "hoodlums" suffering from "kleptomania," according to editorial writers for the leading U.S. business publications *Forbes* and the *Wall Street Journal*.[22] These policies did entail that the country's investors, rather than simply its working class and poor alone, bear some of the costs of this most recent crisis – an obviously unacceptable situation for the U.S. business press. For such free-market proponents, it appears that the only viable long-term solution for Argentina – and here yet again, there are no surprises – is to push the free market program to yet a higher degree. This seems primarily to mean that Argentina establish the U.S. dollar as the official currency of the country. Such an action would presumably remove government authority over the country's economic conditions to an extent even beyond what had been obtained through the 1991 convertibility plan. The neoliberal agenda would also entail selling any remaining public assets, cutting government spending at both the federal and provincial levels, and eliminating any remaining vestiges of trade protection and controls over financial flows.

But how would this policy package work, even assuming a best-case scenario? Argentina would become even more dependent than previously on the good opinion of foreign investors. And even allowing that Argentina could succeed in winning such a seal of approval, any increase in the value of the dollar – over which the Argentine government would obviously have no control – would yet again generate declining exports and rising imports. This would mean a trade deficit and corresponding need for borrowed funds to cover the deficit. It would also mean a weakened domestic industry, and with that, job losses and a contraction of the domestic market. Such a situation would thus bring both more demand for foreign credits and a diminished view, by these same foreign investors, of the profitable opportunities available in Argentina.

The only other reasonable option is for Argentina to return to a model in which the public sector plays a major role in the economy – by actively promoting domestic investment and an expanding domestic market, and by placing limits on the speculative inflows and outflows of foreign financial capital.[23] This does not mean that the import substitution industrialization policies of the 1950s and 1960s should be revived intact. The extent of global integration would make a return to the precise policies of the import substitution era impossible even if they were desirable. But the relative success of the import substitution years does nevertheless demonstrate that the active use of government policy to promote a growing economy and social well-being is clearly possible. Moreover, unlike with the various free-market experiments, the success of this approach does not depend on forcing ever-greater austerity on Argentina's working class and poor.

One year after the December 2001 food riots broke out, no viable policy initiatives were even under discussion for ending what had become the country's worst depression in seventy years. Instead, living amid the ruins of the country's hyper-neoliberal economic model, the Argentine people have taken it upon themselves to find the means to survival. Thus, the *Wall Street Journal* of December 20, 2002 published a story titled, "Self-Reliance Helps Argentines Endure Economic Chaos." The story describes initiatives such as voluntary neighborhood relief efforts, schools growing food for their students, and workers rescuing closed plants from liquidation during the previous year's "economic contraction twice as severe as the one it experienced during the Great Depression...[with] worse...expected." According to the *Journal*, in more than 100 factories, "workers seized control of the plants and kept them operating, saving 13,000 jobs." One educator leading neighborhood relief efforts explained that "You could die waiting for the IMF and government to solve Argentina's problems."

Sweatshops and global manufacturing production

Probably the most widely publicized feature of the landscape of global austerity in recent years has been the spread of sweatshop labor conditions throughout the world, especially in the production of clothing and footwear.

In the U.S., the reports that first attracted widespread media attention were about the production of Nike athletic shoes, beginning with a 1992 story in *Harper's* that described workers in Indonesia assembling nearly fourteen pairs of Nike shoes every day and earning fourteen cents per hour, less than the Indonesian government's standard for "minimum physical need" for a full-time worker. The next heavily reported revelations concerned the clothing line endorsed by TV personality Kathie Lee Gifford, whose popular appeal rested heavily on her wholesome image. In April 1996, Charles Kernaghan of the New York-based National Labor Committee told a U.S. Congressional committee that Gifford's clothes were made by Honduran girls earning 31 cents per hour laboring in sweatshops.[24]

Similar reports have continued. For example, an October 2, 2000 *Business Week* story titled "A Life of Fines and Beatings" described conditions in Chinese factories that make products for Wal-Mart, among other Western companies. One handbag-producing firm profiled in the story employs 900 workers. It charged workers $15 a month for food and lodging in a crowded dormitory, which the article describes as a "crushing sum" given that a newly hired worker would clear $22 in their first month. The company also forced new workers to relinquish their personal identity cards, so "workers risked arrest if they ventured out of their immediate neighborhood."

These news reports detailing conditions in individual production sites are also consistent with more extensive and systematic studies of labor practices in the global apparel and footwear industry sponsored by, among others, the International Labor Organization of the United Nations, and various U.S. university groups. These reports found extremely low pay, dangerous and unhealthy working conditions, and restrictions on workers' basic rights – i.e. all features that we commonly associate with the term "sweatshop" – to be common in the apparel and footwear industry in the developing world.[25]

But certainly an abundance of poorly-paid jobs and bad working conditions are hardly novel phenomena in less-developed countries. Indeed, these are among the main features that define a country as being "less developed." Is there really anything new about the sweatshop labor conditions that have been widely publicized in recent years? Or is it simply a matter of the media in rich countries suddenly paying more attention to a long-standing and pervasive situation?

In fact, the current high level of attention to global sweatshop conditions does reflect more than just a rise in awareness. The underlying reality behind the rise in sweatshops is the extremely rapid increase over the past twenty-five years in less-developed countries producing manufactured products for export markets. We can see this pattern in Figure 5.1, showing the share of manufacturing exports as a percentage of total exports for the less-developed countries. As the figure shows, manufacturing exports amounted to 17.7 percent of total exports for less developed countries as recently as 1980. By 1998, the figure had risen to 71.6 percent. The most rapid growth in exports among these countries has been in Asia – especially China, South

FIGURE 5.1: Manufacturing exports in less developed countries
(manufacturing exports as share of total exports)

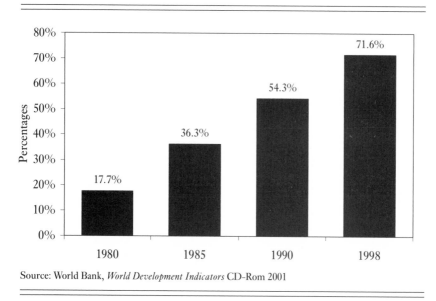

Source: World Bank, *World Development Indicators* CD-Rom 2001

Korea, Taiwan, Thailand, Malaysia, Indonesia and India. But Latin American and African countries have also experienced significant increases in their export markets.

Of course, not all manufactured exports from less-developed countries are produced under sweatshop conditions. But the strategy of many business owners in less-developed countries – just as in the advanced countries – is to gain a competitive advantage through squeezing workers, and thereby driving down labor costs as far as possible. In many countries, business firms are able to proceed unchecked with such "race to the bottom" employment practices because of a lack of reasonable laws governing minimum wages, working conditions, and the basic rights of workers. Perhaps even more frequently, reasonable labor standards do exist on paper in less-developed countries but are not enforced in practice. These are the conditions that have fostered the rapid spread of sweatshops throughout the developing world.

Are sweatshops really so bad?

But recognizing the existence of sweatshops is one thing: is it reasonable to also assume that sweatshops are a problem for less-developed countries? In fact, many well-known economists and other commentators consider the spread of sweatshops in these regions as a highly favorable development. This view is expressed straightforwardly in a September 24, 2000 *New York Times Magazine* article titled "Two Cheers for Sweatshops," by Nicholas Kristof and Sheryl WuDunn, focusing on conditions in Asia. Kristof and WuDunn write:

> Fourteen years ago, we moved to Asia and began reporting there. Like most Westerners, we arrived in the region outraged at sweatshops. In time, though, we came to accept the view supported by most Asians: that the campaign against sweatshops risks harming the very people it is intended to help. For beneath their grime, sweatshops are a clear sign of the industrial revolution that is beginning to reshape Asia.
>
> This is not to praise sweatshops. Some managers are brutal in the way they house workers in firetraps, expose children to dangerous chemicals, deny bathroom breaks, demand sexual favors, force people to work double shifts or dismiss anyone who tries to organize a union. Agitation for improved safety conditions can be helpful, just as it was in 19th-century Europe. But ... the simplest way to help the poorest Asians would be to buy more from sweatshops, not less.

Jeffrey Sachs, a leading economist at Columbia University expresses this same perspective even more emphatically when he says that the problem is "not that there are too many sweatshops, but that there are too few." Also endorsing this view, the Princeton economist and *New York Times* columnist Paul Krugman explains that "the result [of sweatshop employment] has been to move hundreds of millions of people from abject poverty to something still awful but nonetheless significantly better," and thus, that "the growth of sweatshop employment is tremendous good news for the world's poor."

However else one might react to such perspectives, they do bring attention to a simple, but extremely important fact about sweatshops: that the single most important reason that sweatshops exist is that people accept these jobs. True, once workers are hired into sweatshop firms, they are often forced to stay on the job through harsh forms of compulsion, as the *Business Week* story quoted above makes clear. Still, for the most part, workers could escape sweatshop conditions simply by refusing to show up at work. The fact that they do show up means that sweatshop employment represents an option for hundreds of millions of workers in developing countries that is superior to their next best alternative. Presumably, this is the sense in which the Kristof and WuDunn offer "two cheers" for sweatshops, Professor Sachs calls for more sweatshops, and Professor Krugman praises them as "tremendous good news" for the world's poor.[26]

But is it actually true that there is no alternative to creating ever more sweatshops if developing countries are to reduce poverty and succeed economically? In fact, this perspective is seriously misguided, because it ignores some crucial facts about the way that conditions have changed dramatically under neoliberal globalization.

Surplus workers in less-developed countries[27]
At least since World War II, rural workers in developing countries have been migrating out of agricultural employment. This migration has freed up more workers to contribute toward the production of non-agricultural goods and services, which, in turn, has generally contributed positively to economic growth in developing countries. But this migration out of agriculture also created a new problem: that the supply of workers moving out of agriculture was exceeding the demand for these workers in other forms of employment. This pattern led to the formation of a massive pool of "surplus" workers – people who were forced to scramble for a living any way they could. A high proportion of them migrated into the queue for jobs in the manufacturing sectors in developing countries with virtually nothing as an alternative fallback position. These are the conditions under which poor working people might well regard a sweatshop factory job as a better option than any immediately practical alternative.

This pattern has worsened under neoliberal globalization, resulting from the interaction of several factors. First, the reduction or elimination of tariffs on agricultural products has enabled cheap imported grains and other agricultural products to capture a growing share of the developing countries' markets. This has made it increasingly difficult for small-scale farmers in developing countries to survive in agriculture, which, in turn, has accelerated the migration into the non-agricultural labor market. Neoliberal policies have also brought reductions, if not outright elimination, of agricultural subsidies to smallholders, as we saw with the situation in rural India.

As conditions have thus worsened for small-scale agricultural producers, their opportunities for finding jobs in manufacturing have also been limited by several factors also associated with neoliberal policies. The first has been the overall decline in economic growth and average incomes in most developing countries in the neoliberal era. As income growth fell, so did the expansion of domestic markets, and thus also the expansion of jobs producing goods for domestic consumers.

But what about the sharp rise in manufacturing exports by developing countries? In fact, even this development has not generally translated into a comparable rise in jobs producing goods for export markets (with some important exceptions, notably China again, but also Malaysia and Chile). Many of the countries that are now manufacturing exporters – in particular the large Latin American economies, Mexico, Argentina and Brazil – did already have large-scale manufacturing sectors in operation, though these earlier-vintage manufacturing sectors, under the import substitution model, concentrated on producing for their domestic markets. The liberalization of trade policies has therefore produced improvements in their exporting capacity, but, concurrently, a corresponding increase in the penetration of their own domestic markets by foreign imports. Moreover, firms in the relatively new export manufacturing countries have been forced to appropriate higher productivity production methods in order to compete in the global market. This has made their operations more efficient, but has also entailed reducing the number of workers they employ.

Workers in developing countries thus face a double squeeze: diminishing opportunities to continue earning a living in agriculture, but nothing close to a compensating growth of job opportunities outside of agriculture. These are the circumstances that have pushed more working people in developing countries into a desperate situation where they must accept a sweat-shop job to continue to live. But this situation can hardly be construed as "tremendous good news for the world's poor," as Paul Krugman put it. They are simply the raw facts of life for hundreds of millions of people under global neoliberalism.

Sweatshop jobs vs. no jobs: no alternatives?

In fact, there is evidence in considering the pattern of manufacturing pro-duction in less-developed countries that offers grounds for optimism about alleviating sweatshop conditions. The argument that sweatshops are "tre-mendous good news for the world's poor" is based on a simple premise: that if working conditions in developing countries were to become more desir-able – that is, if wages were to rise, workplaces to become cleaner and safer, and workers were able to exercise basic rights – then labor costs in these countries would become excessive. The firms producing in developing coun-tries would then be out-competed on global markets, and job opportunities for the poor would dry up, despite the best intentions of anti-sweatshop activists. But this simple premise is contradicted by the actual patterns be-tween wage and employment growth in the apparel industries of developing countries. Table 5.3 offers evidence that speaks to this question.

More specifically, Table 5.3 gives data on the relationship between real wage and employment growth in the apparel industries for twenty-two de-veloping countries between 1988–97 (these twenty-two developing coun-tries were the only ones for which adequate data were available). I have grouped the countries into four categories, those in which:

1) employment and real wage growth *rose* together;
2) employment and real wage growth *fell* together;
3) employment *fell* while real wage growth *rose*; and
4) employment *rose* while real wage growth *fell*.

As we can see from the table, the countries in which employment and real wages rose together, shown in panel A, is the largest category – both in terms of the total of eight countries included in this category, and in terms of

TABLE 5.3: Relationship between employment and real wage growth in developing countries' apparel industries

	Total apparel employment in 1997	Employment growth average annual rate 1988–97 (percentages)	Real wage growth average annual rate 1988–97 (percentages)
A) Countries in which employment and real wages rose together			
(listed according to total employment levels in 1997)			
1) Indonesia	393,300	+17.4	+1.3
2) India	270,000	+29.9	+0.7
3) Philippines	161,300	+4.8	+1.2
4) Morocco	116,900	+10.3	+2.3
5) Colombia	66,700	+3.7	+1.2
6) Malaysia	60,500	+4.4	+3.8
7) Costa Rica	32,900	+4.1	+2.9
8) Chile	13,800	+1.6	+6.5
Total employment for all countries	1,215,400		
B) Countries in which employment and real wages fell together			
1) Kenya	7,300	-1.2	-1.9
2) Guatemala	1,900	-2.1	-10.3
3) Barbados	1,300	-3.1	-6.1
Total employment for all countries	10,500		
C) Countries in which employment fell while real wages rose			
1) South Korea	151,500	-5.7	+8.3
2) South Africa	126,300	-0.5	+2.1
3) Mauritius	66,400	-1.3	+7.0
4) Mexico	24,500	-2.1	+1.8
5) Puerto Rico	20,100	-3.6	+0.3
6) Singapore	8,100	-11.5	+4.8
7) Panama	4,300	-0.7	+1.8
Total employment for all countries	401,200		
D) Countries in which employment rose while real wages fell			
1) Uruguay	11,300	+0.2	-6.3
2) Jordan	4,900	+8.7	-3.3
3) Ecuador	3,900	+1.5	-10.2
4) Bolivia	2,200	+18.5	-1.9
Total employment for all countries	22,300		

Source: World Bank, *World Development Indicators*, 2001 CD-ROM

the 1.2 million workers employed in these countries as of 1997. These figures clearly contradict the notion, at least in the apparel industry, that developing countries must maintain labor costs as low as possible in order for job opportunities to grow. It is true that wages rose only modestly in most of the eight countries listed. But the fact that they are rising at all demonstrates that factors other than maintaining sweatshop working conditions are contributing to the growth of jobs. Some of these other factors are the productivity levels in the apparel plants, the quality of the local transportation and communications infrastructure, and the effectiveness of the marketing channels through which the newly manufactured clothing items reach retail markets.

Panel B includes three countries – Kenya, Guatemala and Barbados – in which apparel workers' wages fell over 1988–97, but employment nevertheless declined as well. This is a small grouping of countries, which also employs a small number of workers. But it is still useful to observe examples in which pushing wages down did not succeed in stimulating job growth.

Panel C shows the countries in which wages rose while employment declined. But these cases need to be interpreted carefully. South Korea, for example, experienced the fastest real wage growth of the twenty-two countries in the sample, at an average annual rate of 8.3 percent, while the number of jobs in the apparel industry was declining at a 5.7 percent annual rate. Two developments explain this pattern: rising productivity among apparel producers; and growing strength by the country's labor movement, which pushed successfully for higher wages while operating in a democratic environment for the first time. Jobs in which both wages and productivity are rising rapidly should be considered as a positive development. But it does still create a challenge at the same time: that job opportunities be created elsewhere in the Korean economy, to prevent unemployment from rising. We take up this issue in some detail in the next chapter of the book.

The countries in Panel D conform most closely in their experiences to the claims of sweatshop enthusiasts: they experienced employment growth while wages declined. But this grouping consisted of only four countries, employing 22,300 workers.

The overall point is that there is no single formula that will deliver a successful manufacturing sector in developing countries. Maintaining sweatshop working conditions and other "race to the bottom" business practices may indeed be successful in driving down costs and thereby enhancing competiveness. But the evidence presented here also shows that 1) there are other ways to establish a growing manufacturing sector in developing countries; and 2) pushing labor costs down will, in itself, guarantee nothing.

There is another important consideration at play here: the fact that consumers in the United States and other wealthy countries express strong preferences to not purchase products made under sweatshop conditions, the entreaties of sweatshop enthusiasts notwithstanding. Consider the results of a 1999 survey of U.S. consumers sponsored by the National Bureau of Economic Research. This poll found that, on average, consumers were willing to pay 28 percent more on a $10 item and 15 percent more on a $100 item to ensure that the products they bought were made under "good working conditions."[28]

These polling results are especially striking, given the findings from a study I conducted with co-workers Justine Burns and James Heintz. We estimated how much retail prices in the United States would have to rise in order to fully finance a 100 percent wage increase for apparel production workers in Mexico.[29] We recognized that a one-time, 100 percent wage increase for Mexican workers – a doubling of existing wage rates – was well beyond what was likely to result even in a political environment dominated by a broadly shared commitment to eliminating sweatshops. But for the purposes of the exercise, it was important that we not err by underestimating how much labor costs might have to rise to eliminate sweatshops. The result we obtained was that retail prices in the U.S. clothing market would have to rise by only *1.8 percent to fully cover this 100 percent wage increase.* Consider, for example, the case for a $100 sports jacket. To finance a 100 percent wage increase for Mexican workers producing this jacket, the retail price of the jacket would have to rise by $1.80, to $101.80. At the same time, the National Bureau of Economic Research poll finds that U.S. consumers would be willing to pay $115 for this jacket if they could be assured that it had not been made under sweatshop conditions.

Of course, by itself, this simple exercise does not demonstrate that sweatshop labor conditions could be readily wiped out through modest increases in consumer prices. The world is obviously more complex than our exercise allows. Take just one additional layer of complexity. If the jacket's retail price really did rise from $100 to $101.80 in the U.S. market because U.S. consumers want their clothes manufactured under non-sweatshop conditions, how would the consumers actually know whether that extra $1.80 that they spent on the jacket is actually getting channeled back to the production-level workers in Mexico, as opposed to getting pocketed by the owners of their local J.C. Penney outlet? There is no airtight answer to this or several other similar questions. Nevertheless, the exercise still gives important support on behalf of an important conclusion: that the spread of sweatshop working conditions need not be considered as an inevitable, much less desirable, feature of the global economic landscape.

Foreign aid and economic growth

We see that the relentless spread of sweatshops is not the only way to create jobs in developing countries. But what about the broader pathologies in the less developed countries associated with the neoliberal era, i.e. declining growth, increased inequality and lack of progress in reducing poverty? World leaders set clear goals for poverty eradication at the United Nations Millennium Summit: to cut in half by 2015 the proportion of people whose income is less than one dollar a day, who suffer from hunger, or who are unable to reach or afford safe drinking water.[30] Are there any measures through which these goals could conceivably be met?

One obvious and widely discussed initiative would be for the wealthy countries to simply increase the amount of aid they provide for poor countries. This approach has received widespread attention in recent years, most visibly from the admirable, energetic efforts of rock star Bono, the lead singer of the group U2. Bono's mission has led him to, among other things, tour areas of Africa in May 2002 with the first Treasury Secretary of the Bush-2 administration, Paul O'Neill. Bono emphasized the need for increased aid during the Africa tour, while former Secretary O'Neill espoused the virtues of free market economic policies as the single most powerful anti-poverty weapon for the continent.

Of course, what former Secretary O'Neill managed to neglect during this joint tour are the ways in which neoliberal economic policies have worsened poverty and inequality throughout most of Africa, as well as in Argentina, rural India and elsewhere. Indeed it would be illuminating to consider the Bono/O'Neill tour from another perspective. Let's allow that Bono's efforts at persuading the rich countries to substantially increase their aid to developing countries were to completely succeed. How large would the benefits be of this dramatic policy shift relative to the less developed countries pursuing the *opposite* of what former Secretary O'Neill proposed, that is, to abandon neoliberalism in favor of policy measures that could restore growth to something akin to the 1961–80 era of developmental states? Here are some figures that offer a rough answer to this question.

Increasing foreign aid

In the early 1970s, the wealthy countries committed themselves to provide 0.7 percent of their annual GDP for development aid. The March 2002 United Nations Conference on Financing for Development affirmed that a dramatic increase in aid is necessary if there was to be any possibility to achieve the Millennium Summit poverty goals. As U.N. Secretary General Kofi Annan wrote during the Monterrey conference, "all economic studies indicate that to achieve the Millennium Development Goals, we need an increase of about $50 billion a year in worldwide official aid – a doubling of present levels."[31] But as of 1999, the average amount given by the wealthy countries was only 0.32 percent of each country's GDP. The United States was the least generous by a substantial amount, allocating only 0.1 percent of its GDP to development aid.[32]

Indeed, even Annan's call for a $50 billion increase in development aid is well below the amount that would be generated if the wealthy countries did actually uphold their earlier commitment to providing 0.7 percent of GDP in aid. Considering the years 1995–99, the 0.7 percent of GDP foreign aid pledge would have meant an average annual aid contribution of $160 billion/year, an average increase of $105 billion over the approximately $55 billion per year that the wealthy countries did contribute in these years.

Clearly an increase in aid of $105 billion, or even $50 billion, would represent an implausible leap in generosity for most of the rich countries, especially the United States, given their evident willingness to disregard earlier pledges on this matter. But at least we have now established some outer bound figures as to how much additional income to the developing countries could be generated by increased foreign aid – the far outer limit figure being $105 billion, while even the $50 billion called for by Secretary General Annan also representing an improbable goal.[33]

Returning to developmental era growth

The U.N. Conference on Financing for Development was also clear that "a crucial task" for meeting its poverty reduction goals is "to enhance the efficiency, coherence, and consistency of macroeconomic policies."[34] But the official conference document provides no specifics as to what should constitute such "efficient, coherent, and consistent" macroeconomic policies. As a simple starting point for addressing this issue, what if we allowed that the developing countries were able to return to something like their average rate of economic growth during the era of developmental states? As we have seen earlier (see Table 5.1), the less developed countries (excluding China) grew at an average annual rate of 5.5 percent between 1961–80 but this rate dropped to 2.6 percent between 1981–99. The decline in the average growth rate for less developed countries was therefore 2.9 percent per year during the neoliberal era.

To give a rough estimate of how important such a shift in their growth path would be for the less developed countries, I have estimated the effects of raising the average growth rate for these countries by 2.9 percent per year over the years 1995–99 only. The specific question we are asking is: if the poor and middle income countries grew from 1995–99 at an average rate that was 2.9 percent faster than the rate at which they actually grew, how much additional national income would they have generated?

The answer is that, for the full five-year period, the poor and middle-income countries, exclusive of China, would have produced an additional $2.4 trillion in income. The average total income increase over the five-year period would therefore be $480 billion per year – that is, an amount that is nearly five times larger than what would be generated by an implausible outer limit increase of $105 billion in foreign aid. It is important to emphasize that this result does not rely on assuming that the less-developed countries achieve anything unprecedented in their growth performance, but simply that they return to their *average* rates of growth during the era of developmental states. In other words, if the less developed countries abandoned the neoliberal policies that have inhibited their growth for the past generation, and established a new policy environment that promoted growth to an extent comparable to the levels they achieved in the 1960s and 1970s – but to no more than the average levels of this earlier period – they would have generated by 1999 gains in national income nearly five times larger than what they would attain by even an implausibly generous increase in aid from the wealthy countries.

To put it another way: if economic policies concerning less developed countries were to embrace the arguments of both Bono and former Bush Treasury Secretary Paul O'Neill – that is, for aid to dramatically increase while neoliberalism remained the dominant policy approach – incomes in developing countries would still be around $400 billion a year *less* than what could be achieved through eschewing neoliberalism in favor of something approximating the economic policies that guided the era of developmental states. Figure 5.2 summarizes the relative effects of the three options: 1) a Bono-level of increased aid support, versus 2) a return to a developmental state period growth performance, versus 3) Bono-level aid plus continuation of neoliberal rates of growth.

How much does $480 billion matter?

$480 billion is an immensely large figure, but what would it mean concretely for people's lives? How important would this amount be, for example, as a means of reducing poverty in the developing countries? To get some rough sense of this, it will be helpful to examine in a bit more detail the case of a single developing country. Brazil is a good case study for this purpose, since it is a large and important developing economy and because its own growth experience during the developmental state and neoliberal periods parallels the average experience for the developing countries as a whole.

FIGURE 5.2: The relative benefits of aid and growth for developing countries
(average annual gains based on 1995–99 data)

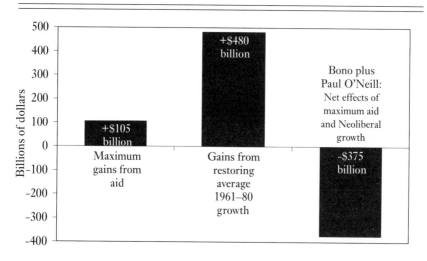

Source: Calculations based on figures in World Bank, *World Development Indicators* CD-Rom, 2001

The average per capita income in Brazil between 1995–99 was about
$4,500 per year. If Brazil's growth rate over these five years rose by 2.9
percent per year over the actual growth experience, this would generate an
average increase in income of $415 per person – that is, the average Brazil-
ian would enjoy roughly a 9 percent increase in income over the five-year
period. But what about the poor specifically? Between 1995–99, the poorest 10 percent of Brazil's population lived on an average of $375 per year,
that is, putting this segment of the population almost exactly at the United
Nations' minimal global poverty threshold of one dollar per day of income
(i.e. $375 per year/365 days). Thus, if Brazil's poorest 10 percent were to
receive a benefit from Brazil's accelerated economic growth equal to the
average for the whole society, their additional $415 in annual income would
represent more than a doubling of their living standard. Note that this
example does not entail that Brazil's poor somehow begin receiving a pro-
portionate share of the country's *total national income*, but only a propor-

tionate share of its *increased* income generated by accelerated growth. Everyone in Brazil would still be better off through this equal distribution of the gains from growth, with the average-income person still enjoying a roughly 9 percent income gain.

But we also need to recognize that Brazil's income distribution is one of the most unequal in the world. Short of major political upheaval, one should not reasonably expect that Brazil's growth dividend would be divided equally. However, even if we assumed that Brazil's poor received a gain from growth only one-fourth as large as the average person, that would still mean that the income of the poor would rise by 28 percent, or roughly $100. The federal government of Brazil defines what it terms as a "basic food basket" for an adult as costing approximately $56 per month. Thus, even the $100 in additional income would mean that Brazil's poor could purchase for themselves nearly two additional months of this basic food basket.

More generally then, even allowing for a highly unequal distribution of the gains from accelerated economic growth, the benefits of returning to something akin to the growth experience of the 1960s and 1970s would bring major benefits to the poor, both in Brazil and throughout the less developed world. At the same time, a major feature of any concerted poverty-reducing effort – an effort, for example, that takes seriously the anti-poverty commitments made at the U.N. Millennium Summit – would include measures for equalizing the gains from accelerated economic growth. In this regard, policies to eliminate sweatshops and guarantee workers decent, if still modest, minimum wages are good examples of measures that would enable the dividends from improved economic growth to be shared equitably.

Is global poverty a cause of terrorism?

Do the pervasive conditions of poverty that we have described in this chapter act as a breeding ground for terrorists? How we answer this question first depends on what we mean by "terrorism." Official government forces throughout the world, including, among others, those under every U.S. president since Harry Truman as well as those under Saddam Hussein in Iraq, have either engaged in or sponsored others in deliberate acts of violence against innocent civilian populations.[35] The military wing of the African National Congress in South Africa under apartheid also conducted acts of violence against innocent civilians. Were they terrorists or freedom fighters? We can ask the same question for scores of other organizations throughout the world.

To focus our discussion, we will examine the relationship between poverty and terrorism as it applies to members of non-governmental organizations engaged in violence against innocent civilians, especially groups such as al-Queda, as opposed to the African National Congress – that is, groups whose claims of high moral purpose are resolutely rejected across a wide range of political opinion.

Of course, the September 11 terrorist attacks brought unprecedented attention to this issue. Indeed, in the months immediately after September 11, virtually every political figure across the spectrum offered support for the position that the contemporary conditions of severe global poverty did indeed contribute to the type of terrorism we witnessed on September 11. Speaking at the March 2002 U.N. Conference in Monterrey, Mexico, even George Bush offered the view that "We fight against poverty because hope is the answer to terror."[36]

The Nobel Prize winning economist Lawrence Klein has provided a deeper perspective on the issue, arguing that we consider not simply the conditions of absolute poverty around the world, but the sharp increases in inequality as well, as inviting young people to contemplate extremist political perspectives. In a paper presented to the American Economic Association meetings in 2002, Klein wrote:

Think of the potential "dead end" future for young people growing up in poor environments. Are these not conditions for putting terrorist activities forward, in the face of disillusioned youth, and even embellishing it in the flagrant demonstration of affluent consumption through the very efficient facilities of information technology?[37]

This broad perspective has also been supported in the most extensive recent analysis of terrorism developed from within mainstream U.S. policy circles, the 2001 book *Terrorism and U.S. Foreign Policy* by Paul Pillar, a former deputy chief of the Counterterrorist Center at the Central Intelligence Agency. Pillar identifies two basic root causes of terrorism. The first is a political controversy that invites extremist efforts at resolution when some groups become convinced that more moderate solutions are unavailing. The second is what Pillar calls "the socioeconomic prospects of populations that are, or may become, the breeding stock for terrorists." Pillar writes as follows concerning these socioeconomic conditions:

> Terrorism is a risky, dangerous, and very disagreeable business. Consequently, few people who have a reasonably good life will be inclined to get into that business, regardless of their political viewpoint. Those who have more desolate lives and little hope of improving them will have fewer reservations about getting into it. The majority of terrorists worldwide are young adult males, unemployed or underemployed (except by terrorist groups), with weak social and familial support, and with poor prospects for economic improvement or advancement through legitimate work.[38]

Pillar also reports that recognizing these socioeconomic factors has provided a straightforward method of getting some low-level recruits to renounce terrorism: "Tell the young man that if he cuts all ties with his current organization he will receive assistance in finding a job and a new place to live." Here then, according to this former CIA expert, is a simple approach to counterterrorism that has demonstrated its effectiveness in the field: provide low-level terror recruits with decent jobs and housing that would otherwise have been unattainable to them. He does also recognize that "not every terrorist or potential terrorist can be bought off in this way." Still, Pillar is clear that poverty does breed terrorism and that attacking poverty – even at the level of providing minimally decent life opportunities on a case-by-case basis – is an effective counterterrorist tool.

But this consensus position has been recently challenged in a widely cited paper by the distinguished Princeton economist Alan Krueger and Jitka Maleckova, a Middle East specialist at Charles University in the Czech Republic.[39] Krueger and Maleckova developed a formal statistical model to evaluate the backgrounds of the 129 Lebanese Hezbollah terrorists killed during the 1980s and early 1990s. They found that, relative to the overall population of Lebanon at the time, these people were neither especially poor nor uneducated. Rather, they were more likely to have incomes above the poverty line and to have received a better than average amount of education. In an analysis of opinion polls in Palestine in 2001, Krueger and Maleckova similarly found that the poor and uneducated were not especially likely to support terrorist attacks against Israel.

These are valuable and thought-provoking findings. But they should not be regarded as surprising. We are well aware that Osama bin Laden is a scion of one of Saudia Arabia's wealthiest families. Mohammad Atta, the on-site leader of the 9/11 attacks, came from an upper middle-class Egyptian family. He had earned a degree in architecture from Cairo University and had also done graduate studies in urban planning in Germany. More generally, it is of course true that terrorist groups could not function effectively without intelligent, self-confident, articulate leaders. Such people are far more likely to be drawn from relatively privileged backgrounds than from the poor.

But what about the foot soldiers in the terrorist armies? Krueger and Maleckova's formal evidence says that even these people are not especially recruited from the poor. However, this result is based on considering only one such group, the Lebanonese Hezbollah. Moreover, even here, what Krueger and Maleckova actually show is not that the terrorist group members are from affluent backgrounds, but only that they are modestly more advantaged than the general population which is itself generally underprivileged. For example, Krueger and Maleckova report that the official poverty rate among the general Lebanese population at that time was 33 percent, while it was 28 percent among the Hezbollah members – a difference which, as they recognize, is not meaningful in their statistical model.

Pillar also offers relevant evidence – if not a formal statistical model – on this question, also focusing on the Middle East. He writes that "most members of the extremist Palestine Islamic Jihad are of low social origin and live in poverty in the bleak neighborhoods or refugee camps of the Gaza Strip. Hamas also does its most successful recruiting in Gaza (p. 31)." This description does not suggest that the Palestinian terrorists should necessarily be from *worse off* backgrounds than the average resident of Gaza, but only that they should broadly reflect the characteristics of the social groups whose cause they claim to champion. Of course, even among the poor, the recruits to terrorism necessarily represent a distinct minority precisely because they pursue extreme political solutions. By definition, this makes them more aggressive in responding to their social conditions than the average among their cohort. It should therefore not be surprising that they should also be somewhat better educated than the average. Most poor people do not have the wherewithal to advance an aggressive political response of any kind to their privation.

In any case, there is a more fundamental point to consider which can easily get neglected amid debates about headcounts in terrorist organizations. Krueger and Maleckova are themselves clear that relatively privileged people are drawn to terrorism because they hold strong political convictions. These convictions do not arise from thin air. In however destructive and self-defeating a fashion, terrorist groups are responding to what they perceive as egregious injustices that are not being corrected through nonviolent political channels. Certainly the existence of severe poverty – especially, as Lawrence Klein points out, amid flagrant demonstrations of opulence – is one such injustice that will serve to attract such politically committed recruits. The terrorists' chosen solutions will almost certainly produce further injustice and suffering. But this point is separate from how the terrorist groups recruited their membership in the first place.

This returns us to the broader challenge. If neoliberalism in less developed countries has produced more extensive poverty and greater inequality, can we advance viable alternatives to neoliberalism that will reverse these trends? It would be preposterous to anticipate that developing such alternatives to neoliberalism would eradicate terrorism on their own. Moreover, there is no shortage of obvious justifications for attacking poverty regardless of their impact on terrorism. But it also should not be a stretch of the imagination to expect, very simply, that when we sow fewer seeds, we will produce a correspondingly smaller crop.

CHAPTER SIX

Another Path Is Possible

"The world can and has been changed by those for whom the ideal and the real are dynamically contiguous."

— WILLIAM JAMES

"Too often a vehicle for mystification, economics can best become an instrument for enlightenment if we see it as the means by which we strive to make a workable science out of morality."

— ROBERT HEILBRONER

The neoliberal economic agenda – of eliminating government deficits and inflation, sharply cutting back government spending, deregulating labor and financial markets, and opening national economies to free trade and multinational capital investments – has become so dominant throughout the world over the past generation that even thinking through serious alternatives presents itself as a daunting task. Not surprisingly, supporters of neoliberalism regard such efforts as exercises in economic illiteracy or mere foolishness.

The experience under the Clinton presidency stands out as a prime example of the obstacles one faces in attempting to advance alternatives. This is because Clinton did actively tout his policy agenda as an alternative to neoliberalism – as the "third way" between "those who said government was the enemy and those who said government was the solution." But, as we have seen, Clinton offered only a mildly less severe version of neoliberal orthodoxy, adhering fundamentally to all its basic tenets. And while the Clinton period did produce gains in GDP and productivity growth relative to Reagan/Bush, Carter and Nixon/Ford, we have also seen how these favorable developments were the result of an unprecedented financial bubble that government regulators, Alan Greenspan chief among them, were perfectly willing to wave along. Moreover, under the full eight years of Clinton's presidency, even with the bubble ratcheting up both business investment and consumption by the rich, we have seen that average real wages remained at a level 10 percent below that of the Nixon/Ford peak period, even though productivity in the economy was 50 percent higher under Clinton than Nixon and Ford. The poverty rate through Clinton's term was only slightly better than the dismal performance attained during the Reagan/Bush years. In short, rhetoric aside, the Clinton economy was never an alternative to neoliberalism, but rather a variation on the orthodox model that illuminates powerfully why a real alternative is so badly needed.

But the Clinton framework did also serve the crucial function of defining a left boundary for the neoliberal model against which George W. Bush could retreat rightward. Thus, Bush entered office attacking the minimally worker-friendly labor regulations and workplace safety standards that were held over from Clinton's term, provoking *Time* magazine's observation that Bush was advancing an "unwaveringly pro-business, anti-labor agenda." And even amid the stock market collapse and steady stream of big business scandals, Bush has been unwilling to entertain any serious proposals for reigning in these excesses and creating a financial regulatory framework that encourages productive investment over speculation and fraud. He has also been unwilling to budge from his single overarching economic commitment of delivering tax cuts to the rich. Instead, Bush is drawing on the anti-deficit obsession promulgated under Clinton as a basis for cutting revenue sharing to state and local governments, even while expanding the military budget.

The inability to envision alternatives to neoliberalism has even more severe consequences in the less-developed countries. We have seen how neoliberal restructuring has brought slower economic growth, greater inequality and more poverty for most low and middle-income countries. As specific examples of neoliberalism in action, we have discussed the desperation among poor farmers in India after the Indian government cut agricultural subsidies, the global spread of sweatshop labor conditions, and the deep depression in Argentina as a consequence of the government there following policies prescribed by the International Monetary Fund.

Throughout the less-developed world, the policies of the International Monetary Fund have acted as a crucial locus of neoliberalism, since it is the vehicle through which the U.S. government's commitment to these policies is transmitted globally. The bitter irony here is that the mission intended for the IMF when it was first created was the opposite of what it has now become. It was during the Latin American debt crisis of the 1980s that the IMF's transformation became complete: to use the governments' economic policy tools to deliberately impose austerity conditions – otherwise known as an economic depression – on less-developed countries as a "solution" to their economic problems, rather than to use government policy to *prevent* depressions. In its initial incarnation, the IMF saw depressions as the sickness to be prevented. It now sees depressions as the medicine to cure other illnesses, like balance of payments difficulties, fiscal deficits and inflation. These problems evidently take higher priority under contemporary neoliberal practice than preventing depressions and mass unemployment.

The prevailing logic of neoliberalism is so firmly implanted at the IMF at present that when confronted with a powerful critique of its policies by Professor Joseph Stiglitz, a Nobel Laureate in Economics and former Chief Economist at the World Bank, the response of the IMF's Director of Research was to assert that Stiglitz couldn't possibly be thinking like a rational earth-bound human being, but must rather be receiving signals from some alternative "Gamma Quadrant."[1]

I have observed the effects of this IMF mindset first hand, most recently at a conference in April 2002 in Johannesburg, South Africa, sponsored by an agency of the African National Congress government in power. The African National Congress, of course, is the political party which, under Nelson Mandela's leadership, led South Africa's transition out of apartheid to a non-racial democracy. The focus of the conference was how to reform the country's financial system to better meet the needs of the country's working people and poor. My University of Massachusetts colleague Gerald Epstein and I came to the conference with proposals on how to mobilize the country's well-developed, sophisticated financial system to directly attack the country's unemployment rate, estimated to be as high as 40 percent, and other related, and equally severe, problems. Our proposals received enthusiastic receptions from labor officials and community leaders, and even some favorable responses from business representatives. But the government economists participating in the conference from the Treasury Department and Central Bank were far less receptive. These officials were mostly highly competent economists. Nevertheless, they argued that our proposals were out of step with the basic neoliberal package of deregulating financial markets and tightly limiting government spending.

On the last afternoon of the meetings, I had a lunchtime conversation with one of the most impressive government economists at the conference. At one point, I blurted out in frustration that "you and your colleagues certainly know your economics. But it seems to me that you are using your abilities to rehash all the many reasons why the orthodox textbooks tell us that pursuing an aggressive attack on unemployment is not possible. I would much rather see you focusing your energies on the ways in which advancing an employment policy can be made workable."

The response by this official sent shivers through my body. He said, "You're right. If we don't start now doing something about 40 percent unemployment, in five years South Africa will make Rwanda look like a picnic." He was of course referring to the ethnic slaughtering that took place in Rwanda in 1994, which claimed, as a low estimate, an unfathomable 800,000 lives in a country whose population was 7.5 million in 1993. This economist was no doubt exaggerating for effect the severity of the social tensions building in South Africa relative to those that had produced the slaughter in Rwanda. But at least he made clear that, even amid the economic models and stacks of computer printouts that are the normal sensory stimulants of government economists, he hadn't lost touch with the realities transpiring daily just outside his Treasury ministry office. And still, despite his blunt recognition of South Africa's deepening unemployment crisis, he immediately retreated back to affirming the verities of the country's neoliberal policy commitments. Thus, straight from having just compared conditions in South Africa with Rwanda, he returned to insisting that there was no getting around that the government must continue to support financial deregulation and tight limits on government spending – that is, major components of the standard neoliberal prescription. He was convinced that the IMF-neoliberal package was the only viable approach for South Africa for the foreseeable future. Meanwhile, of course, the unemployment crisis advances, undermining all the enormous achievements over two generations of the African National Congress and its supporters.

There are alternatives

While egalitarian alternatives to neoliberalism – focusing on increasing employment opportunities at decent wages and stable financial markets – may seem infeasible to orthodox economists, and even to well-meaning and competent African National Congress Treasury officials, in fact, fundamental shifts in the direction of economic policy could be implemented immediately, under existing conditions, and relying only on conventional policy tools. This is the case both for the United States and less-developed countries, where we have focused our attention, but it is also true more generally. Of course, the details as to what would constitute a viable egalitarian policy approach will vary according to the specific conditions facing any given country. Still, we can build from perspectives that start from a recognition of the Marx, Keynes and Polanyi problems to develop egalitarian alternatives to neoliberalism that will have broad applicability. I will try to show this first in discussing the U.S., then the situation in less-developed countries.

Sketching an egalitarian program for the U.S. economy

Since I am attempting to present only a mere sketch of an alternative program, I will focus on what I consider some of the most basic considerations. The cornerstone of an alternative policy approach in the United States is to return to the basic commitment that emerged out of the Great Depression, the New Deal, and World War II, and was sustained, for the most part, through the 1960s. This is to promote full employment at decent wages. The corollary to a policy of full employment at decent wages is that workers can afford to spend money, which then maintains overall spending in the economy at a high level.

This creates the further benefit of businesses wanting to increase their investments to meet the demands of an expanding market.

Since the 1980s, U.S. economic policy has been focused on "inflation targeting" – which means to either completely stamp out inflation or at least to contain it at a negligible level of 2 percent or less. Eliminating federal deficits was added to inflation-targeting in the 1990s as a first-tier policy concern. A shift back to what we may call "employment targeting" does not mean ignoring either inflation or excessive government deficits, which would be self-defeating. But it does mean that the goal of expanding the supply of jobs at decent pay should receive at least as much, if not more, consideration among policy makers as controlling inflation or the federal deficit. In other words, employment targeting means that when Alan Greenspan and other Federal Reserve officials recognize that U.S. workers are experiencing "a heightened sense of job insecurity," as Greenspan put it in 1997, this should not be celebrated as a positive development because it inhibits inflationary pressures. It should rather be attacked as a problem requiring a solution.

The last years of the Clinton presidency did illustrate how powerful a tool low unemployment can be. With unemployment having fallen below 4.5 percent for three straight years, average real wages finally began to rise and poverty fell. The last time unemployment fell this low in the U.S. was when Lyndon Johnson was President in the second half of the 1960s. The benefits in this period of approaching full employment were even more dramatic. As Arthur Okun, a member of the Council of Economic Advisors under President Johnson wrote about those years:

> Prosperity has been the key to the reduction of the number of people below the statistical poverty line from 40 million in 1961 to 25 million in 1968. It has meant jobs for those formerly at the back of the hiring line ... . It has made economic security a reality to millions of middle-income families.[2]

Of course, both under Clinton in the 1990s and Johnson in the 1960s, there were severe problems with the way low unemployment was attained. Because workers had experienced the "heightened sense of job insecurity" under most of Clinton's tenure, when wages did finally start to rise significantly in 1997, this was from an extremely low base. Moreover, the injection of increased spending under Clinton that produced low unemployment came from the stock market bubble which, as has now become transparently clear, was unsustainable. In the 1960s, the catalyst driving the economy to full employment was government spending on the Vietnam War – that is, a source of economic stimulus that was also unsustainable and even more undesirable than the 1990s market bubble.

The central challenge for an employment-targeted policy in the U.S. today would therefore be to identify alternative sources of job expansion that do not require waging war or destabilizing the financial system. The Bush-2 plan for huge military spending increases obviously does not qualify any more than the Vietnam War as a desirable source of job expansion. But an alternative plan is staring the Bush administration in the face: to expand substantially federal government support for state and local governments programs. This would enable the state and local governments to reverse the severe spending cuts they experienced in the aftermath of the 2001 recession, and beyond this, to expand their commitments in education, childcare, health, environmental protection, and public infrastructure investments. Increasing spending in these areas would have a double benefit, in that they stimulate overall spending in the economy in the short run while also promoting higher productivity and general well-being in the long run.

But if an employment-targeted federal spending program could be crafted around expanding such socially desirable projects, that still wouldn't prevent, on its own, a return to the afflictions that accompanied the expansion of the 1990s, i.e. destabilizing financial practices, along with rising inequality and wage stagnation for most of the decade. The employment-targeted spending program would therefore have to be buttressed by new forms of regulation of both labor and financial markets. How to proceed in these areas?

Labor regulations

One of the most basic elements of a new regime of labor regulations in the U.S. has already been powerfully advanced since the mid-1990s by the so-called "living wage" movement. By the end of 2002, some version of a "living" minimum wage standard has become law in around ninety U.S. municipalities, while similar such measures are being debated elsewhere throughout the country. The guiding principle behind the U.S. living wage movement is very simple: that the minimum wage should be high enough such that workers can support themselves and their families at least at a modestly decent standard. This means a wage which offers workers "the ability to support families, to maintain self-respect, and to have both the means and the leisure to participate in the civic life of the nation," as the historian Lawrence Glickman describes the concept as it initially emerged during political struggles early in the twentieth century.[3] In practical terms, it is impossible to identify a single hourly wage rate to which this notion of a "living wage" corresponds. But municipal governments around the country have passed ordinances setting the minimum within a range of $8–$11 plus benefits. This contrasts with the current national minimum wage of $5.15.

But workers also deserve the right to organize themselves to achieve more than a decent minimum – that is, to promote gains in wages, benefits and workplace conditions more broadly, not just for those near the bottom of the pay scale. This will entail strengthening the legal rights of workers to organize and form unions. In his powerful 2001 Presidential Address before the Industrial Relations Research Association, Sheldon Friedman surveyed ways in which workers in the U.S. "who seek to form a union nearly always face a broad array of well-honed and devastingly effective employer tactics designed to suppress their freedom to organize." Among other evidence, Friedman reports on a 2000 study by Human Rights Watch that documented the exploding rate at which workers in the U.S. face job discrimination, harassment and discharge for attempting to form unions. In the 1950s, only hundreds of workers suffered such reprisals. But by the 1990s, just the number of cases recognized by the National Labor Relations Board had risen to over 20,000 per year. Clearly, advancing an egalitarian policy agenda will not be sustainable unless employers and government regulators respect workers' fundamental rights to organize themselves as they wish. Indeed, the very notion of an egalitarian policy project absent this basic right is a contradiction in terms.

Defending workers' rights to organize can also produce broader benefits, since workers receiving decent wages through union contracts will also
be able to stimulate overall demand in the economy through their own
enhanced ability to spend. A well known, though probably apocryphal en-
counter between Henry Ford and Walter Reuther, the first President of the
United Auto Workers union, captures this point. Ford and Reuther were
said to have been together watching as one Ford plant became more auto-
mated. As the new machinery rolled into the plant, Ford said to Reuther,
"Well Walter, how will you organize those machines?" Reuther responded,
"Yes, that will be a problem Henry. But how will you get them to buy Fords?"

Financial regulation

U.S. politicians began deregulating the financial system in the 1970s based
on the contention that the regulatory structure devised during the 1930s
Depression – the so-called Glass-Steagall system – was not appropriate to
contemporary conditions. Bill Clinton, Alan Greenspan and Treasury Secretary Robert Rubin maintained that same position through the 1990s, as
they presided over the final dismantling of Glass-Steagall.

Given that the financial system has become infinitely more complex
since the 1930s – including in its capacity to circumvent regulations – there
is no question that the Glass-Steagall system was becoming increasingly out-
moded. However, the conclusion that the financial system should therefore
be deregulated – as Greenspan, Clinton and virtually all other policy makers
have claimed over the past thirty years – never followed from this fact. After
all, the Keynes problem – that, if left to their own devises, financial markets
will inevitably be overtaken by destabilizing speculative forces – did not disappear over the past thirty years. Rather, the symptoms of the Keynes problem only became more virulent as deregulation proceeded. Recognizing the
flaws of the old regulatory system should therefore have led not to deregulation, but to constructing a new regulatory system appropriate to these contemporary symptoms.

Because the contemporary regulatory system has become so complex
and nimble in its capacity to circumvent regulations, an effective regulatory
system should be guided by a few basic premises that can be applied flexibly

and broadly across market segments, including the stock, bond, foreign currency and derivative markets (these last including the markets for options and future contracts on financial instruments). In this spirit, one principle around which a new system should be structured is that the regulations be applied consistently across the various institutions and financial instruments that make up the overall market. A major problem over time with the Glass-Steagall system was that there were large differences in the degree to which, for example, commercial banks, investment banks, stock brokerages, insurance companies and mortgage lenders were regulated, thereby inviting clever financial engineers to invent ways to exploit these differences. Beyond this, an egalitarian system of regulations would clearly also promote the aim of fairness as well as economic stability.

One measure for promoting both stability and fairness is a small sales tax on all financial transactions – that is on the sale of all stocks, bonds, derivatives and foreign currencies. Proposals of this type have become well-known through the specific case of taxing foreign currency transactions. This is the so-called "Tobin Tax," named for the late Nobel Laureate economist James Tobin who first proposed it. The idea behind the financial transaction sales tax – whether it applies to foreign currency transactions or to stocks, bonds, or other instruments – is that it raises the costs of speculative trading and therefore discourages the types of excesses that occurred in the U.S. stock market in the 1990s, since the tax would have to be paid every time a trade takes place. The tax will not discourage investors who intend to hold onto their assets for a longer time period, since, unlike the speculators, they will be trading infrequently. A tax of this sort will also raise lots of revenue, even if one assumes a sharp decline in trading occurs after the tax is imposed. Two colleagues and I have estimated that a consistently applied tax of this sort in the U.S. – starting at a 0.5 percent rate for stocks and sliding down from there for bonds and other instruments – would generate approximately $100 billion per year in revenue, even after factoring in a significant decline in the amount of trading due to the tax. The funds generated by this tax, in other words, would fully cover *all* the cuts in state and local spending for 2003 that are likely to occur due to shortages of revenue sharing funds from the federal government.[4]

A second type of measure that would be important for promoting both stability and fairness in the financial system is what are called asset-based reserve requirements. These are regulations that require financial institutions to maintain a supply of cash as a reserve fund in proportion to the other, riskier assets they hold in their portfolios. Such requirements can serve both to discourage financial market investors from holding an excessive amount of risky assets, and as a cash cushion for the investors to draw upon when market downturns occur. One example of an asset-based reserve requirement that is already in operation is the so-called margin requirements on stocks purchased with borrowed funds. As we have discussed, Alan Greenspan acknowledged in September 1996 that he could have prevented the speculative market bubble at that time by raising margin requirements. A simple proposal would therefore be for Greenspan or his successors to actually make use of this policy tool as the next incipient bubble begins to form.

The same policy instrument can also be used to push financial institutions to channel credit to projects that promote social welfare. One major example of this was that from the 1930s to the 1970s, savings and loan institutions in the U.S. were permitted to only lend money to households to finance the purchase of private homes. This requirement channeled massive pools of credit toward supporting the goal of middle-class home ownership, and everything that goes with that. This same policy measure could be used to promote the construction of low-cost housing over more vacation homes. Policy makers could stipulate that, say, at least 5 percent of banks' loans portfolios should be channeled to low-cost housing. If the banks fail to reach this 5 percent quota of loans for low-cost housing, they would then be required to hold this same amount of their total assets in cash. The banks would therefore not necessarily have to meet the 5 percent low-cost housing threshold, but they would have a strong incentive to do so rather than to hold cash, which would generate no interest for them.[5]

Implications for trade policy

If the U.S. successfully implemented a complimentary set of egalitarian policies such as these, an important additional result would follow: that the costs to U.S. workers would fall sharply from opening the economy to exports, in particular, from poor countries. From the workers' standpoint, trade protectionist policies are actually a form of social protection. They aim to preserve U.S. workers' jobs and bargaining power over wages by reducing the pool of foreign workers that effectively compete to produce products for the U.S. market. But trade protectionist measures are a poor substitute for direct forms of social protection, including the measures we have discussed in the areas of employment targeting and increasing overall demand as well as labor and financial regulations. Thus, contrary to the neoliberal perspective on globalization, the case on behalf of an open trading system actually becomes stronger when effective social protections work to promote standards of fairness and social solidarity that a free market economy undermines.

But didn't this all fail before?

Although I have presented only a sketch of some features of an alternative program for the U.S. economy, one can nevertheless, at the outset, raise legitimate questions about the underlying approach itself. One basic question jumps out immediately: aren't these pretty much the same social democratic-type policies that, following both Keynes and Polanyi, were predominant among Western countries from the end of World War II through the 1960s? And weren't these policies supplanted by Thatcherism, Reaganism and other variants of neoliberalism precisely because the resulting contradictions of big government and inflation proved insurmountable?

There are indeed problems associated with running a capitalist economy at something approximating full employment and, moreover, these problems become magnified under globalization.[6] The most basic issue here is the Marx problem, though now operating in reverse. If, as we discussed in Chapter 1, employers increase their bargaining power when the reserve army of unemployed workers is growing, it then follows that workers will gain in bargaining strength in an economy committed to full employment. This means workers will have the power to bid up their wages, and that businesses will respond, as much as possible, by raising prices. Strong inflationary pressures can then emerge, though this does not inevitably occur. In Chapter 3, we discussed why, under Clinton, U.S. workers remained insecure about their job situation even as unemployment kept falling. Inflation thus remained dormant even at low unemployment.

But what happens in cases where full employment does indeed generate strong inflationary pressures? Many social groups within a full-employment economy would still almost always benefit from these circumstances, including in particular the workers holding jobs who otherwise would have been unemployed. But other segments of society will experience costs. Among those bearing the costs would be groups that do not receive full cost-of-living adjustments when inflation rises. This would include retired people on fixed-income pensions and the lowest-paid workers, whose wages are generally not adjusted upward to account for inflation. But the most powerful losers from inflation are banks and other financial institutions whose major source of income is interest on loans and bonds. For the most part, the interest payments on bank loans and bonds are not indexed to rise with inflation. This is why financiers are usually adamant in their opposition to inflation, and why they frequently welcome increases in the unemployment rate that diminish inflationary pressures.

But nonfinancial businesses that face global competition can experience equally serious problems from inflation. Because of the foreign competition, these businesses will have limited ability to mark up prices to cover their increased wage costs in a full employment economy. As such, these businesses are more likely to experience a fall in profitability in a full employment economy than the firms that are not exposed to foreign competition.

These problems of a low-unemployment economy did in fact emerge to varying degrees in the U.S. and Western Europe by the end of the 1960s and into the 1970s. Focusing on the U.S., we saw in Chapter 2 that wages rose quickly in the 1960s, faster, in fact, than the rate at which productivity improved. This both squeezed profits and created inflationary pressures. Foreign competition for U.S. firms also intensified in this period, first from the Western European economies which had by then fully recovered from World War II, then increasingly from Japan and the emerging Asian Tiger economies. This also pushed corporate profits down. The two oil price "shocks" initiated by the Oil Producing and Exporting Countries (OPEC) –

an initial fourfold increase in the world price of oil in 1973, then a second fourfold price spike in 1979 – cut still further into corporate profits.[7]

These were the conditions by the end of the 1970s that led to the demise of full employment-targeting as a basic goal of economic policy. The fundamental aims of the Thatcher/Reaganite neoliberal alternative emerged out of that historical moment of high inflation and declining profitability.[8] These aims were to cut taxes on businesses and the rich, so that at least *after-tax* profits could begin rising; and to weaken both regulations on corporations and social protections for workers, to shift bargaining power in favor of business.

Would policies such as I have sketched inevitably produce the same outcome? There is no question that programs such as I have sketched need to take account of the problems associated with inflation. But how serious are these problems? Answering that question accurately is clearly the first requirement.

The neoliberal commitment to "inflation targeting" is based on the premise that inflation needs to be held at no more than 2 percent. Consider, however, the basic matter of how inflation affects economic growth. The preponderance of evidence on this question finds that, as long as inflation remains moderate, its effect on growth is negligible. This conclusion has been supported by the work of several economists. Among them is Michael Bruno, who, as Chief Economist at the World Bank in the mid-1990s, directed a study that examined the relationship between inflation and economic growth for 127 countries between 1960 and 1992. Bruno and his colleagues found that average growth rates fell only slightly as inflation rates moved up to 20–25 percent. Of particular importance for our concerns here, Bruno found that during 1960–72, economic growth increased among all the countries he studied as inflation rose from negative or low rates to the 15–20 percent range. This is because, as Bruno explains, "in the 1950s and 1960s, low-to-moderate inflation went hand in hand with very rapid growth." In the United States in particular, the pressures of rapid growth and near full employment tied to the Vietnam War were clearly responsible for the rise in inflation in those years. But even with this, the average rate of inflation between 1965–69 was 4.4 percent, which deserves recognition as a matter of concern, but hardly a calamity.[9]

One highly innovative approach to tackling this problem was implemented in Sweden from the 1950s to 1970s, following the work of the brilliant Swedish trade union economists Rudolph Meidner and Gösta Rehn.[10] Meidner and Rehn did support employment-targeted policies aimed at expanding the number of decent-paying jobs. But they also favored limiting such policy interventions, to the point where, through these measures alone, the economy still maintained a positive unemployment rate of about 3 percent. Meidner and Rehn opposed job expansion measures that, on their own, aimed to bring the economy all the way to full employment, since they held that unacceptably high inflation could indeed result if full employment was achieved through such stimulus measures alone. In other words, Meidner and Rehn supported maintaining some slack in the economy to keep upward wage pressure from producing headlong inflation. At the same time, alongside this commitment to maintaining restraints on job stimulus policies, they also supported active labor market interventions by the government aimed at getting as many as possible of the remaining unemployed workers into jobs. These labor market interventions included both travel allowances to help workers physically get to new jobs and retraining programs to increase workers' qualifications. Through this overall approach – combining restrained employment-targeting measures with active labor market interventions – Meidner and Rehn argued that the economy could achieve something close to full employment at decent wages while still maintaining control over inflation.

Following some reasonable approximation of the Meidner-Rehn approach most of the time, Sweden succeeded at maintaining unemployment at an average rate below 2 percent between 1951–2000 while still holding inflation at a 4.4 percent average rate. Now of course, Sweden is a small, rich, egalitarian, white suburb, nestled in a safe, far-northern corner of the world. But this is the point: Sweden was not prosperous and egalitarian when they first began developing this approach. It was the success of the Meidner-Rehn model – not by itself, but certainly as a major contributing factor – that enabled Sweden to grow into what it became. Robert Heilbroner of the New School University has written insightfully about applying more broadly the lessons of what he terms "slightly imaginary Sweden."[11] For the case of the United States, the key lesson to extract from slightly imaginary

Sweden would be this: if workers were living within a framework of basic social protections such as those I have sketched, they should then be much more amenable to moderating their wage demands in situations where inflationary pressures threatened prospects for economic stability and growth.

And while this is indeed a crucial lesson for considering realistic possibilities for an egalitarian alternative to neoliberalism in the U.S., we must emphasize again that the actual problems in the U.S since the 1970s – as opposed to the hypothetical dangers of excessive inflation – have been of a completely different nature: that average real wages actually fell even as productivity was increasing. So creating an economy in which average and low-wage workers receive pay increases at a rate just equal to the economy's productivity growth rate – and no more than that – would itself represent a major advance, both in terms of the need for inflation control and the more basic requirements of social justice.

Egalitarian alternatives for the less-developed countries

The general approach I have sketched for the U.S. – focusing on employment-targeted macroeconomic policies along with regulation of financial and labor markets, while also maintaining watchfulness about inflation – does have broad applicability among less-developed countries. Indeed, some of the specific measures I discussed are already in place or have been employed during the recent past in many less-developed countries. But the ascendancy of neoliberalism throughout the less-developed world has meant that these policies have either been abandoned or greatly diminished in their effectiveness over the past twenty years. To some extent, the major departure for less-developed economies from a neoliberal model would simply entail renewing old policy approaches within a supportive global policy framework, as opposed to the current hostility of the U.S. government and IMF. At the same time, there are obvious ways in which conditions are dramatically different in less-developed countries relative to rich countries like the U.S. Any egalitarian policy agenda – even just in its focus on employment targeting and the regulation of labor and financial markets – would have to take account of these to have any chance of success. Let me briefly mention a few such matters.

Perhaps the most stark difference between the advanced and less-developed countries is that between roughly 35–50 percent of the working people in less-developed countries are working in what is called "informal" jobs. This category includes, for example, agricultural day laborers, urban street vendors or at-home producers of clothing. Women are disproportionately employed in such informal jobs. For the most part the jobs pay poverty-level wages or worse. The other defining characteristic of informal jobs is that they fall outside the sphere of any sort of government labor interventions. The people filling these jobs are obviously badly in need of work. They form the pool of workers that I discussed in Chapter 4 who line up to be hired in sweatshops. Their prominence in less-developed countries raises an obvious question: does a program such as I have sketched for the U.S., focused on job expansion at decent wages and regulation of labor markets, have any relevance to this situation?

In fact, such policies could be effective at improving conditions for workers with informal jobs, in particular via the *complimentary* effects of a job expansion program and enhanced labor market regulations. Ongoing research by many economists, including my University of Massachusetts colleague James Heintz and myself, suggests that the process of "informalization" – i.e. the expansion in the proportion of informal jobs in less-developed economies – has occurred both because of the slowdown in economic growth that we observed in Chapter 4 and due to the weakening of government regulations accompanying neoliberal restructuring programs. Thus, for example, data from the International Labor Organization for Latin America shows that from 1990–97, the proportion of informal jobs rose when countries were experiencing both growth and recessions, though the rate of informalization did accelerate during slumps. Other evidence from the years 1980–99, i.e. roughly spanning the neoliberal era in less-developed countries, suggests that rapid average rates of economic growth in the range of 5 percent or more can produce a decline in the rate of informalization. However, more moderate average growth rates did not prevent informalization from spreading, though again, on average, the rate of informalization did fall in countries where economic growth was faster. This result suggests that increasing average growth rates will at least create the possibility for improved labor market regulations to operate effectively to raise the proportion of people who work at jobs with minimally decent standards of pay and working conditions.[12]

As for the task of establishing workable labor market regulations themselves, we have seen in Chapter 4 that the burden of achieving this does not need to fall on government policy makers alone. Rather, consumers in the United States (and, evidence suggests, other high-income countries as well) are willing to pay higher prices if they can be assured that the products they buy are not made under sweatshop conditions. As the movement underlying this sentiment continues to spread, the incentives will strengthen for both businesses and policy makers in less-developed countries to establish and enforce decent standards.

There are also distinct aspects to financial market regulations when they apply to less-developed economies. The single most important fact to highlight here is the formidable success achieved by many less-developed countries – or, as with South Korea or Taiwan, what were formerly less-developed countries – through maintaining a tightly regulated financial system. The key feature of these policies was that governments aggressively channeled credit at subsidized rates to industries and firms that were successful at expanding the country's industrial capacity and export markets. At the same time, the governments tightly controlled the inflow of funds from foreign investors and the development of speculative markets in financial instruments. These successful regulatory policies could not contrast more sharply with the debacle of IMF-directed financial deregulation in Argentina that we have reviewed. In short, less-developed countries committed to breaking from the neoliberal policy model have a clear, workable alternative from which they can constructively proceed.[13]

Finally, there are numerous reasons why trade policies need to be considered distinctly in the case of developing countries. But we may boil these down to two basic and interrelated points. The first is that developing countries need access to the markets in rich countries like the U.S. more than U.S. firms need protection from third world producers. Less-developed countries should grow increasingly over time on the basis of expanding their domestic markets – i.e. with their own people earning wages high enough to be able to buy the products they themselves produce. This expansion of domestic markets will be a crucial result of a successful jobs expansion program in less-developed economies, just as it is in the U.S. But this does not gainsay the fact that, at present, less-developed economies can benefit greatly through selling products on the much larger markets in rich countries. How could it be otherwise? As Alice Amsden of MIT aptly points out, "Consider an old colonial couple, the Netherlands and Indonesia. The population of Indonesia is 13 times greater than that of the Netherlands, but the market in the Netherlands … is almost three times greater than Indonesia's."[14] Here then, it again becomes evident that creating a strong system of social protections in the U.S. will have major ramifications for the rest of the world as well, because it will create an environment in which U.S. workers are not forced to unjustly bear the costs of developing countries successfully selling to export markets.

The second interrelated point is that governments in less-developed countries need to maintain some tariffs and other forms of protection over their domestic markets more than businesses in rich countries need to compete for a share of these markets. Precisely because these are *less-developed* economies, their producers cannot always be expected to compete on an even basis with firms in rich countries. We saw how opening markets in India for agricultural products created a disaster for some of the country's most vulnerable farmers. Moreover, as Ha-Joon Chang of Cambridge University has clearly demonstrated in his new book *Kicking Away the Ladder*, the countries of the world that are now rich themselves developed their national economies on the basis of protecting their markets and nurturing their so-called "infant industries."[15] Of course we are in a new era of globalization. But this only means that the lessons of history should be appropriately adapted to the current circumstances, not ignored altogether.

There is of course the real danger of corruption and favoritism – popularly known since the 1997 Asian financial crisis as *crony capitalism* – becoming the predominant political force when governments in less-developed countries actively partake in subsidizing and protecting their local businesses. Crony capitalism should hardly be an alien concept for those who observe the unflagging obeisance of U.S. policy makers – all the way up to Clinton, Bush and Greenspan – to the agendas of corporate America. Nevertheless, it remains true that developing a successful alternative to neoliberalism in less-developed countries – no less than in the United States – hinges on the ability of governments to exercise discipline over their country's capitalist class. No set of egalitarian policies, however well designed, can be made workable if government policies are allowed to become simply another venue through which a country's most privileged groups are permitted to enrich themselves further. But establishing the protections against such an eventuality moves us beyond the realm of economic policy, and into the spheres of politics, culture, and as Adam Smith himself expressed it, of moral sentiments.

Adam Smith's dictum which served as the epigram for Chapter 1 deserves reflection in these closing pages. The corruption of moral sentiments through "the disposition to admire, and almost to worship the rich and powerful, and to despise or at least neglect persons of poor and mean condition" is an unavoidable, ever-present peril in any large, complex society, regardless of whether it is called capitalist, socialist, or something else, and independently of the extent to which the society is integrated into the global economy. But this danger is naturally compounded under a neoliberal economic regime, given that the premise of neoliberalism is that the market determines society's winners and losers in a fair and efficient way. It further follows within a neoliberal framework that the rich and powerful – those that have either been the biggest winners in the market or at least have had close relatives or friends within this gilded circle – should also be responsible for establishing the boundaries of a society's acceptable political debate and economic policy interventions.

The priority of serving the rich and powerful was obviously foremost during the Clinton presidency. How else to explain, among other things, Clinton and Greenspan's energetic advocacy of deregulating the financial system when Greenspan knew full well that the stock market had become a dangerous bubble? Then there is the Bush-2 administration. Can anyone doubt what its priorities are, given Bush's unwavering dedication to cutting taxes for the rich, converting both a national security emergency and a recession into opportunities to shower more gifts on the overprivileged? The

International Monetary Fund has also made no secret of its own fealty to the premises of neoliberalism as expressed in its Washington Consensus policy model for less-developed countries. The fact that this model has failed to promote economic growth and financial stability, or to reduce poverty and inequality, appears beside the point to Washington Consensus insiders when the fundamental premises of neoliberalism are at stake. This is the corruption of moral sentiments on a global scale.

Adam Smith was clear that a market economy will not be sustainable without a commitment to social solidarity as its undergirding. But creating this foundation of solidarity does not mean eradicating markets, competition and inequality of wealth. We do not yet have the self-knowledge or wherewithal to organize a society in a fair and effective way without these basic elements of capitalism. We can debate whether it might be possible to do so within a longer-term historical horizon. But as that debate proceeds, we have the capacity now to push the institutions of liberal capitalism to their limit in allowing democratic politics and egalitarian goals to gain ascendancy over acquisitiveness. Economics, moreover, need not continue in its present role as the insurmountable fortress defending the moral sentiments of neoliberalism. Economics is fully capable of serving now, as it has in the past, as one useful tool among many that creates the pathway toward a more just society.

APPENDIX I

U.S. Macroeconomic Trends 1960–2000 by NBER Cycle Data Groupings

This appendix reports on U.S. macroeconomic data trends through grouping the data according to National Bureau of Economic Research (NBER) cycle dates, rather than on the basis of presidential eras, as I did in Chapter 2. Grouping time-series data according to cycles is the most analytically appropriate technique, though it is obviously less evocative historically and politically than the groupings by presidential era reported in Chapter 2. As we see in this appendix, the macroeconomic patterns we observe for presidential eras correspond closely to the patterns that emerge through the NBER cycle groupings as well. The results here thus give support to the validity of the patterns we describe in Chapter 2.

The NBER cycle dates are organized on a peak-to-peak basis. I have derived peak dates from the NBER monthly peaks. When the NBER peak month falls between January–September of a given year, that year becomes the cyclical peak year. If the monthly peak falls between October–December, the following year becomes the peak year. In addition, I have merged two sets of cycles into a single cycle – those for 1970–73/1974–79 and 1980–81/1982–90.

TABLE A1.1: Macroeconomic performance indicators *(percentages)*

	1960–69	1970–79	1980–90	1991–2000
GDP real growth (pct.)	4.4	3.3	2.9	3.2
Productivity growth (pct. for non-farm business sector)	2.8	1.9	1.4	2.0
Unemployment rate (pct.)	4.8	7.1	7.1	5.6
Inflation rate (pct. measured by CPI)	2.3	6.2	5.5	2.8

Source: National Income and Product Accounts (NIPA); Bureau of Labor Statistics

TABLE A1.2: Components of GDP *(percentages)*

	1960–69	1970–79	1980–90	1991–2000
Consumption	61.4	62.3	64.5	67.0
Government	22.4	21.2	20.6	18.6
Investment	15.5	16.7	16.7	15.8
Net exports	0.3	-0.3	-1.7	-1.4

Source: National Income and Product Accounts (NIPA); Economagic website

TABLE A1.3: Financial market indicators

	1960–69	1970–79	1980–90	1991–2000
S&P 500 real average annual growth rate (pct.)	4.6	-5.9	8.3	14.5
S&P 500 real growth minus GDP real growth (pct. gap)	+0.2	-9.2	+5.4	+11.3
Total household debt/disposable personal income (pct.)	67.3	67.6	77.2	95.6
Total household debt/ financial assets (pct.)	17.5	20.5	23.1	22.8
Household bank deposits plus govt. securities/total financial assets (pct.)	23.0	25.9	26.7	18.8
Corporations internal funds/total debt (pct.)	96.3	85.2	94.7	95.5
Corporations debt/ equity (pct.)	59.3	122.0	165.7	90.2
Real interest rate (10-year Treasury bond minus CPI rate)	2.3	0.4	4.9	3.6

Source: Economagic website; Flow-of-Funds Accouunts

Table A1.4: Real wage trends

	1960–69	1970–79	1980–90	1991–2000
Average wage for nonsupervisory workers (in 2001 dollars)	13.60	15.22	14.04	13.55
Average wage for 10th percent decile (in 2001 dollars)	—	7.07	6.22	6.11
Ratio of 90th/10th percent decile wages	—	3.6	4.1	4.4

Source: Bureau of Labor Statistics; Mishel, Bernstein and Boushey, *State of Working America 2002-03.*

Notes: Wage data for decile groupings begins in 1973.

Table A1.5 Individual poverty rates

1960–69	1970–79	1980–90	1991–2000
17.5	11.8	13.8	13.5

Source: Current Population Survey

APPENDIX 2

A Phillips Curve Model With Unit Labor Costs

The discussion here is drawn from my 2003 paper, "Wage Bargaining and the U.S. Phillips Curve: Was Greenspan Right About 'Traumatized Workers' in the 1990s?" presented at the January 2003 Allied Social Science Association annual meetings.

The model is derived from the so-called NAIRU triangle model, which is an extension of the traditional Phillips curve analytic framework. According to Robert Gordon (e.g. 1997, 1998: full references for Appendix 2 on pp. 206–207), the leading developer of the triangle NAIRU model, the model holds that the inflation rate depends on three basic determinants (thus the "triangle"): aggregate demand pressures, supply shocks such as oil price increases and inertial inflation. According to Gordon, the precise specification of these explanatory variables should be flexible. For example, both the unemployment rate and the rate of capacity utilization are valid measures of the level of aggregate demand. Lown and Rich of the New York Federal Reserve Bank (1997) extended the Gordon NAIRU triangle model by including unit labor costs as an additional independent variable explaining inflation. They found that incorporating labor costs into the model could, to a substantial extent, explain the lack of inflationary pressures at low rates of unemployment between 1990–95. Rich and Rismiller (2000), among others, presented descriptive evidence that also showed the importance of import price changes as affecting the NAIRU for the 1990s.

This exercise is an extension and variation on the Lown and Rich model. It also formally incorporates the Rich and Rismiller findings regarding the effects of import prices.[1] (Notes for Appendix 2 on p. 206.) The changes I have made relative to Lown and Rich are as follows. First, I define the full sample period to 1960.2–2000.4. This enables us to consider how well the model that incorporates unit labor costs as a variable holds up through the entire 1990s. I have also specified the full sample as beginning at a business cycle peak quarter, according to the NBER dating methodology, and ending in a quarter just prior to the last business cycle peak of 2001.1. In testing the forecasting capacity of our model for the 1990s, I define our estimation period as ending in 1990.2, a quarter prior to a peak quarter, and our forecast period as beginning with the 1990.3 peak quarter.

I have tested the model with various specifications of the three explanatory variables. But in the tests reported here, I utilize the unemployment rate as the measure of aggregate demand pressure, while Lown and Rich use a measure of capacity utilization, the ratio of actual to potential GDP. Using this "GDP gap" ratio rather than the unemployment rate does not alter the results in any significant way.

I defined the quarterly inflation rate as the (annualized) change in the CPI relative to its value of the previous quarter (i.e. the inflation rate for 1990.1 is DCPI (1990.1–1989.4)). Lown and Rich measured the quarterly change in the CPI based on a four-quarter lag (the inflation rate for 1990.1 is D(CPI 1990.1–1989.1)). The four-quarter lag technique does generate a smoother time series. But, as such, it also suppresses potentially meaningful sources of variation.[2] Beyond this in terms of variable specification, I was flexible in terms of specifying variables either in levels or rates of change; and in terms of lag structures. No important analytic issues rest on these matters. I report here only the specifications that yielded the best fit according to the individual t-statistics. In these reported regressions, I also constrained to zero all lagged variables that were statistically insignificant.

The summary results of this exercise are shown in Table A2.1, while the full definitions of the variables are presented at the end of this appendix. The full results from the exercise – including specifications in which variables are not constrained to zero if their coefficients are insignificant – are shown in my 2003 paper.

The dependent variable in all equations is the core CPI-U inflation rate, i.e. the rate that excludes fluctuations in food and energy prices. Equation 1 presents the basic triangle NAIRU model, including the unemployment rate, two lagged values of inflation, and positive changes in oil prices[3] as the independent variables. All the explanatory variables are highly significant and with theoretically appropriate signs.

In equation 2, I simply add unit labor costs as an explanatory variable. The unit labor cost measure incorporates the three components of labor cost – wages, benefits and productivity growth. As the table shows, unit labor costs are significant as a current value, as well as through one and two period lags. This result confirms what Lown and Rich had found with data through 1995 – that incorporating labor costs as an additional factor does add explanatory power to the NAIRU model over the full 1960.2–2000.4 period.

As a more targeted test of the relative explanatory power of equations 1

TABLE A2.1: Estimating a "triangle" NAIRU model
with unit labor costs and import prices

Dependent Variable is Core CPI-U Inflation Rate – with one-quarter lags
1960.2–2000.4 (absolute values of t-statistics are in parentheses)

Independent variables, summary statistics	(1)	(2)	(3)	(4)	(5)	(6)
Constant	0.003 (1.25)	0.004 (2.03)	0.002 (0.98)	0.004 (1.98)	0.005 (2.26)	0.006 (2.59)
Unemployment rate – one quarter lag	-0.016 (4.28)	-0.016 (4.41)	-0.015 (3.73)	-0.15 (4.07)	-0.016 (4.47)	-0.016 (4.36)
Inflation – one quarter lag	0.528 (7.04)	0.408 (5.39)	0.636 (8.40)	0.453 (5.89)	0.401 (5.27)	0.417 (5.45)
Inflation – two quarters lag	0.358 (4.66)	0.27 (3.63)	0.312 (3.85)	0.226 (2.96)	0.291 (3.78)	0.283 (3.64)
Oil prices – no lag	0.047 (4.60)	0.033 (3.29)	——	——	0.026 (2.10)	——
Unit labor costs – no lag	——	0.062 (2.04)	——	0.079 (2.56)	0.053 (1.72)	0.054 (1.70)
Unit labor costs – one quarter lag	——	0.090 (2.90)	——	0.109 (3.48)	0.084 (2.70)	0.089 (2.82)
Unit labor costs – two quarters lag	——	0.081 (2.59)	——	0.094 (2.92)	0.076 (2.39)	0.077 (2.40)
Import prices	——	——	——	——	0.026 (1.11)	0.053 (2.74)
Adjusted R^2	.78	.80	.75	.79	.80	.80
Durbin-Watson statistic	2.16	2.13	2.07	2.06	2.13	2.10

Source: See variable definitions in text of appendix

and 2 for explaining the experience of the 1990s, I conducted ex post forecasts for the 1990.3 to 2000.4 period. I used forecasted, as opposed to actual, out-of-sample values of the inflation rate for the forecast period. This dynamic forecasting exercise is a more stringent test of a model's forecasting effectiveness than a static forecast utilizing actual out-of-sample values.

The results of this forecasting exercise are shown in Figure A2.1. Equation 1, the basic NAIRU triangle model, begins to consistently and increasingly overpredict inflation by the third quarter of 1993. By 2000.4, equation 1 predicts an 8.3 percent inflation rate while the actual rate was 2.5 percent. Equation 2 predicts a 4.6 percent inflation rate for 2000.4. This is also an overestimate, but at 2.1 percentage points above the actual inflation rate, it is still fully 3.7 percentage points closer to the actual rate than the equation 1 forecast. For the full 1990.3–2000.4 forecasting period, the average error of the two forecasts, as measured by root mean squared errors, was 2.5 percent for equation 1 and 1.1 percent for equation 2. That is, the average equation 1 error was more than twice as large as that for equation 2.

One factor that could potentially weaken the predictive power of the models for the 1990s was that there were no oil supply shocks in this period comparable to the 1970s. To test the importance of this, in equations 3 and 4, I constrain to zero the oil price variable, and otherwise test the same specifications as in equations 1 and 2. These equations generate a small decline in overall explanatory power, as measured by the adjusted R^2 values. But all the included explanatory variables remain highly significant.

I then repeated the ex post inflation forecasting exercise for 1990.3–2000.4 with equations 3 and 4. We do get more accurate forecasts for both the equations that exclude and include unit labor costs as an explanatory variable. But as with equations 1 and 2, we also see – and now to a greater extent – that equation 4, which includes unit labor costs, performs much better during the forecasting period. This is evident in Figure A.2.2, showing the inflation forecasts generated by equations 3 and 4 along with the actual inflation rate. The root mean squared error for equation 3 is 2.5 percent, while that for equation 4 is 0.8 percent – in other words, the overall forecast which includes unit labor costs is now more than three times more accurate than the equation excluding unit labor costs. More generally, as Figure A2.2 shows, the equation including unit labor costs now does a consistently good job of predicting inflation with the exception of the period 1998.1–1999.1, during which a bulge emerges between the actual and predicted rates generated by equation 4. Still, by 2000.4, equation 4 predicts a 2.7 percent inflation rate, quite close to the actual 2.5 percent rate.

FIGURE A2.1: Inflation forecasts including:
* *unemployment, inertial inflation, oil shocks only*
* *unit labor costs as additional factor*

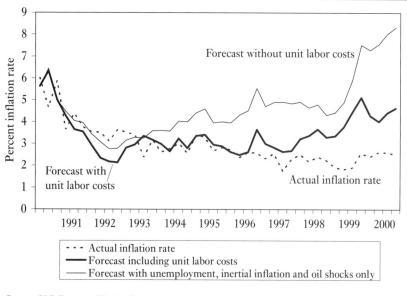

Source: U.S. Bureau of Labor Statistics

As a last consideration, I examine the effects of import prices on the model. But in equation 5, we see that import prices are not statistically significant in a specification in which no other variables have been constrained to zero. At least in part, this result is due to multicollinarity between import prices and oil prices, since oil imports are a large component of the overall U.S. import bill. The correlation coefficient between the variables is 0.53. In equation 6, I therefore constrain the oil price variable to zero. This generates a result in which import prices are highly significant.

As a final exercise, I then use equation 6 to again forecast inflation from 1990.3–2000.4. The results are shown in Figure A2.3. Here we see a consistently strong fit between the actual inflation rate and that predicted by the model that includes both import prices and unit labor costs. In particular, much of the bulge for 1997–99 that we observed with the equation 4 forecast is absent with equation 6. The root mean squared error for this forecast is 0.7 percent, in

FIGURE A2.2: Inflation forecasts excluding oil shocks:
* *unemployment, inertial inflation only*
* *unit labor costs as additional factor*

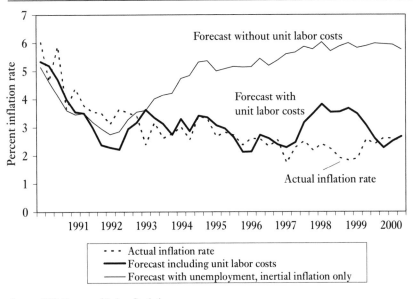

Source: U.S. Bureau of Labor Statistics

contrast, again, with the 2.5 percent figure for equation 3, which excludes both unit labor costs and import prices.

Overall, these results show that, in understanding how labor market conditions affect inflation, it is clearly inadequate to rely on the unemployment rate alone – or some similar aggregate demand proxy – as a measure of workers' capacity to bid up wages that lead to inflation. Rather, workers' relative bargaining power to achieve wage and benefit gains relative to the rate of productivity growth changes over time. This shift in the relative power of workers, in turn, has a major independent influence on the unemployment/inflation relationship. In addition, the effects of import prices also grew in the 1990s relative to the effects of oil prices specifically. This factor fits more readily within the triangle model that allows for supply shocks. Yet the fall of import prices, bound up with the deepening of U.S. integration in the global economy, is more difficult to characterize as a "supply shock" per se than the

FIGURE A2.3: Inflation forecasts including import prices:
* *unemployment, inertial inflation only*
* *unit labor costs and import prices as additional factors*

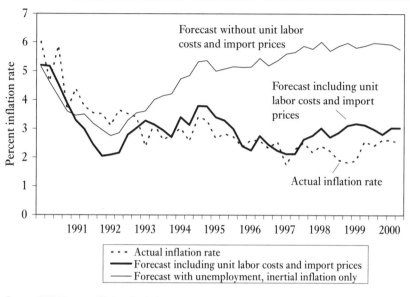

Source: U.S. Bureau of Labor Statistics

1970s experience with oil. But focusing on the labor market relationship that has always been at the heart of the Phillips curve type analyses, we see here that the breakdown in the 1990s of the unemployment/inflation relationship that had held from the 1960s to the 1980s is no mystery. To a considerable extent, it can be traced directly to the weakening relative bargaining power of workers at low unemployment rates.

Definition of variables in eonometric model

Core CPI-U Inflation Rate – Percent change in the quarterly core CPI from the previous quarter's value, measured as log differences, $\log X - \log X_{t-1}$. The core inflation rate excludes changes in food and energy prices.

Unemployment Rate – Percentage change in the quarterly rate of unemployment from the previous quarter's value, measured as log differences.

Oil prices – The net positive change in the real price of oil, calculated as the percentage change in the current real price of oil from the previous year's maximum (if that change is positive, zero otherwise). The methodology is adapted from Lown and Rich (1997), who in turn followed the work of Mork (1989). Mork's model reflects corrections for the effects of price controls during the 1970s. The real price of oil is defined as the nominal oil price index deflated by the GDP deflator.

Import prices – Percent change in the quarterly relative price of imports, i.e. import prices divided by the core CPI. Quarterly changes are from the previous quarter's value, measured as log differences.

Unit labor costs – Percent change in quarterly unit labor costs from the previous quarter's value, measured as log differences.

Data source for all variables is the U.S. Bureau of Labor Statistics.

Notes for Appendix 2

1.   My approach bears a resemblance to that developed by Ball and Moffitt in "Productivity Growth and the Phillips Curve," in Krueger and Solow, op. cit. They explain the time-varying NAIRU based on the idea, advanced initially by Joseph Stiglitz, that changes in the NAIRU are caused by changing aspirations of workers. As a general case, they assume that wages rise with the growth of labor productivity. But they allow that when productivity growth changes, lags may occur in workers' demands relative to the new productivity rate. When aspirations are relatively high, this leads to a higher NAIRU, and the NAIRU falls when aspirations are low. Empirically, the fundamental empirical problem with this argument is that it ignores the fact which we discussed above, that since 1973, productivity has persistently risen – albeit at a varying *growth rate* – while real wages have fallen in absolute dollars. I discuss this point in some detail in my 2003 paper.

2.   I did however also run the model with a four-quarter lag structure. This did not produce any substantive difference in the results.

3.   This specification generated more significant results over the full period than the more general measure of oil price changes, including both increases and declines.

References for Appendix 2

Ball, Laurence and Robert Moffitt (2001) "Productivity Growth and the Phillips Curve," in Alan Krueger and Robert M. Solow eds., *The Roaring Nineties: Can Full Employment Be Sustained?* New York: The Russell Sage Foundation and the Century Foundation, pp. 61–90.

Gordon, Robert J. (1997) "The Time-Varying NAIRU and its Implications for Economic Policy," *Journal of Economic Perspectives* (11:1), 11–32.

Gordon, Robert J. (1998) "Foundations of the Goldilocks Economy: Supply Shocks and the Time-Varying NAIRU," *Brookings Papers on Economic Activity*, #2, pp. 297–346.

Lown, Cara S. and Rich, Robert W. (1997) "Is There An Inflation Puzzle?" *Reserve Bank of New York Economic Policy Review*, December, 51–69.

Mork, Knut A. (1989) "Oil and the Macroeconomy When Prices Go Up and Down: An Extension of Hamilton's Results, *Journal of Political Economy*, 97:3, pp. 740–744.

Rich, Robert W. and Donald Rissmiller (2000) "Understanding the Recent Behavior of U.S. Inflation," *Federal Reserve Bank of New York Current Issues In Economics and Finance*, July, http://www.newyorkfed.org/rmaghome/curr_iss/ci6-8.pdf.

Stiglitz, Joseph (1997) "Reflections on the Natural Rate Hypothesis," *Journal of Economic Perspectives*, Winter, pp. 3–10.

Measuring the impact of alternative influences on the federal fiscal budget

To estimate what government receipts would have been if real growth rates had differed from their actual values in the 1990s, a simple bivariate regression analysis was used in which the growth rate of nominal federal receipts was modeled as a function of the growth rate of nominal gross domestic product (GDP). The data came from the Office of Management and Budget's *Historical Tables 2002* and the National Income and Product Accounts of the Bureau of Economic Analysis. The annual difference in the logarithms of nominal receipts and nominal GDP were used to calculate growth rates from 1980 to 2000. From the regression analysis, the simple OLS estimate of the elasticity of receipts with respect to economic growth was 1.004 (p-value = 0.016). That is, a 1 percent increase in the nominal growth rate roughly corresponded to a 1 percent increase in the growth rate of receipts.

The estimated growth rates of receipts were then used to calculate the actual dollar value of revenues the federal government would receive in each year under consideration. Actual receipts one year before the projections began were used as the initial starting point (for example, if the estimates of revenues ran from 1996–99, receipts in 1995 were used as the base year). Federal revenues in the second half of the 1990s grew at a faster rate than could be explained by economic growth alone. Therefore, when actual growth rates were used to predict revenues in this period, positive residuals would be observed. Since these residuals could be interpreted as capturing the impact of unobserved factors other than economic growth, all projections with alternative growth rates were adjusted using the residuals. In this way, only the variation that could be attributed to changes in the underlying growth rates would be reflected in the estimates – all other factors influencing nominal revenues were assumed to remain the same.

To illustrate the impact of factors such as growing capital gains revenues, higher federal receipts to GDP ratios, and a reduction in federal spending relative to GDP, the hypothetical impact on the federal surplus/deficit was calculated in which these variables remained at their 1992 levels. Data for outlays and receipts were taken from the OMBs *Historical Tables 2002* while capital gains tax revenues came from the Office of Tax Analysis of the U.S. Department of the Treasury. In 1992, the ratio of outlays to GDP was 22.2 percent, the ratio of receipts to GDP (less capital gains revenues) was approximately 17.0 percent, and capital gains tax revenues to GDP was 0.46 percent. These 1992 ratios were used with actual GDP figures for subsequent years to determine the impact on spending and revenues had these ratios remained unchanged.

NOTES

Chapter One

1.   News of the Cheney promotional video for Arthur Andersen was reported by the BBC on 7/10/02.

2.   See Clinton address on Social Security 2/9/98.

3.   Dornbusch is quoted in the *Journal of Commerce*, 1/7/99. The quote was reprinted in *Left Business Observer* #88, 2/99.

4.   Figures for the average wages of nonsupvisory workers comes from the U.S. Bureau of Labor Statistics. The data on CEO compensation for 1991 and 2001 are from *Business Week* 3/30/92 and 4/15/02.

5.   I develop this analytic approach in greater depth, including relevant references, in Robert Pollin, "Globalization and the Transition to Egalitarian Development," Political Economy Research Institute Working Paper #42 <http://www.umass.edu/peri/pdfs/WP42.pdf>.

6.   Karl Polanyi, *The Great Transformation: The Political and Economic Origins of Our Time*, Boston: Beacon Press, 1944, p. 231.

7.   James Boyce, "Inequality as a Cause of Environmental Degradation," *Ecological Economics*, vol. 11, 1994, p. 17< http://www.umass.edu/peri/pdfs/PS1.pdf>. For a fuller discussion of this same issue, see James Boyce, *The Political Economy of the Environment*, Northampton, MA: Edward Elgar, 2002.

Chapter Two

1.   The quotes are from Bob Woodward, *The Agenda*, New York: Simon & Schuster, 1994, pp. 165 and 91.

2.   *The Agenda*, op. cit., p. 239.

3.   Many of these same themes are explored by Michael Meeropol in *Surrender: How the Clinton Administration Completed the Reagan Revolution*, Ann Arbor: University of Michigan Press, 2000 (paperback edition).

4.   According to Steven Greenhouse and Joseph Kahn of the *New York Times* (3/12/99), Clinton's interview with the *Seattle Post-Intelligencer*, in which he suggested that the WTO might at some point employ sanctions to enforce core labour rights around the world, "stunned the delegates, and even his own negotiators."

5.   See the interesting discussion of these issues, specifically as they apply to NAFTA, by Meherene Larudee, "Integration and Income Distribution under the North American Free Trade Agreement: The Experience in Mexico," in Dean Baker, Gerald Epstein and Robert Pollin (eds), *Globalization and Progressive Economic Policy*, Cambridge 1998.

6.   The ERP for 1998 states that the Administration has "made significant reform of the existing trade adjustment assistance program a priority"; in reality, these programs were minimal.

7.   David Howell, "Theory-Driven Facts and the Growth in Earnings Inequality," *Review of Radical Political Economics*, Winter 1999, pp. 54–86. See also David Card and John E. DiNardo, "Skill Biased Techological Change and Rising Wage Inequality: Some Problems and Puzzles," NBER Working Paper No. w8769, February 2002.

8.   Interview with Moberg by Josh Mason in November 1999.

9.   See Robert Pollin and Stephanie Luce, *The Living Wage: Building a Fair Economy*, New York: The New Press, 2000 (paperback edition), for a discussion of the historical trends in the minimum wage.

10.   Data on EITC coverage comes from IRS, "Individual income tax returns, 2000, preliminary data," Internal Revenue Service *Statistics of Income* (SOI), Winter 2001/2, pp. 163–73.

11.   For discussion of the declining use of food stamps, see Sharon Parrott and Stacy Dean, "Food Stamps Can Help Low-Income Families Put Food on the Table," Center on Budget and Policy Priorities, Washington D.C. 1999 <http://www.cbpp.org/3-31-99fs.htm>; Andrew Revkin, "A Plunge in Use of Food Stamps Causes Concern", *New York Times* 25/2/99; Rebecca Blank and David Ellwood, "The Clinton Legacy for America's Poor," National Bureau of Economic Research Working Paper 8437; and James P. Ziliak, Craig Gundersen and David N. Figlio, "Food Stamp Caseloads Over the Business Cycle," *Southern Economic Journal*, forthcoming 2003.

12.   The EITC, in short, is a variation on the Speenhamland system of Poor Law used in Britain in the eighteenth and nineteenth centuries. See the excellent discussion on this by Barry Bluestone and Teresa Ghilarducci, *The American Prospect*, May–June 1996, pp. 40–46. According to the brilliant historical analysis of the Poor Laws themselves in E.J. Hobsbawm and G. Rudé, *Captain Swing*, New York: Pantheon, 1968, as a result of these measures, "the distinction between worker and pauper vanished."

13.   The "Gramm" of Gramm-Leach-Bliley was former Senator Phil Gramm of Texas. Sen. Gramm's wife is Professor Wendy Gramm, who served as Chair of the Commodity Futures Trading Commission from 1988–93 and was called the "Margaret Thatcher of financial regulation" by the *Wall Street Journal*. Wendy Gramm is now best known for

having served as a director of Enron during the disgraced firm's heyday of cooking its books and, still more damaging, if less spectacular, converting the provision of energy supply from a public utility into yet another vehicle for financial speculation.

14.   See Robert Pollin, "Financial Structures and Egalitarian Economic Policy," *New Left Review*, December 1995, for a survey of such proposals.

15.   William Greider describes the September 24, 1996 Federal Reseve meeting in *The Nation*, 3/25/02, p. 6. For a fuller discussion of Greenspan's changing explanation as to why he was unwilling to raise margin requirements to slow down the rampaging stock market, see Tom Schlesinger, "Dealing with Asset Bubbles: The Fed's Changing Story and the Historical Record," *Financial Markets Center* <http://www.fmcenter.org/pdf/marginupdate091402.pdf>.

16.   The *Wall Street Journal* (1/4/00), for example, announced on the occasion of Clinton's renomination of Greenspan as Chairman of the Federal Reserve, "The U.S. economy is enjoying its best performance in more than a generation with low unemployment and low inflation. If the current expansion lasts through February, something generally expected, it will surpass the 1960's as the longest period of uninterrupted economic growth in U.S. history."

17.   On a more technical note, revisions in the methods used for measuring inflation and investment also made the Clinton record look better than was true with the pre-revision statistics. For a discussion of the problems and potential biases in the new statistical methods, see Dean Baker, "Something New in the 1990s? Looking for Evidence of an Economic Transformation," in *Unconventional Wisdom: Alternative Perspectives on the New Economy*," in Jeff Madrick ed., New York: Century Foundation, 2000.

18.   The quote from *The Economist* is from a 5/12/01 story, p. 80. The follow-up story was published on 8/11/01, pp. 55–56.

19.   The arguments and evidence cited here come specifically come from Chapter 1, "The Making of the New Economy," from the 2001 *Economic Report of the President*.

20.   Gordon's argument is presented in "Does the New Economy Measure Up to the Great Inventions of the Past?" *Journal of Economic Perspectives* 14 (2000): 49–74. The specific quote was reported in James Grant, "Wired Office, Same Workers," *New York Times*, May 1, 2000, p. A27.

21.   Wynne Godley provided a prescient analysis as to why these financial patterns in the household sector are unsustainable. See *Seven Unsustainable Processes: Medium-Term Prospects and Policies for the United States and the World*, Levy Institute, Annandale 1999, as well as more recent updates based on this same analytic framework, including Wynne Godley and Alex Izurieta, "The Case for a Severe Recession," *Challenge*, March–April 2002, pp. 27–51.

22.   For historical figures on interest rates, see Robert Pollin and Gary Dymski, "The Costs and Benefits of Financial Instability: Big Government and the Minsky Paradox," in Dymski and Pollin (eds), *New Perspectives in Monetary Macroeconomics*, Ann Arbor: University of Michigan Press, 1994, pp. 369–402.

23. The Krugman quote is from "Does Third World Growth Hurt First World Prosperity?" *Harvard Business Review*, July–August, 1994. The data presented in Figure 2.1 are the official figures provided by the U.S. Bureau of Labor Statistics. Nevertheless, the precise movements of the average real wage and productivity trends are sensitive to a series of disputable technical considerations. For example, Alan Blinder and Janet Yellen claim that the figures showing a trend decline in average real wages are "misleading" because they "overdeflated by using the 'old' CPI and they excluded fringe benefits, which grew faster than real wages." See their essay "The Fabulous Decade," in Alan Krueger and Robert Solow eds., *The Roaring Nineties*, New York: The Russell Sage Foundation and Century Foundation, 2001, p. 148. But the figures reported here are derived from the revised CPI-U figures. The Bureau of Labor Statistics has developed another series, CPI-U-RS that attempts to use the current revised methods for estimating inflation back to 1978. Thus, we cannot use CPI-U-RS to measure wage trends for our full 1960–2000 period. Moreover, the BLS itself acknowledges methological problems with this series as well. In any case, the downward movement of average real wages would still persist using this series, though it would be more moderate. Nor would including fringe benefits in this trend significantly alter the overall pattern if one works with an appropriate Bureau of Labor Statistics data series on benefits (e.g. the benefit series for "Blue Collar Occupations"). All such technical issues aside, Blinder and Yellen still acknowledge that "real wages had been doing miserably for years … . During the decade ending in 1992, real wages failed to keep up even with the sluggish growth of productivity," (p. 92). In short, the basic conclusion one obtains from the official government statistics remains in force: that, over the period 1973–93, average real wages were falling or, at best, stagnant, while productivity was rising, even if at a relatively slow pace.

24.   In recent years, many researchers and government officials have questioned the adequacy of this method for establishing poverty thresholds. The most extensive scientific survey of these issues was that sponsored by the National Research Council (NRC), Constance F. Citro and Robert T. Michael, eds., *Measuring Poverty: A New Approach*, Washington, D.C.: National Academy Press, 1995. According to the NRC study, establishing overall poverty thresholds on the basis of food costs alone presents many problems. For one thing, there are large variations in housing and medical care costs by region and population groups. In addition, food prices have fallen relative to those for housing. As noted above, child care costs have also not been adequately accounted for. The NRC study reports on six alternative methodologies to the current official method for measuring absolute poverty for a two adult/two child family. The thresholds generated by these alternative methodologies are all higher than the official threshold, ranging between 23.7 and 53.2 percent above the official threshold.   The average value of these alternative estimates is 41.7 percent higher than the official threshold. The NRC study also includes consideration of "relative" as well as "absolute" measures of poverty. Relative poverty, as the term suggests, takes account of problems resulting from pronounced inequality in a society, even if that society's average living standard is relatively high. We focus here only on absolute poverty measures. For an

insightful overview on these both poverty measures as well as current poverty trends throughout the world, see Keith Griffin, "Problems of Poverty and Marginalization," *Indicators*, 2 (2), Spring 2003, pp. 22-48. Also available at <http://www.umass.edu/peri/pdfs/WP51.pdf>.

25.   This conclusion broadly reflects the assessment of the careful and balanced study, "The Clinton Legacy for America's Poor," by Rebecca Blank and David Ellwood, both of whom held high policy positions during Clinton's presidency (published in Jeffrey A. Frankel and Peter R. Orszag, *American Economic Policy in the 1990s*, Cambridge, MA: MIT Press, pp. 749–800). For example, Blank and Ellwood's evaluation of the situation for female-headed poor families is that "the modest income gains over the late 1990s for mother-headed families in the bottom of the income distribution suggest that anything that disrupts their earnings (such as a future recession), could sharply increase poverty rates if public assistance is no longer readily available," (p. 787).

Chapter Three

1.   The full title is *The Fabulous Decade: Macroeconomic Lessons from the* 1990s, New York: The Century Foundation Press, 2001. Alan Blinder, Professor of Economics at Princeton, was both a member of the Council of Economic Advisors under Clinton and Vice-Chair of the Federal Reserve. Janet Yellen, Professor of Economics at UC Berkeley, served as a governor of the Federal Reserve and Chair of the Council of Economic Advisors.

2.   Robert Gordon, "The Time-Varying NAIRU and its Implications for Economic Policy," *Journal of Economic Perspectives*, 1997, 11:1, pp. 11–32; and "Foundations of the Goldilocks Economy: Supply Shocks and the Time-Varying NAIRU," *Brookings Papers on Economic Activity*, 1998, 2, pp. 297–334.

3.   Douglas Staiger, James Stock and Mark Watson, "The NAIRU, Unemployment and Monetary Policy," *Journal of Economic Perspectives*, 1997, 11:1, pp 33–50, and "Prices, Wages, and the U.S. NAIRU," in Alan Krueger and Robert Solow eds., *The Roaring Nineties*, New York: The Russell Sage Foundation and Century Foundation, 2001.

4.   "The Time-Varying NAIRU," p. 30.

5.   These results are developed in more depth in Robert Pollin, "Wage Bargaining and the U.S. Phillips Curve: Was Greenspan Right About 'Traumatized Workers' in the 1990s?" a work in progress that I initially presented at the January 2003 Allied Social Science Association.

6.   See *Business Week* 27/12/99.

7.   Greenspan's testimony can be found on the Federal Reserve site at <www.bog.frb.fed.us.boarddocs/ hh/1997/July/testimony.htm>. Yellen's comments from the 9/26/96 Federal Open Market Committee Meeting are at: <http://www.federalreserve.gov/FOMC/Transcripts/1996/19960924Meeting.pdf>, p. 21.

8.   Kate Bronfenbrenner, "The Effects of Plant Closing or Threat of Plant Closing on the Right of Workers to Organize," Report to the U.S. Department of Labor 1997 and "Uneasy Terrain: The Impact of Capital Mobility on Workers, Wages, and Union Organizing," Report Submitted to the U.S. Trade Deficit Review Commission, June 2001.

9.   Minsik Choi (2001) "Threat Effect of Foreign Direct Investment on the Labor Union Wage Premium," Amherst, MA: Political Economy Research Institute Working Paper Number 27 <http://www.umass.edu/peri/pdfs/WP27.pdf>.

10.   The figure reports the same time series that Schiller presents in his book. This includes his technique of measuring the denominator of the ratio as a ten-year backward moving average of earnings. Some controversy exists as to whether earnings should be smoothed in this way, or at all. In any case, the overall pattern for the P/E ratio does not change if contemporaneous values for earnings are used in the denominator of the ratio.

11.   The history of this bogus fact is told well in Yochi J. Dreazen, "Fallacies of The Tech Boom," *Wall Street Journal*, 9/26/02.

12.   "The United States," *Monthly Review*, July 1999, p. 129.

13.   See especially Kindleberger, *Manias, Crashes and Panics: A History of Financial Crisis*, New York 1977.

14.   In saying "probably," as opposed to "certainly," I am acknowledging the countervailing possibility that worsening conditions in overseas markets might have driven foreign investment in the U.S. upwards still further. But it is still difficult to imagine the bubble continuing had the demise of Long-Term Capital Management been permitted to play out without Federal Reserve crisis management.

15.   See Daniel Larkins, "Note on the Profitability of Domestic Nonfinancial Corporations, 1960–2001," *Survey of Current Business*, September 2002, pp. 17–20.

16.   There are tax implications for some shareholders through which they would benefit by selling their shares back to the corporation as opposed to receiving dividends. If shareholders have held their shares for more than one year, the capital gains they receive from the sale is taxed at the lower capital gains rate than if they had to pay ordinary income taxes on a dividend payment. But because the details of how this tax effect would work varies for individual shareholders, one would not expect that this factor alone could drive up share prices through a buy-back strategy.

17.   Scott Weissbenner of the Federal Reserve Board research staff conducted a careful recent analysis of the link between corporate buy-back strategies and paying top executives through stock option opportunities. Weissbenner found that option grants for top executives are indeed associated with increased share buy-backs as well as a reduction in the corporations paying out of dividends. See Scott Weisbenner, "Corporate Share Repurchases in the 1990s: What Role Do Stock Options Play?" Federal Reserve Board Finance and Economics Discussion Series <http://www.federalreserve.gov/pubs/feds/2000/200029/200029pap.pdf>.

18. Robert Rubin, of course, was an unequivocal champion of financial deregulation while at the Treasury, before becoming the most prominent early beneficiary of the latest bout of deregulation as co-chairman of the newly formed Citigroup. Rubin's successor as Treasury Secretary, Lawrence Summers, was no less fervent a promoter of deregulation, even though as an academic economist he once showed apprehension of its dangers: see Lawrence and Victoia Summers, "When financial markets work too well: a cautious case for a securities transaction tax," *Journal of Financial Services Research*, 1989.

19. The U.S. government supplies data on foreign asset ownership from two separate sources: the Department of Commerce's annual report on "International Investment Posiiton of the U.S. at Yearend," published in the *Survey of Current Business*; and the Federal Reserve quarterly *Flow of Funds Accounts*. The two sources report different total figures. But this is primarily because the *Flow of Funds Accounts* excludes "market value of foreign equities held by U.S. residents" in its calculation of total liabilities, while the *Survey of Current Business* accounting does include this category as a liability. The *Survey of Current Business* approach is more consistent, given that foreign holdings of U.S. corporate equities are included as an foreign asset under both the *Survey of Current Business* and *Flow of Funds* accounting procedures.

20. One source of potential confusion as to the magnitude of the foreign ownership effect on U.S. stock prices is that, in the U.S. *Flow of Funds Accounts*, foreign "portfolio" equity purchases – i.e. purchases of less than a 10 percent ownership share – remained fairly constant over the 1990s (data from Table L213). But as Lawrance Evans shows in *Why the Bubble Burst*, when one properly includes "foreign direct investment" – i.e. ownership purchases of more than 10 percent – in the total foreign asset position, the rise of foreign equity purchases is in step with the overall increase in the foreign net asset position.

21. Dean M. Maki and Michael G. Palumbo, "Disentangling the Wealth Effect: A Cohort Analysis of Household Savings in the 1990s," Board of Governors of the Federal Reserve System <http://www.federalreserve.gov/pubs/feds/2001/200121/200121pap.pdf>.

Chapter Four

1. Edmund Phelps, "Europe's stony ground for the seeds of growth: Continental nations must cast off corporatism if they are to emulate thriving economies," *Financial Times*, August 9, 2000.

2. Cheney appeared on "Meet the Press," 12/3/00; as reported in Richard Stevenson, "Contesting The Vote: The Republican Running Mate; History Will View Gore 'In a Better Light' If He Quits Soon, Cheney Says," *New York Times*, 12/4/00.

3. William D. Nordhaus, "The Recent Recession, the Current Recovery and Stock Prices," *Brookings Papers on Economic Activity*," 1:2002, p. 199–220.

4.   Michelle Conlin, "The Big Squeeze on Workers: Is There a Risk to Wringing More from a Smaller Staff?" *Business Week*, 5/13/02.

5.   See U.S. Conference of Mayors website, <http://www.usmayors.org/uscm/news/press_releases/documents/hunger_121802.asp>.

6.   In an 8/1/02 *Wall Street Journal* opinion article "Dow 36,000 Revisited," Glassman and Hassert held that, based on economic reasoning, 36,000 was still the most appropriate level for the Dow (rather than, say, its closing of 7,892 at the end of February 2003). But they claimed in their opinion piece that they had never actually stated in their book *when* the Dow would reach this appropriate level. In fact, however, Chapter 1 of the book's paperback edition, published in 2000, ends with this passage: "The case is compelling that 36,000 is a fair value for the Dow *today* (emphasis in original). And stocks should rise to such heights very quickly." The last defense for their claims would thus seem to hinge on their definition of "very quickly." See James K. Glassman and Kevin A. Hassett, *Dow 36,000*, New York: Three Rivers Press, 2000, p. 19.

7.   John Kenneth Galbraith, *The Great Crash – 1929*, Boston: Houghton Mifflin, 1954, p. 138.

8.   Blodget quote is in Saul Hansell, "'Buy' Was Cry, as Stock Bubble Burst," *New York Times*, March 4, 2001, p. A1; Herbert Stein mentions what he terms "Stein's law" in, among other places, his *What I Think: Essays on Economics, Politics, and Life*, Washington, DC: The AEI Press, 1998, p. 19.

9.   William Nordhaus op. cit. correctly points out that the capacity utilization index for industry takes account of only 20 percent of the economy, and therefore does not adequately reflect possible constraints on growth coming out of a recession. Despite this, the figure is still a reasonable indicator of the severity of a cyclical downturn, especially for the industrial sector itself, but more broadly, if more indirectly, as well.

10.   These foreign investment figures are drawn from the Federal Reserve Board Flow of Funds Accounts, Table F.107. Following the same calculation approach as that discussed in Chapter 3, footnote 20, I have added here figures for both "U.S. corporate equities," and "foreign direct investment in the United States."

11.   The McCain quote is from *Financial Times*, 1/6/00, p. 27.

12.   Ruth Simon and Michelle Higgins, "Stretched Buyers Push Mortgages to the Limit," *Wall Street Journal* Online, 6/17/02; and Terri Cullen, "The Dangers of Buying a Home at the Top of a Market Bubble," *Wall Street Journal Online*, 6/18/02.

13.   Dean Baker, "The Run-Up in Home Prices: Is It Real or Is It Another Bubble?" Center for Economic and Policy Research, 8/5/02 < http://www.cepr.net/Housing_Bubble.htm>.

14.   These calculations apply to average refinancing costs across households. They therefore do not reflect the evidence showing the costs of refinancing are consistently higher

for non-white households, even after controlling for differences in income levels. This form of racial discrimination in credit markets has been documented most recently in the study by Calvin Bradford, "Risk or Race? Racial Disparities and the Subprime Refinance Market," Center for Community Change, May 2002.

15. This 6 percent negative wealth effect is somewhat larger than the estimated 4 percent figure associated, as we discussed in Chapter 3, with stock values. The 6 percent wealth effect estimate is from Karl Case, Robert Shiller and John Quigley, "Comparing Wealth Effects: The Stock Market versus the Housing Market," National Bureau of Economic Research Working Paper #w8606.

16. See Alan Beattie, "Fed Seeks to Reassure on Economic Eventualities," *Financial Times*, 12/4/02, p. 9 for Greenspan's perspective on the Fed's alternative policy options. As the article discusses, Greenspan's views on this were amplified at the time by Fed Governor Ben Bernanke, who is also a well-known Princeton University macroeconomist. The technique that Greenspan and Bernanke discussed for reducing long-term interest rates would entail that the Fed specifically target long-term U.S. government bonds for purchase. When the Fed deliberately increases the demand for these bonds, their price rises, which means that the effective interest rate yield on them falls. When the Fed thus lowers the interest rate on long-term government bonds, the assumption is that this will also push down long-term private market rates such as the corporate Baa bond rate. But again, the effectiveness of this sort of intervention is likely to be diminished if businesses and households are already carrying excessive debt loans and if the financial markets are dominated by highly speculative practices.

17. This characterization is further supported by the findings from a survey by Matthew Shapiro and Joel Slemrod, "Consumer Responses to Tax Rebates," National Bureau of Economic Research Working Paper #w8672, 12/01. Shapiro and Slemrod found that only 22 percent of households receiving rebate checks intended to spend the money they received. Most households reported that they were rather planning to use the money to pay off debts or increase their savings. If Shapiro and Slemrod's findings are accurate, it suggests that the stimulus effects of the measure were likely to have been weaker still, indeed, virtually undetectable. However, these survey findings are not consistent with evidence we discussed above, showing that households actually increased their borrowing during the recession. In any case, these survey findings certainly support the overall conclusion that, at best, the rebates provided only a mild stimulus during the recession.

18. These figures are presented in Citizens for Tax Justice, "House GOP 'Stimulus' Bill Offers 16 Large, Low-Tax Corporations $7.4 Billion in Instant Tax Rebates," 10/26/01 <http://www.ctj.org/html/amtdozen.htm>.

19. "Most of Bush's Proposed New 2003 Tax Cuts Would Go To Top 10 percent," Citizens for Tax Justice, 1/8/03 <http://www.ctj.org/stim03.pdf>.

20. R. Glenn Hubbard, "Bigger Pie, Bigger Pieces," *Wall Street Journal*, 2/12/03; Michael J. Mandel, "Is It Class Warfare?" *Business Week*, 1/20/03, pp. 28–30.

21. Figure is quoted from the 2003 *Economic Report of the President*, Table B-95, p. 386.

22. J.M. Keynes, *The General Theory of Employment, Interest, and Money*, op. cit., p. 159.

23. Russell Gold and Robert Gavin, "Falling Short: Fiscal Crises Force States to Endure Painful Choices," *Wall Street Journal*, 10/7/02.

24. Rhea Borja, "Oregon Rejects Tax Hike That Would Have Helped Schools," *Education Week*, 2/5/03.

25. Federal Funds Information for States, "Major Discretionary and Mandatory Funding Programs," 2/4/02.

26. Max Sawicky, "Budgeting Beyond the Beltway: How the Federal Budget Imperils State and Local Finances," *EPI Issue Brief #175*, Economic Policy Institute, 2/14/02 <http://www.epinet.org/>.

27. David Rodgers, "Director Picks Small Fights Over Budget: As Election Approaches, Daniels and GOP Struggle to Address the Federal Deficit," *Wall Street Journal*, 6/12/92, p. A4.

28. Increasing long-term interest rates in anticipation of future inflation is known as incorporating an "inflation premium" in long-term rates to reflect the perceived "inflation risk." But increased inflation risk may not be the only factor contributing to rising long-term rates in any given situation, and in particular, was not the only factor in 2001–02. When financial markets become increasingly volatile, as we have observed, one would also expect the markets to respond to the increased "default risk" or "speculation risk" through raising long-term rates. In fact, however, the evidence suggests the markets were primarily responding to their perception of increased inflation risk in 2001–02. As one important piece of evidence on this, the rates on short-term U.S. Treasury bills – financial instruments that are effectively free of both inflation and default risk – did fall in correspondence with the Greenspan-induced decline in the Federal Funds rate. But long-term Treasury bonds, which also carry no default risk but do face the same inflationary risks as corporate bonds, declined in a pattern much closer to the gradual decline of the Baa corporate bond rate. Indeed, we obtain a sense of the extent to which increased default risk was important through the observing the rate of decline in the Baa corporate bond rate relative to both the safer Aaa corporate rate and the Treasury bond rates. Between 7/00 when Greenspan began cutting the Federal Funds rate, and 12/02, the ten-year Treasury Bond rate fell by 2.02 percent, the Aaa corporate bond rate fell by 1.44 percent and the Baa bond rate fell by 0.9 percent. Meanwhile, the three-month Treasury Bill rate fell by 4.97 percent.

29. One of the more thoughtful analyses of this issue, which recognizes the logic of various perspectives and attempts to weigh their relative strength, is by two Federal Reserve economists, Douglas W. Elmendorf and David L. Reifschneider, "Short-Run Effects of Fiscal Policy with Forward-Looking Financial Markets," *National Tax Journal*, September 2002.

30. Indeed, it has been the explicit position of some free market proponents – the Nobel Laureate economist Milton Friedman most prominently – that federal deficits serve a useful purpose precisely because they create powerful pressures to cut government spending programs. See, for example, Milton Friedman, "What Every American Wants," *Wall Street Journal*, 1/15/03, p. A10.

31. U.S. Office of Management and Budget, *The Budget for the Fiscal Year 2004, Historical Tables*, Table 3.1 <http://www.whitehouse.gov/omb/budget/fy2004/pdf/hist.pdf>.

32. See Dean Baker, Robert Pollin, and Elizabeth Zahrt, "The Vietnam War and the Political Economy of Full Employment," *Challenge* May–June 1996, pp. 35–45.

33. William Nordhaus, "Economic Consequences of War with Iraq," in *War With Iraq: Costs, Consequences and Alternatives*, Cambridge, MA: American Academy of Arts and Sciences, 2002, pp. 51–86.

34. See the candid pre-invasion article in *Business Week*, 2/10/03, "Its Not 'All About Oil' But…" on the benefits of overthrowing Saddam Hussein for U.S. oil interests, including oil-service firms such Haliburton Co, the company that Vice President Cheney headed as CEO before becoming Vice President. The *New York Times* editorial page described the awarding to Bechtel of the first reconstruction contract as "sending a deplorable message to a skeptical world," 4/19/03 <http://www.nytimes.com/2003/04/19/opinion/19SAT1.html>.

35. See "Wishy-Washy: The SEC Pulls its Punches on Corporate-Governance Rules," *The Economist*, 2/1/03, p. 60.

36. Karen Tumulty, "From W. With Love," *Time*, 3/26/01, pp. 46–48. The quote from Steve Rosenthal in the next paragraph is also from this same article.

37. For example, Randy Johnson, Vice President for Labor Policy at the United States Chamber of Commerce said in March 2001 "All that Bush has done so far is to really level the playing field back to where it was when Clinton took office," Steven Greenhouse, "Unions See Bush Moves as Payback for Backing Gore," *New York Times*, 3/25/01, p. 33.

38. See, for example, on this issue, Jeanne Cummings and Carlos Tejada, "Taft-Hartley Could Bloody Labor and Bush," *Wall Street Journal*, 10/11/02, p. A4.

39. "Dancing With Hardhats: Bush's Strategy Starts to Work," *Business Week*, 4/15/02, p. 51.

40. See Chapter 7, "Supporting Global Economic Integration," of the 2002 *Economic Report of the President*. As with the Clinton *Economic Report of the President* presentation, this discussion neglects to mention that even the orthodox Heckscher-Ohlin theoretical argument on behalf of free trade rests on highly restrictive assumptions of full employment and uniform production methods and, even after allowing for those as-

sumptions, recognizes that trade opening produces losers as well as net gains in efficiency. See the discussion in Chapter 2, pp. 22–24.

41. The effective subsidy here would be less than 18 percent when U.S. firms are able to purchase relatively cheap foreign products as inputs in their production processes and, equivalently, when foreign firms buy U.S. goods at prices that are relatively high in terms of their own domestic currencies.

42. Even under a regime of adequate social protections, there could still be a need for trade protection. The two most compelling reasons for trade protection are to encourage the development of new industries, the so-called "infant-industry" argument for trade protection; and as a means of generating government revenues. But both of these cases would apply almost entirely to developing countries.

Chapter Five

1. The literature on the alternative development models in less developed countries is voluminous. Some important examples include Alice Amsden, *The Rise of "the Rest": Challenges to the West from Late-Industrializing Economies*, New York: Oxford University Press, 2001; Ha-Joon Chang, *Kicking Away the Ladder: Development Strategy in Historical Perspective*, London: Anthem Press, 2002; Walden Bello and Stephanie Rosenfeld, *Dragons in Distress*, San Francisco: Institute for Food and Development Policy, 1990; and Robert Pollin and Diana Alarcon, "Debt Crisis, Accumulation Crisis and Economic Restructuring in Latin America," *International Review of Applied Economics*, vol. 2, No. 2, 1988, pp.127–154. Alexander Cockburn and I tried to summarize some of the main historical lessons and myths in the transition to ascendent neoliberalism in "Capitalism and its Specters: The World, The Free Market, and the Left," *The Nation*, 2/25/91, pp. 224–36. The quotations from Ronald Reagan and Michael Manley presented in this section are taken from this earlier article.

2. Tony Smith, "Brazil's President Elect Picks a Central Banker," *New York Times*, 12/13/02, p. W1. The previous quote reporting the message Lula sent to financial markets is from Agence France Presse, 10/28/02.

3. See Minqi Li, *Three Essays on China's State Owned Enterprises: Towards an Alternative to Privatization*, doctoral dissertation, University of Massachusetts Amherst, 2002, for an outstanding analysis of China's economic policy directions since the 1980s, as well as a discussion of the alternatives being considered for the future.

4. Mark Weisbrot, Dean Baker, Egor Kraev and Judy Chen present a similar data analysis on growth in less developed countries in, "The Scorecard on Globalization: Twenty Years of Diminished Progress," Center for Economic and Policy Research, July 2001, <http://www.cepr.net/globalization/scorecard_on_globalization.htm>.

5. It is also true that when we include China within the group of low and middle income countries, the overall growth patterns we observe are modified but do not change dramati-

cally. Thus, per capita GDP growth for low and middle income countries including China is 3.2 percent for 1961–80 and 1.4 percent for 1981–99. This same conclusion also correspondingly holds for the figures on relative distribution patterns presented in Table 5.2.

6.   These considerations are drawn out more fully in Francis Stewart and Albert Berry, "Globalization, Liberalization, and Inequality: Expectations and Experience," in Andrew Hurrell and Ngaire Woods eds., *Inequality, Globalization and World Politics*, New York, Oxford University Press, pp. 150–186. See also Christian E. Weller and Adam Hirsh, "The Long and the Short of It: Global Liberalization, Poverty, and Inequality," Economic Policy Institute, October, 2002.

7.   Bob Sutcliffe, "A More or Less Unequal World? World Income Distribution in the 20th Century," *Indicators,* forthcoming 2003, <http://www.umass.edu/peri/pdfs/WP54.pdf>. The figures in Table 5.2 on global distribution exclusive of China are not based on figures in Professor Sutcliffe's paper. Professor Sutcliffe kindly supplied the necessary underlying figures to me on request. Professor Sutcliffe has also pointed out correctly that the figures in Table 5.1 and the top panel of Table 5.2 do not adjust national income figures based on calculations of purchasing power parities (PPP) between national currencies, while the figures in the lower panel of Table 5.2 are adjusted based on PPP. This inconsistency in methodologies was unavoidable because of gaps in the availability of PPP-adjusted data for the 1961–80 period. Moreover, as Prof. Sutcliffe pointed out in a private exchange, from the PPP-adjusted data we do have for these years, it appears that this methodological inconsistency does not have any significant effect on the data patterns presented in Tables 5.1 and 5.2.

8.   The world "average" figure is the median expressed in 1990 dollars after adjusting for purchasing power parities. The figures for the richest and poorest 1 percent are means for their groupings in 1990 dollars adjusted for purchasing power parities. I am grateful to Professor Sutcliffe for supplying these figures to me on request.

9.   Sanjay G. Reddy and Thomas W. Pogge, "How Not to Count the Poor," version 4.4, August 15, 2002, p. 4, < http://www.columbia.edu/~sr793/count.pdf>.

10.   Shaohua Chen and Martin Ravallion, "How Did the World's Poorest Fare in the 1990s?" <http://www.worldbank.org/research/povmonitor/pdfs/methodology.pdf>; and International Monetary Fund, *World Economic Outlook*, May 2000, Chapter 4, p. 1, <http://www.imf.org/external/pubs/ft/weo/2000/01/pdf/chapter4.pdf>.

11.   Basic sources on the suicide deaths include Vamsicharan Vakulabharanam, "The Dark Side of 'White Gold': Globalization and Cotton Farming in Telangana," Prospectus for a Dissertation, Department of Economics, University of Massachusetts, Amherst, 2001; Utsa Patnaik, "Deflation and *Déjà Vu*: Indian Agriculture in the World Economy," Centre for Economic Studies and Planning, Jawaharlal Nehru University, January 2002; G. Parthasarathy, "Suicides of Cottom Farmers in Andhra Pradesh: An Exploratory Study," *Economic and Political Weekly*, 3/28/98, pp. 720–726; *Farmers' Suicides in Andhra Pradesh: Report of the People's Tribunal*, July 1998; Rajani X. Desai, *What The Peasant*

Suicides Tell Us, Bombay: Radical Union for Political Economy; C. Shambu Prasad, "Suicide Deaths and Quality of Indian Cotton: Perspectives from History of Technology and Khadi Movement," *Economic and Political Weekly*, 1/30/99, pp. 12–19.

12.   Prabhat Patnaik and C.P. Chandrasekhar, "India: *Dirigisme*, Structural Adjustment and the Radical Alternative," in Dean Baker, Gerald Epstein and Robert Pollin eds., *Globalization and Progressive Economic Policy*, Cambridge, UK: Cambridge University Press, 1998, p. 67. See also the critical evaluation of the Patnaik/Chandresekhar paper by Keith Griffn in the same volume. Despite differences between Patnaik/Chandresekhar and Griffin, they all agree that 1991 did represent a sharp turning point toward toward a neoliberal policy agenda.

13.   C.P. Chandrasekhar and Jayati Ghosh, *The Market That Failed: A Decade of Neoliberal Economic Reforms in India*, New Delhi: LeftWord Books, 2002. Among other sources, Chandrasekhar and Ghosh cite the following assessment on the 1990s growth experience by the Reserve Bank of India: "Filtering the data on real GDP growth to eliminate irregular year-to-year fluctuations indicates the presence of a growth cycle in the Indian economy and a discernible downturn in the second half of the 1990s." (p. 44)

14.   The quotes in this paragraph are taken from Ken Silverstein, "Stop the Press: Why The Media Missed Latin America's Collapse," *The American Prospect*, 2/25/02, pp. 15–17.

15.   The quotes in this paragraph are taken from Doug Henwood, "Casualties: Argentina," *Left Business Observer*, #99, February, 2002, < http://www.leftbusinessobserver.com/Argentina.html>.

16.   The discussion in this section draws from three primary sources: Robert Pollin and Eduardo Zepeda, "Latin American Debt: The Choices Ahead," *Monthly Review*, February 1987, pp. 1–16; Robert Pollin and Diana Alarcon, "Debt Crisis, Accumulation Crisis and Economic Restructuring in Latin America,"op. cit; and David Felix, "Debt Crisis Adjustment in Latin America: Have the Hardships Been Necessary?" in Gary Dymski and Robert Pollin eds., *New Perspectives in Monetary Macroeconomics: Explorations in the Tradition of Hyman P. Minsky*, Ann Arbor: University of Michigan Press, 1994, pp. 169–200.

17.   See Miguel Teubal, "Argentina: The Crisis of Ultramonetarism," *Monthly Review*, February 1983, pp. 18–26.

18.   The same James Baker who went on to become Secretary of State under George Bush-1 and majordomo of George Bush-2's successful effort at preventing the State of Florida from properly counting its 2000 Presidential election ballots.

19.   The details as to how to implement such a plan in a viable way were presented by Professor David Felix of Washington University in St. Louis with his usual incisiveness in "How to Resolve Latin America's Debt Crisis," *Challenge*, November/December 1985.

20.   This section draws substantially from Manuel Pastor Jr. and Carol Wise, "Stabilization and its Discontents: Argentina's Economic Restructuring in the 1990s," *World Development*, 1999, pp. 477–503; David Felix, "After the Fall: The Argentine Crisis and Repercussions," *Foreign Policy In Focus Policy Report*, August 2002, <http://www.fpif.org/pdf/reports/PRargentina2.pdf>; Arthur MacEwan, "Economic Debacle in Argentina: The IMF Strikes Again, *Foreign Policy In Focus Global Affairs Commentary*, 1/2/02, < http://www.fpif.org/pdf/gac/0201argentina.pdf>; and Mark Weisbrot and Dean Baker, "What Happened to Argentina," *Briefing Paper*, Center for Economic and Policy Research, 1/31/02, < http://www.cepr.net/IMF/what_happened_ to_argentina.htm>.

21.   Quoted in Pastor and Wise, op. cit, p. 493, from *Latin American Weekly Report*, 8/3/95.

22.   Mary Anastansia O'Grady, "Argentina Never Really Earned its Good Marks in the 1990s," *Wall Street Journal*, 2/22/02.

23.   In addition to the works cited, see Lance Taylor, ed., *After Neoliberalism: What Next for Latin America?*, Ann Arbor: University of Michigan Press, 1999; and Dani Rodrik, "Reform in Argentina, Take Two," *The New Republic*, January 14, 2002, <http://thenewrepublic.com/011402/rodrik011402.html>.

24.   The rise of anti-sweatshop activism in the U.S. is chronicled in Randy Shaw, *Reclaiming America: Nike, Clean Air, and the New National Activism*, Berkeley: University of California Press, 1999.

25.   This literature is summarized briefly in Robert Pollin, Justine Burns and James Heintz, "Global Apparel Production and Sweatshop Labor: Can Raising Retail Prices Finance Living Wages, *Cambridge Journal of Economics*, forthcoming 2004,<http://www.umass.edu/peri/pdfs/WP19.pdf>; and more fully in Robert Pollin and James Heintz, *The Political Economy of Global Sweatshops* [working title], New York: The New Press, 2004 forthcoming.

26.   The quotations from Sachs and Krugman are cited in an excellent essay by Professor John Miller of Wheaton College, "Why Economists Are Wrong About Sweatshops and the Antisweatshop Movement," *Challenge*, January–February 2003, pp. 93–122.

27.   These issues are developed more fully, with citations, in Robert Pollin, "Globalization and the Transition to Egalitarian Development," Political Economy Research Institute Working Paper #42, <http://www.umass.edu/peri/pdfs/WP42.pdf>.

28 .   The poll results are in Elliot, K. A. and R. B. Freeman (2000) "White Hats or Don Quixotes? Human Rights Vigilantes in the Global Economy," National Bureau of Economic Research Conference on Emerging Labor Market Institutions, <http://www.nber.org/~confer/2000/si2000/elliot.pdf>.

29.   Pollin, Burns, and Heintz, op. cit. Our study examined the case for Mexico only because, among developing countries, it provides the most comprehensive government statistics on production costs in its apparel industry.

30. The U.N. Millennium goals are presented at <http://www.un.org/millenniumgoals/index.html>.

31. Kofi A. Annan, "Trade and Aid in a Changed World," *New York Times*, 3/19/02, <http://www.un.org/News/ossg/sg/stories/sg-19mar2002.htm>.

32. Figures for development assistance provided by OECD countries is at <http://www.oecd.org/pdf/M00022000/M00022968.pdf>.

33. This $105 billion figure does not take account of a long-standing controversy regarding the effects of foreign aid, i.e. whether a dollar of aid to a poor country will actually produce something close to a dollar of additional income for the recipient country. Critics of aid programs from both the political right (e.g. Milton Friedman and Peter Bauer) and left (e.g. Keith Griffin and Teresa Hayter) have argued, for different reasons, that aid inhibits the development of productive activities in a less developed country. An alternative perspective, taking account of standard "multiplier effects" of increased income, would suggest that a dollar of aid could increase development by something more than the dollar of aid provided. The most recent formal statistical studies on this question acknowledge that they are unable to reach any firm conclusions, though they provide suggestive, if fragile, evidence that aid may enhance growth in the short run but that such positive effects could turn negative within a longer-term framework. (Henrik Hansen and Finn Tarp, "Aid and Growth Regressions" *Journal of Development Economics*, 64, 2001, pp. 547–570 and Robert Lensink and Howard White "Are there negative returns to aid?" *Journal of Development Studies*, 37(6), 2001: 42–65.) Taking account of these arguments and findings, the most reasonable working assumption for our purposes is also the simplest: that a dollar of aid will produce roughly a dollar of additional national income – that is, a dollar of aid will have the same proportional effect on national income as an increase in the country's growth rate generated by some other means.

34. United Nations, *Report of the International Conference on Financing For Development*, Monterrey, Mexico, March, 2002, p. 3, <http://ods-dds-ny.un.org/doc/UNDOC/GEN/N02/392/67/PDF/N0239267.pdf?OpenElement>.

35 . This point is well documented in Alexander George ed., *Western State Terrorism*, New York: Polity Press, 1991. For a history of terrorism by the U.S. government in particular, see especially the essay by Richard Falk in this volume, "The Terrorist Foundations of Recent U.S. Foreign Policy," pp. 102–120.

36. Similar to President Bush, Colin Powell remarked at the 2002 World Economic Forum that "terrorism really flourishes in areas of poverty, despair and hopelessness, where people see no future," *New York Times*, 2/2/02. p. A1. A representative sampling of post September 11 expressions on the link between poverty and terrorism by global leaders is presented in Evelyn Leopold, "UN Told Poverty Breeding Ground for Terrorism," *Reuters News Service*, 9/11/01; Peter Ford, "Injustice Seen as Fertile Soil for Terrorists," *Christian Scientist Monitor*, 9/28/01; and Andrew Johnson, "Disparities of Wealth Are Seen as Fuel for Terrorism," *International Herald Tribune*, 12/20/01.

37. L.R. Klein, "International Economic Performance and Security," Department of Economics, University of Pennsylvania, p. 3.

38. Paul Pillar, *Terrorism and U.S. Foreign Policy*, Washington, D.C.: Brookings Institution Press, 2001, p. 31.

39. Alan B. Krueger and Jitka Maleckova, "Education, Poverty, Political Violence and Terrorism: Is There A Causal Connection?" National Bureau of Economic Research Working Paper 9074, <http://www.nber.org/papers/w9074>. Among the press stories prompted by the Krueger and Maleckova paper were Nicholas Kristof, "Behind the Terrorists," *New York Times*, 5/7/02; and Sebastian Mallaby, "Does Poverty Fuel Terror?" *Washington Post*, 5/20/02.

Chapter Six

1. Stiglitz' critique is presented most extensively in *Globalization and its Discontents*, W.W. Norton, 2002. The 7/2/02 speech which both denounces and mocks Stiglitz by IMF Director of Research Kenneth Rogoff is at <http://www.imf.org/external/np/vc/2002/070202.htm>.

2. Arthur M. Okun, *The Political Economy of Prosperity*, Washington, DC: The Brookings Institution, 1970, p. 124.

3. Lawrence Glickman, *A Living Wage: American Workers and the Making of a Consumer Society*, Ithaca, NY: Cornell University Press, 1997, p. 66. For a contemporary analysis of the living wage approach, see Robert Pollin and Stephanie Luce, *The Living Wage: Building a Fair Society*, New York: The New Press, 2000 (paperback edition).

4. See Robert Pollin, Dean Baker, and Marc Schaberg, "Securities Transaction Taxes for U.S. Financial Markets," *Eastern Economic Journal*, 2003 forthcoming.

5. In the S&L case, the regulation effectively created a 100 percent asset reserve requirement for these institutions. See the discussion in Robert Pollin, "Public Credit Allocation Through The Federal Reserve: Why It Is Needed; How It Should Be Done," in G. Dymski, G. Epstein and R. Pollin eds., *Transforming the U.S. Financial System: Equity and Efficiency for the 21st Century*, Armonk, NY: M.E. Sharpe, 1993, pp. 321–354.

6. The first person to clearly recognize these problems was the great Polish economist and contemporary of Keynes, Michal Kalecki, initially in his brief essay, "The Political Aspects of Full Employment," in Ch. 12 of his *Selected Essays on the Dynamics of the Capitalist Economy*, Cambridge, UK: Cambridge University Press, 1971, 138–145. For a comparison of Kalecki and Marx's ideas on unemployment with the current mainstream notions about a "natural rate of unemployment," see Robert Pollin, "The 'Reserve Army of Labor' and the 'Natural Rate of Unemployment': Can Marx, Kalecki, Friedman and Wall Street All Be Wrong?" *Review of Radical Political Economics*, Summer 1998, pp. 1–13.

7.   Two recent works by Robert Brenner, "The Economics of Global Turbulence," *New Left* Review, #229, May–June 1998 and *The Boom and the Bubble*, Verso, 2002, offer an insightful history of these developments in the U.S. economy through the 1970s and provides a useful context for understanding the evolution of the U.S. in the subsequent two decades. Thus, Brenner begins *The Boom and The Bubble* by observing that, "It cannot be emphasized enough that the revitalization of the U.S. economy from around 1993 took place against a backdrop of economic stagnation in the U.S. and on a world scale lasting at least two decades, beginning in the early 1970s." (p. 7)

8.   In characteristically provocative fashion, Professors Michael Howard and John King argue that the fundamental roots of neoliberalism lie elsewhere, and indeed are an out-growth of the rapid pace of technological change. See Michael Howard and John King, "The Rise of Neoliberalism in Advanced Capitalist Economies: Towards a Materialist Explanation," *International Papers in Political Economy*, vol. 9, no. 3, 2002.

9.   See Michael Bruno, "Does Inflation Really Lower Growth," *Finance and Develop-ment*, September 1995. For a more recent analysis of the same question, considered specifically within the context of a critique of inflation-targeting policies, see Gerald Epstein, "Employment-Oriented Central Bank Policy in an Integrated World Economy: A Reform Proposal for South Africa," Political Economy Research Institute Working Paper #39,<http://www.umass.edu/peri/pdfs/WP39.pdf>. On the Vietnam experi-ence, see Dean Baker, Robert Pollin and Elizabeth Zahrt, "The Vietnam War and the Political Economy of Full Employment," *Challenge* May–June 1996, pp. 35–45.

10.   The main features of the model are surveyed insightfully in Lennart Erixon, "A 'Third Way' in Economic Policy: A Reappraisal of the Rehn-Meidner Model in Light of Modern Economics," *International Papers in Political Economy*, 9:2, 2002. See also the fascinating interview with Rudolf Meidner by Bertram Silverman, "The Rise and Fall of the Swedish Model: Interview with Rudolf Meidner," *Challenge*, 41:1, pp. 69–91.

11.   See Robert Heilbroner, *Twenty-First Century Capitalism*, New York: W.W. Norton, 1993.

12.   See James Heintz and Robert Pollin, "Informalization, Economic Growth and the Challenge of Creating Viable Labor Standards in Developing Countries," Political Economy Research Institute Working Paper #60, May 2003, <http://www.umass.edu/peri/pdfs/wp60.pdf>.

13.   The literature on the East Asian financial market model is voluminous. See, for example, Alice Amsden, *The Rise of "The Rest": Challenges to the West From Late-Indus-trializing Economies*, New York: Oxford University Press, 2001, and Joseph Stiglitz, "From Miracle to Crisis to Recovery: Lessons from Four Decades of East Asian Experience," in J. Stiglitz and Shahid Yusif eds., *Rethinking the East Asian Miracle*, Washington, DC: World Bank, 2001. For a comprehensive analysis of the various methods through which developing countries can mitigate the negative effects of international capital flows into and out of their countries, see Gerald Epstein, Ilene Grabel and K.S. Jomo "Capital

Management Techniques In Developing Countries: An Assessment of Experiences from the 1990's and Lessons For the Future," Political Economy Research Institute Working Paper #56, 2003, <http://www.umass.edu/peri/pdfs/WP56.pdf>. This study was prepared by commission for the G-24, an organization of finance ministers of developing countries under the auspices of the United Nations.

14.   Alice Amsten, "Fair Trade," *Milken Institute Review*, First Quarter 2002, p. 9.

15.   Ha-Joon Chang, *Kicking Away the Ladder: Development Strategy in Historical Perspective*, London: Anthem Press, 2002.

INDEX